The Search for a New Order

The Search for a New Order

Intellectuals and Fascism in Prewar Japan

by William Miles Fletcher III

The University of North Carolina Press Chapel Hill

© 1982 The University of North Carolina Press
All rights reserved
Manufactured in the United States of America

Library of Congress Cataloging in Publication Data

Fletcher, William Miles, 1946–
The search for a new order.

Bibliography: p.
Includes index.
1. Japan—Politics and government—1926–1945.
2. Intellectuals—Japan. 3. Shōwa Kenkyūkai.
I. Title.
DS888.5.F58   320.952   81-16198
ISBN 0-8078-1514-4   AACR2

To Michèle

Contents

Preface
ix

Chapter 1
Politics and Intellectuals in Prewar Japan
3

Chapter 2
Striving for Social Reform
7

Chapter 3
Perceptions of Crisis
28

Chapter 4
A Turn to the State
51

Chapter 5
Confronting Fascism and Nationalism
71

Chapter 6
The Early Years of the Shōwa Research Association
88

Chapter 7
Designing a New Order
106

Chapter 8
Political Mobilization
134

Chapter 9
Intellectuals, Fascism, and the Quest for Power
155

Notes
163

Selected Bibliography
191

Index
213

Preface

This book could not have come into being without the help of many people, to whom I am indebted. I want first to thank James B. Crowley, whose advice, criticism, and support have been invaluable from the beginning. In addition, John W. Hall, Thomas R. H. Havens, Gerhard L. Weinberg, Lawrence D. Kessler, and Sheldon M. Garon made thoughtful comments about the entire manuscript. I am grateful to them and to others who have read parts of my manuscript in various stages.

While I was in Japan, I received advice and cooperation from many Japanese scholars and former colleagues of Ryū Shintarō, Rōyama Masamichi, and Miki Kiyoshi. Hosoya Chihiro and Fujiwara Akira of Hitotsubashi University gave me helpful suggestions and aided my research in many ways. Baba Shūichi of the University of Tokyo introduced me to the materials of the Shōwa Research Association, which were under his supervision, and he shared his knowledge of the association with me. Ebata Kiyoshi, editor in chief of the *Asahi* newspaper, kindly aided me in arranging interviews with many of Ryū's former colleagues. Doi Akira, Gotō Ryūnosuke, and other members of the Shōwa dōjinkai consented to interviews and cooperated fully with my research. I appreciate the kindness of Mrs. Ryū Hatsue and her family for agreeing to meet with me. I would like to thank collectively all those who took time out from busy schedules to answer my questions.

I benefited greatly from help provided by the staffs of the following libraries where I conducted much of my research: the Ohara Social Problems Research Institute at Hōsei University; the National Diet Library in Tokyo; the Harvard Yenching Library; and the Library of Congress. Kaneko Hideo of the Sterling Memorial Library at Yale University was also very helpful, as was Edward Martinique at the Wilson Library at the University of North Carolina at Chapel Hill.

Financial support from several sources enabled me to complete this project. A Fulbright-Hays Grant enabled me to conduct research in Japan, and a grant from the University Research Council at the University of North Carolina at Chapel Hill and a Reynolds Industries Junior Faculty Development Award facilitated additional research and final revisions.

Ms. Julie Perry, Rosalie Radcliffe, and Susan Hicken deserve a special word of thanks for diligently typing several drafts of the manuscript.

The Association for Asian Studies has granted permission to use material from "Intellectuals and Fascism in Early Shōwa Japan," *Journal of Asian Studies* 39, no. 1 (November 1979): 39–63. The University Research Council at the University of North Carolina generously provided a grant to aid publication.

Finally, I want to acknowledge the patience and understanding of my wife, Michèle, who has encouraged me in pursuing this project.

Japanese names are given in the standard Japanese format with the family name first. The titles of all cited books and articles are translated in the bibliography; titles of items not noted separately there—for example, unpublished documents—are translated in the footnotes.

The Search for a New Order

1. Politics and Intellectuals in Prewar Japan

The 1930s in Japan are usually seen as a "dark valley" of domestic oppression and foreign aggression, but, in fact, many responsible Japanese viewed this era as one of unique opportunity, a time to effect important changes both at home and in Asia.[1] Although studies of Japan's diplomacy during this period abound, few scholars have attempted to explain the complicated internal dynamics that produced the nation's policies. In particular, the role and influence of popular and politically active intellectuals have received little attention.

This neglect is all the more surprising given the participation of many well-known intellectuals in the Shōwa Research Association (Shōwa kenkyūkai), a brain trust for Prince Konoe Fumimaro, the dominant political personality in Japan during the late 1930s. As premier in 1938, Konoe declared the establishment of a new order in Asia, a concept that soon evolved into the vision of the Greater East Asian Coprosperity Sphere. Two years later, Konoe launched the domestic New Order Movement as a radical reform of the parliamentary system and the market economy and as a program of mobilization for war.

When Konoe asked his academic and journalistic advisers to draft plans for the new order, the Shōwa Research Association responded by proposing sweeping changes in the political structure established by the Meiji Constitution of 1889. That constitution had granted the Diet the authority to pass judgment on government legislation and had made the military Supreme Command independent of the civilian cabinet. Japanese citizens had the right to vote directly for representatives in the Diet, and through elections, political parties had emerged to dominate that body. The association recommended the concentration of authority to make national policies in a "planning organ" that would not be responsible to the elected Diet. This body, in turn, was to supervise a "national organization" that would function as a comprehensive mass party. The proposed reforms would reduce the power of the existing political parties, build popular support for the planning organ, and coordinate the policies of the civilian government and the military. If the New Order Movement succeeded, the government would assume responsibility for centralized economic planning through corporate groups and the national organization would replace the Diet as the main conduit of communication between the masses and the government.

The leaders of the Shōwa Research Association in 1940 thus attempted to guide the premier of Japan in the building of a political system patterned after European fascism, that is, the Italian corporate state and Nazi economic policies. Three intellectuals were especially enthusiastic about this vision: Rōyama Masamichi (1895–1980), Ryū Shintarō (1900–1967), and Miki Kiyoshi (1895–1945).[2] By advocating a single mass party, state economic control based on corporative organizations, and inculcation of a national service ethic, these men devised a fascist movement that was neither antimodern nor promodern.[3] It was a radical challenge to the established political and economic systems, and it failed.[4] By investigating the intellectuals' motives and the reasons for their adoption of fascist ideas, it is possible to explain the appeal of fascist ideology and a phenomenon that has plagued Japanese scholars since 1945—the relatively little protest by eminent Japanese writers against their government's policies during the 1930s.[5]

The writings of Rōyama, Ryū, and Miki helped provide the intellectual framework that enabled prominent intellectuals to support the ideology of the Greater East Asian Coprosperity Sphere and a fascist new order in Japan. These writers illuminate a more general pattern of thought and behavior of activist intellectuals during the transition from the 1920s, when political parties controlled the Japanese cabinet and attempts to cooperate with the Western powers shaped Japanese diplomacy, to the jingoism and attacks on parliamentary government that marked the 1930s.

A careful reading of the published works of these writers reveals much continuity in their ideas from 1920 to 1940 and the absence of sudden changes or "apostasy." Moreover, their ideas were rationally conceived and were certainly critical of the basic principles of the parliamentary system.[6] The participation of these men in a fascist movement was due to their professional position as academics and journalists in Japanese society, their own definition of their goals, and their basic intellectual orientation.

One problem for Rōyama, Ryū, and Miki was the conflict between their desire to influence national policies and their distance from centers of political power. Their status as members of a tiny elite of highly educated Japanese made this isolation particularly frustrating.[7] Previously, scholars had played an important role in the building of modern Japan. After the Meiji Restoration of 1868, the government had eagerly accepted the services of writers who were knowledgeable about the West, and these men had had a great impact on national policies. Then, the introduction of civil service examinations in the late nineteenth century began to rigidify career paths and to reduce the accessibility of noncareer personnel to official posts, and the separation of civil and bureaucratic intellectuals became much sharper. As "civil" intellectuals, such as writers, scholars, and journalists, were further estranged from the political establishment, they lost interest in political problems.[8] Rōyama, Ryū, and Miki, however, were different. Perhaps as a result of their experiences with activism on college campuses during the early 1920s, each of them had become intensely concerned with contemporary political and economic issues.[9] Their dilemma was to find a means to end their isolation and get the attention of policymakers, a search which led first to a flirtation with the incipient socialist movement and then to an infatuation with fascist ideology in the Shōwa Research Association.

In any society intellectuals who want direct political impact, either as advisers to national leaders or as public officials, must often appeal to those who hold political power and therefore must adapt to the basic policies of a government. To a great extent, these intellectuals risk sacrificing much of their independence of thought in exchange for the chance to affect national policies.[10] In the 1930s, Rōyama, Ryū, and Miki became convinced that as proponents of fascist ideas, they could appeal to policymakers and direct the nation toward utopia.

These writers sought to influence government policies because they believed that the faults of contemporary party politics and free-market economics demanded radical reforms. Their main fear was that clashes among different interest groups—between political parties and between unions and capitalists—would weaken Japan. Each of the three had the conviction that he should help create a new society that would be less contentious, more just, and more efficiently administered. As they observed the rise of union activity and the apparent ineptitude of the parties, they strengthened in this belief, thus forming the basis for cooperation in the Shōwa Research Association.

The basic intellectual orientation of Rōyama, Ryū, and Miki also helped to determine their attraction to fascism. First, like many Japanese intellectuals since 1868, they were determined to keep abreast of the latest trends in the West, and they defined their main task as interpreting and adapting Western ideas and policies. One striking characteristic of their writings is the lack of reference to Japan's own intellectual past; their works are almost all concerned with European writers or the policies of European nations. For these men fascist ideology in the 1930s was simply one more set of Western ideas to digest, as they had guild socialism and Marxism in the 1920s. They believed that one's ideas should be eclectic and change in response to new problems and new blueprints for utopia.

Rather than defend the notion of individual rights, these men supported the use of the power of the state to carry out reforms. This mirrored one of the major developments in twentieth-century politics—the growing reliance on a central state bureaucracy to solve social problems and to intervene in the economy. This trend was especially prominent in Germany and Italy, where it was linked to a desire to prevent social conflict and to build national strength. During the late nineteenth century the German government, under Bismarck's leadership, enacted welfare legislation for industrial workers to forestall social unrest. The requirements of mobilization for World War I brought the first attempts to impose a planned economy on German industry.[11] After the defeat of Germany a strong Social Democratic party demanded national legislation to establish workers' councils to help manage factories, and some prominent officials advocated a corporatist collective economy which would force private companies into special cartels that would cooperate with state planners in achieving national goals.[12] Although this scheme failed, the Nazis later drew on it for their own domestic economic policies. Coming to power in the wake of severe labor disturbances, Mussolini's fascist regime in Italy sought to bring both industrialists and workers under national control through the creation of state-sponsored "corporations."[13]

Meanwhile, Rōyama, Ryū, and Miki witnessed increased attempts by the Japanese government to extend the authority of the state bureaucracy. These efforts included new programs to inculcate the population with nationalistic values, laws to limit freedom of speech, measures to regulate the economy, and finally mobilization for war against China. The organization of the state, the process of formulating policy, and the proper scope of the state's authority became crucial issues to these writers. As they considered national political and economic reforms, they saw in the state-directed corporatist programs of Germany and Italy viable models that Japan might emulate.

European fascism intrigued the three men because they saw it as employing state power and the irrational emotion of nationalism in the service of rational political and economic reform. Although they held great aspirations for Prince Konoe, they overtly glorified neither a charismatic leader nor violence for its own sake. Fascism had great intellectual appeal because it promised a "new society." The influence of fascism on these writers thus underscores an aspect of fascism as an intellectual movement that deserves more attention.[14]

2. Striving for Social Reform

As intellectuals, Rōyama, Ryū, and Miki felt a special responsibility to confront and discover solutions to the major problems facing Japan. This attitude was common among writers of their day. By 1920 many Japanese intellectuals, survivors of the rigorous competition of the education system and possessors of specialized knowledge, had come to regard their position in society as an elite status, not just an occupation. Journalists, in particular, often believed their mission was to guide the masses.[1]

Rōyama, Ryū, and Miki considered themselves members of Japan's elite for good reason, because they had graduated from top universities. Rōyama and Miki graduated from Tokyo and Kyōto, respectively. The oldest and most prominent imperial universities, these institutions produced leaders for all sectors of Japanese society. For example, since the late nineteenth century attendance at the University of Tokyo had often been a stepping-stone to high government office. Ryū attended Hitotsubashi, a national institution that trained leaders for Japanese business. Moreover, each of the three men had studied with outstanding mentors: Rōyama with political scientist Yoshino Sakuzō, Miki with philosopher Nishida Kitarō, and Ryū with historian Miura Shinshichi. They had received the best education that Japan could offer, and they and their college classmates expected to become the future leaders of Japan.

The early careers of these three men showed great promise. After graduating from Tōdai in 1920, Rōyama continued his study of political science there and within seven years became a full professor. Miki too stayed at his alma mater for graduate study and compiled a brilliant record. His biographers are still mystified about the reasons for his departure in 1927. Some rumors suggest that an illicit love affair doomed his chances for an appointment at Kyōto; other rumors blame academic politics.[2] At any rate, he quickly became chief lecturer in philosophy at Hōsei University, a well-regarded private institution in Tokyo. After pursuing graduate work at Hitotsubashi from 1925 to 1928, Ryū left for Ōsaka, where he joined the Ohara Social Problems Research Institute (Ohara shakai mondai kenkyūjo), the most prestigious private research organization in Japan. Here he joined a staff of prominent liberal and socialist intellectuals, including Professor Takano Iwasaburō, the president of the institute; Professor Morito Tatsuo, who had been purged from the University of Tokyo because of his study of Western radical thought; and Kushida Tamizō, a star pupil of Kawakami Hajime, Japan's first major interpreter of Marxism.

The first writings of Rōyama, Ryū, and Miki revealed a preoccupation with their role as elite intellectuals. Their constant reference to the problems of "intellectual elements," the "intelligentsia," the "intellectual class," and "intellectuals" indicated their strong self-identity as members of a special group in society. They also feared that they would be cut off from significant influence. Miki, for example, openly lamented the "skepticism" prevalent among what he viewed as a demoralized intelligentsia during the 1920s and worried that his peers would retreat from dealing with complex contemporary economic and political problems.[3] His hope, which Ryū and Rōyama shared, was that intellectuals could unite with the emerging proletariat in a sweeping reform movement. A peaceful but complete restructuring of the economic and political system remained their ideal throughout the prewar period.

Responses to the Dilemmas of Industrialization

Since the middle of the nineteenth century each generation of Japanese intellectuals has faced a new set of concerns pertaining to drastic changes occurring within Japan and the impact of Western ideas. During the 1860s and 1870s Japanese scholars strove to understand and explain Western ideas. Discovering what Japan could profitably learn from the West was a major task for many writers. The next few decades saw young Japanese, the "new generation of Meiji," agonize over the pace and extent of Westernization in Japan. Whereas the first leaders of Meiji were intent upon making Japan a strong nation to fend off Western imperialism, this generation turned from a worship of the West to a desire to prove Japan's own greatness.[4]

The turn of the century, however, brought new issues. Japan had adopted a Western parliamentary form of government, and political parties had emerged as increasingly powerful political bodies. The economy was industrializing rapidly and even seizing markets from Western competitors. Although these accomplishments were sources of new pride, they also caused problems. Government officials worried about signs of class antagonisms—unions and strikes—that had accompanied industrialization in Europe and which were appearing in Japan.[5] The challenge to young Japanese intellectuals of the early twentieth century was to design theories of analysis that could explain these changes occurring within Japan and to suggest remedies to the tensions caused by industrialization.

The prosperity brought by World War I, when Japan provided munitions for her wartime allies and exports to the European colonial markets, only accentuated social conflict. First, different sectors of the economy began to experience different rates of growth.[6] The chemical, machine, and metal manufacturing industries grew more rapidly than the previous mainstays of the Japanese economy, textiles and agriculture. Japan's economy evolved into a "dual structure," in which a small number of large, heavily capitalized enterprises coexisted with many small, labor-intensive concerns.

This pattern of growth continued during the 1920s. New industries prospered, as did their workers, and Japan's industrial base approached that of European nations. However, production in other sectors of the economy lagged, and many Japanese workers were still employed in small-scale enterprises with less than five workers. This dual structure understandably spurred criticism of Japanese capitalism and uncertainties as to how the disparities in growth and prosperity could be rectified.

In 1918 the soaring price of rice provoked spontaneous nationwide demonstrations that both frightened the government and revealed how quickly mass protests could spread throughout urban Japan. Moreover, in the expansion of Japanese industry during World War I, organized labor had made great strides. In 1919 the Friendly Society (Yūaikai), originally a mutual-aid society for workers, became a federation of trade unions (Nihon sōdōmei) dedicated to protecting workers' rights. The Friendly Society was the largest union, but it was only part of a general union movement. There were only four trade unions in 1915; by 1919 the number had increased to seventy-one.[7] Labor disputes erupted during the summer and fall of 1919 and became increasingly violent as anarchists and syndicalists gained greater influence within the unions and struggled for leadership with moderate socialists.[8] The spring and summer of 1921 witnessed protracted and violent strikes against the Ōsaka Electric Light Company and the Kawasaki and Mitsubishi shipyards.[9]

The formation of workers' unions and their striving for power made a strong impression on Rōyama, Ryū, and Miki during their early careers, and devising ways of satisfying the demands of unions and ensuring social peace became one of their central concerns. For them, the reform of the political system to accommodate the power of the emerging industrial working class was essential to this effort.

As Rōyama and his peers looked at Japanese politics in the early 1920s, they saw trends both hopeful and ominous. On the one hand, the prospects for a more open parliamentary democracy seemed promising, as the autocratic features of the Meiji monarchy showed signs of softening. New scholarly interpretations of the 1889 Meiji Constitution augured the adoption of universal manhood suffrage and of the principle of ministerial responsibility to the Diet. In the political realm, Hara Kei of the Seiyūkai, the majority political party, formed a party cabinet in 1918, and seven years later the Diet enacted the Universal Manhood Suffrage Act. The authority of the famous Meiji oligarchy—the *genro*—also rapidly dwindled, as did their numbers. These indices of political liberalism coincided with a policy of cooperation with the Anglo-American sea powers, which was reflected at the Washington Conference in Japan's commitments to naval limitations and the "Open Door" principle in China.

On the other hand, state officials were adopting authoritarian policies by limiting the range of legal dissent and encouraging collectivist values in the schools. Numerous private nationalistic groups arose to protest the influx of Western ideas, and the government desired to maintain the social order by controlling as much as possible the spread of radical ideas within Japan. During the Taishō era (1912–26) the government's revised ethics textbooks stressed the values of patriotism and loyalty to the throne. The Ministry of Justice sought to intimidate dissenters by prosecuting Professor Morito Tatsuo for writing an article that explicated the anarcho-syndicalist theories of Kropotkin. The culmination of the government's efforts to control public opinion legally was the Peace Preservation Law of 1925. This act outlawed thought that threatened private property and the "national polity" (*kokutai*); a special police force of the Home Ministry was empowered to search out "thought criminals." In passing this law the Diet made the advocacy of ideas contrary to the national polity an illegal act without specifically defining the meaning of that term. The law was to provide the legal basis for the prosecution of communists and the subsequent suppression of many forms of "dangerous thought" during the 1930s.[10]

The power of the state increased in other ways as well. The Imperial Army organized an Imperial Reserve Association (Zaigo gunjinkai) in order to augment its political influence and support in rural areas. The army also encouraged the formation of a national Youth Association (Seinendan) and infiltrated reservists into the leadership of the local branches.[11] Thus, state organizations penetrated into the smallest hamlets.

Even given the growing authority of government organizations, however, the opening up of the political system raised the possibility of substantial change. The dominant mood in academia during the Taishō era reinforced this hope. In 1917 the Bolshevik Revolution in Russia sparked great interest in socialist theory among scholars. In the same year, Kawakami Hajime's critical analysis of economic inequality in Japan, *A Story of Poverty* (*Bimbō monogatari*), became a best-seller. The term *reform* (*kaizō*) became the byword of the period, and the Russian Revolution and independence movements in India and Turkey were interpreted to signify demands for "social reform" all over the world.[12] A decade later, Rōyama, too, remarked on the wave of reform which had then swept the world "like a flood." The deluge came in the form of the doctrines of "democracy, guild socialism, syndicalism, and Marxism." Tired of war and eager to eradicate its causes, the youth of the world, Rōyama wrote, naturally "sympathized with these ideas of reform which tried to cleanse the society and the nation of the past and to build something new."[13] In espousing change, Rōyama and others were convinced that they were following an irresistible international trend.

Rōyama Masamichi's Attraction to Guild Socialism

An important influence on Rōyama and his interest in reform was his teacher, Yoshino Sakuzō. Yoshino was the best-known advocate of democratic reforms in Taishō Japan. Well aware that republicanism was illegal, Yashino avoided a challenge to the sovereignty of the emperor, but argued that Japanese politics should approach the British parliamentary model as much as possible. He believed that because the "major aim of any state is the general welfare of the citizens," the Japanese constitution should allow for more expression of the popular will.[14] His specific agenda of reforms cited the need for universal suffrage, firmer guarantees of the people's rights, a clearer separation of powers between the executive, the legislature, and the judiciary, and popular election of both houses in the Diet.

Yoshino's invocation of the British parliamentary model and his insistence on "government based upon the people" (*minponshugi*) helped inspire his students to conceive of even more extensive reforms. In 1918, Rōyama and his peers formed the New Men's Society (Shinjinkai), a group which has been termed "Japan's first student radicals."[15] This society embodied the belief then popular among students in the inevitability of reform. Undergraduates in 1918, these students aspired to be the "new men" who would pioneer the economic and social rebirth of Japan. Eager to go beyond mere political reform to alter the fundamental values and structure of the society, they pledged "to eradicate the system of materialistic competition which stands in the way of love and peace and to liberate mankind from the state of materialistic struggle."[16]

In search of guidelines for these lofty goals, Rōyama and other New Men's Society members explored all the current waves of Western reformist thought —democracy, syndicalism, socialism, and communism. Enthusiasm and "amorphous rhetoric rather than a set of ideological dogma," characterized the early society, and its supporters were "perhaps more fickle idealists than effective reformers."[17] Although Rōyama remained flexible in absorbing different Western ideologies of reform and was unable to effect many of his proposals for political reform, he was not a fickle idealist. Throughout the 1920s and 1930s he consistently channeled his intellectual energies toward defining and implementing what he regarded as feasible and effective programs of political change within the context of the existing constitutional government.

After graduation from Tokyo University, Rōyama helped form another organization dedicated to reform, the Social Thought Association (Shakai shisōsha). This body split off from the New Men's Society because of friction between the society's founders, like Rōyama, and younger members who favored the theories of revolutionary Marxism.[18] Following its members' interest in Western thought, the Social Thought Association concentrated its activities on exploring theories of Western social democracy.[19] The members' hope was to outline methods to achieve peaceful and moderate reforms in Japan. For this purpose the group published a journal, *Social Thought*, which included regular reports on the social democratic movements in Germany and England, as well as articles on domestic issues.

The first issue of *Social Thought* boldly proclaimed the association's goal of "realizing a new society," for which the journal was to be a "beginning step."[20] In calling for a new society, this declaration reflected the arrogance of youth. It also revealed an elitist attitude befitting recent graduates of Japan's most eminent university, because they assumed that the first step on the road to meaningful reform was an exchange of ideas among themselves. As the association at its peak encompassed no more than forty regular members, including many university professors who had no direct political ties, the efficacy of this strategy was questionable. Nonetheless, the organization provided intellectuals like Rōyama a forum for developing their analyses of society and their ideals for social and political change.

Rōyama soon became obsessed with the theory of what he called "functionalism" (*shokunoshugi*) as the solution to contemporary political problems. Its implementation required the centralization of government administration, the efficient division of that administration into specialized tasks, and the institution of occupational representation in assemblies. Rōyama's academic specialization was in administrative theory, and he equated politics and public administration and stressed their positive role. In 1924 he claimed that "politics or administration have the same character as war. They have a tendency to direct and to intensify the cooperative relationships between all elements of society to a high degree."[21] Politics, then, should be a well-ordered structure centered on the state bureaucracy and not an unruly process of compromise between separate interest groups.

Rōyama viewed modern European history as proving the inevitable centralization and functionalization of government administration. Surveying the postwar governments of Germany and Eastern Europe, Rōyama identified the "completion of central administrative authority" as a crucial characteristic of industrial countries. This trend had "gathered the authority of the whole country into a huge bureaucratic organization. . . . When we see how efficiency has expanded, we feel that cries for so-called decentralization are no more than poetic liberalism or nostalgia."[22] Associating the growth of parliamentary democracy with the increasing centralization of the power of the state, Rōyama pointed to the administrative role of a parliament "in the national supervision of the executive government rather than its character as a legislative body." In European industrial countries where parliamentary cabinets were being established, "the legislative function, in fact, [was] passing to the cabinet and its subordinate organs. . . . Thus [the parliament's] function as an organ of the national supervision of government and administration [was] rapidly increasing."[23]

Just as Britain was a model of parliamentary democracy to Yoshino Sakuzō, that nation was a model of centralization and functionalization to Rōyama. In particular, Rōyama cited as his prime illustration of functionalization of administration the report in 1903 of Lord Esher's War Office Committee, which curtailed the independence of the British military. The committee abolished the post of commander in chief of the War Office and located the responsibility for strategic planning in the Committee of Imperial Defense (CID) under the prime minister.[24] Rōyama contended that with the Esher report the British military had lost its political autonomy and had been reorganized according to specific functions as part of the national bureaucracy under parliamentary authority. "Because parliament has already somehow or other obtained the support of the masses, its authority cannot be transferred to military cliques. British military officers have already ceased to be a powerful class of military cliques and have become technocratic specialists."[25]

Once again, he identified administration with politics, specifying that "a trend from authoritarianism to functionalism is the drift of modern politics." He was convinced that all political issues ultimately related to the organization and operation of the national bureaucracy. In this regard, he explicitly rejected Yoshino's supposition that constitutional modifications should be the focus of political reforms. Instead reformers should discern within Japanese society the deep "flowing changes in power relations" that would mandate the gradual evolution of an entirely new political structure in Japan.[26]

Rōyama's belief in the centralization and functionalization of state administration was closely linked to his perception of basic changes occurring in industrial societies all over the world. For him, the rise of the proletariat meant that society was splitting into occupational groups which a new political system would have to incorporate. In this, the British concept of guild socialism seemed to influence him most. G. D. H. Cole, the most active spokesman for guild socialism in England at that time, called for the realization of an industrial democracy governed by the workers, who would be organized by guilds. The central problem, in Cole's view, was not only the elimination of capitalists and the capitalist system but the creation of an economic system in which workers would gain control over their own economic lives in order to escape from what he called the slavery of wages.

Cole's *Self Government in Industry* specifically outlined a "guild constitution" in which workers, divided by industries into guilds, would elect the foremen of their workshops and the leaders of their individual factories and enterprises. Workers would elect representatives of their industrial guild to serve on district committees, which would include delegates of all guilds in a district. Workers in each guild would also select the members of the national executive of that guild. The district committees and each national guild executive would be responsible for determining the basic economic policies of the nation.[27] Cole's original conception of guild socialism presumed that industrial guilds would coexist with the established forms of parliamentary government.

The idea of functional (occupational) representation was central to Cole's guild socialism. Workers would control the enterprises in which they worked, and they would elect representatives to district and national councils that would decide economic policies. Cole's *Guild Socialism Restated* (1920) expanded functional representation into a comprehensive social and political system, a "guild commune." In this version, guilds would dominate the society: "In addition to the Guilds of producers and the corresponding organizations of consumers, there were to be Civil Guilds for such activities as education and health, and these in turn would be paralleled by Cultural and Health Councils to represent the citizen's point of view, with all these various bodies being coordinated at local, regional, and national levels."[28] Cole thought that comprehensive national economic planning could coordinate the policies of the various guilds.

Although radicals like Yamagawa Hitoshi and liberals like Yoshino disparaged the visionary quality of guild socialism, it shaped Rōyama's basic perception of social trends. Cole's doctrine affirmed that industrial society produced new occupational groups which would demand functional representation in a democratic system. In Rōyama's view the "development of this principle of functional representation is a reflection of the reality of the emergence of functional groups. Separate from the background of such groups, existence as a simple individual has become practically impossible."[29] Individualism was no longer a realistic social principle. Looking at trends in Europe, Rōyama became convinced that occupational units would soon become the most important elements in Japanese society and that their role, rather than issues relating to individual liberties, should be the central concern of his writings.

Events on the European continent encouraged Rōyama's belief in the inevitability of occupational representation. The institution of advisory economic councils with representation from both business and labor in the new constitutions of Germany and Czechoslovakia heartened him. He noted too that the Soviet Union had partially adopted the principle of functional representation in the formation of the All-Russian Congress of Soviets. Indeed, he predicted that the Soviet political structure under the New Economic Policy would eventually have to reflect the power of "unions, farmers' organizations, capitalist trusts, and groups of intellectuals and technocrats."[30] His ranking of intellectuals with other groups also indicated the importance that he accorded to the role of intellectuals as a distinct group in modern society.

Guild socialism attracted Rōyama because it invoked a Western model and allowed him to predict gradual change without the violence of class warfare. The rise of new occupational groups in an industrializing Japan—leaders of newly emerging corporations (*zaibatsu*), organized workers, and even alienated intellectuals—was obvious. Because he thought these groups would inevitably demand political power, Rōyama could argue confidently that through "pragmatic compromise" Japanese politics would evolve toward a guild socialist utopia. The crucial question to Rōyama from his viewpoint as a specialist in administration was whether or not representatives of functional groups could "manage the politics of society as a whole that transcends their groups."[31] In his later years, G. D. H. Cole turned increasingly to the state as a mediating force in his visions of utopia;[32] Rōyama, too, would soon look to the state as a major force for reform.

Miki Kiyoshi's Interpretation of Marxism

The fever for reform also affected Miki Kiyoshi. Although Miki's career in pursuing philosophical studies was quite different from Rōyama's, there were important parallels between their basic ideas. Like Rōyama, Miki concentrated on interpreting Western thought into Japan and soon came to regard the rise of the proletariat and industrial strife in Japan as major issues. For Miki, Marxism, which explained the progress of history as a product of changes in the economic structure of society, provided the answer to this problem.

During the late 1920s Marxism swept "through the Japanese intelligentsia like a whirlwind . . . drawing the academic world, too, into its turbulence."[33] The appeal of Marxism in Japan was its "startling freshness of vision as an integrating, systematic science."[34] Many Japanese students of Marxism found it useful not as an ideology of revolution but as an analytical methodology that offered a comprehensive approach to examining society. Miki, and later Ryū Shintarō, approached Marxism as a philosophy to interpret rather than as a guide for revolutionary political action.

In 1927, seeking to provide an original analysis of Marxism, Miki began a series of articles which explained Marxist theory through the concepts of *experience* and *anthropology*.[35] He derived his idea of experience from the concept of *pure experience* set forth by his mentor at Kyōto University, Nishida Kitarō. In stressing pure experience as the basis of all knowledge, Nishida had affirmed the importance of intuition over the rational intellect and had attempted to bridge the artificial division between subject and object. He defined pure experience as "direct knowledge," or the "will to know reality as it is, to abandon the narrow acts of the self and to know according to reality."[36] Nishida believed that one could not interpret reality through abstract and rational hypotheses; one could know only what one experienced directly through "intellectual intuition." Because in pure experience one merged with the world, one could grasp the true basis of reality without mechanical rationalizing. Pure experience embraced everyone and everything.

During his study with Martin Heidegger in Germany, Miki's interest in experience broadened into a consideration of the "interpretation of existence" and the "problem of anthropology."[37] Miki asserted in 1926 that anthropology had to be the "basis of all scholarship which is labeled the science of culture or so-called science of the spirit." As "scholarship which concerned human existence," anthropology, he said, emphasized the "study of 'methods of existence [*sonzai no shikata*].' "[38] Abstract concepts of philosophy could not be studied separately from the concrete existence or life experience of man. Miki stated that his own method was to "understand experience within concepts and concepts within experience." If this formulation was abstract, it still provided him with a novel and controversial approach to interpreting the revolutionary doctrine of Marxism.

The central concept in Miki's approach was that of *basic experience* (*kiso keiken*). Its definition was vague, as Miki postulated that it constituted the fundamental and total reality for human existence. Miki asserted, though, that he was not attempting to introduce a mystical concept, because he defined experience as the immediate fact that "I exist, I exist with other people, and among other things."[39] Man constantly tried to define himself in relation to his basic experience which itself constantly changed. Miki called this process of self-definition the "primary logic" of anthropology. This "human self-definition," which occurred on a social as well as an individual level, changed during successive eras, as the basic experience of man himself altered. To Miki, this sort of development was "dialectical" because one era was constantly evolving into another in a process that constituted the basic dynamic of history.

According to Miki, the creation of ideas or ideology was a "secondary logic" dependent upon the primary logic of anthropology. As Miki phrased it, the "philosophical consciousness" or the "scholar consciousness of an age serves as a mediator of 'basic experience.' "[40] All thought systems in a society —religious, historical, or academic—were man's attempts to understand and articulate his relationship to his basic experience. Therefore, the secondary logic of ideology, the dominant consciousness of an era, could change rapidly with developments in the primary logic of anthropology.

One such metamorphosis, in Miki's schema, occurred during the nineteenth century with Karl Marx's creation of the historical view of materialism. This theory outlined a progression of historical stages, culminating in a proletarian revolution, owing to economic forces. Miki argued that the historical view of materialism was an "ideology" and not just a "set dogma" as many Japanese Marxists believed. Historical materialism was, in fact, a "Marxist form of an anthropology." Just as Aristotle's and Machiavelli's writings responded to the basic experiences of their eras, Marx's theories responded to the demands of his era. "One completely new basic experience was developed. This was the basic experience of the proletariat."[41] In other words, Marx had created the theory of the historical view of materialism because of the rise of the proletariat to power in mid-nineteenth-century Europe. Ultimately, Marxism represented to Miki not an unquestioned theory of the stages of historical development but one ideology that arose in a particular era.

Raising the crucial question of whether Marxism was a perpetually valid theory, Miki wondered whether "the basic experience of the proletariat is really placed in a position of not changing because it has definitely been understood in the historical view of materialism?" He provided his own unequivocal answer: "This is absolutely impossible because of the special character of this basic experience [which shaped Marxism]."[42] When the basic experience of the revolutionary proletariat changed, it would require modifications of the revolutionary ideology of Marxism. Because reality and ideology would continue to develop and to affect each other, one could not predict the future. Instead, dialectical theory, which formed the core of both Hegel's and Marx's thought, suggested to Miki the unlimited possibility of change. "The fundamental definition of real existence is possibility. The character of reality is the character of possibility."[43] "People must not consider a fixed dogma as the basis of the concepts of Marxism; on the other hand, they must understand [it] always [as] a realistic theory in the process of development."[44]

Marxism structured Miki's view of contemporary issues. He agreed with its basic analysis of the problems of capitalist society—that man was becoming alienated from his self, because his labor had become just one more impersonal commodity to be sold on the market.[45] The proletariat, he concurred, had to assume the role of a critic in society because of the superior position of the bourgeoisie. Like Rōyama, however, Miki rejected the tactics of strikes and revolutionary violence as advocated by radicals.[46] He reminded his readers that the most distinctive and superior aspect of Marxism was the dialectical method, which guaranteed eventual economic change, and that Marxism would have to remain a flexible doctrine.[47]

Miki's assertions about the development of Marxism implied a relativistic philosophy that assumed constant change. There could be no universal principles of truth or philosophy to guide the individual, because all thought systems were ideologies that could vary with the different demands of each era. Given this premise, no single doctrine could claim to be the only correct interpretation of historical development. Miki argued too that the individual by himself embodied no ultimate values outside of his social and historical context.

Miki de-emphasized the importance of the individual in society. He claimed, for example, that Nishida's concept of pure experience had thrilled him as a young student because it provided a means of "escaping the theory of the independent self."[48] The idea that, in his words, the individual did not produce experience but that experience produced the individual impressed Miki so much that he later claimed that this insight "fundamentally changed my theory of knowledge." Heidegger's notion of a human being as "being-in-the-world" reinforced Miki's disavowal of the individual. Miki stressed that a "human being is in a relationship of communication with others and, because of this relationship and in it, being has complete meaning. . . . Existence becomes real in our connections (kōshō)." Man was thus "being-in-the-world."[49] This definition mirrored Miki's own understanding of Heidegger's concept of *being* (*sonzai*). As one scholar has explained, to Heidegger being was "created out of history, culture, and human relations. Whatever man does, he does within a cultural-historical-social context that gives him a domain which defines what is significant and meaningful." Miki shared this belief and found it compatible with Marx's assertion that man's social being, as reflected in the relations of production, determined man's consciousness and the basis for historical change.[50]

While Rōyama asserted that man as an individual no longer existed, Miki defined man as a being-in-the-world. Neither writer touted the view of the independent self, but each stressed, in his own way, the importance of social bonds. These conclusions about the relationship of the individual to society placed Miki and Rōyama in a difficult position regarding one central political issue of the 1920s—whether or not the freedom to dissent would increase. Many Japanese officials and private citizens rejected the principle of individual rights as alien and believed that the individual should subordinate his wishes to those of the nation. Although Rōyama and Miki saw themselves as critics of government policies, they failed to elaborate a defense for individual liberties. As elite intellectuals, they wanted the right to voice their opinions, but they did not emphasize the right of every citizen to do so.

Although Rōyama once wrote that the "inner life" of an individual should be free from state control,[51] he consistently argued that the occupational group was the basic unit of industrial society. Miki described the individual as entwined with society as a whole. Miki and Rōyama did not at this time exalt the nation, but they stressed the allegiance of the individual to a larger group. Only a slight shift in their focus would be required for them to elevate the needs of the nation over those of the individual for the purpose of restructuring society.[52]

Ryū Shintarō: From Spengler to Marx

In several important ways, Ryū's early intellectual development was similar to Rōyama's and Miki's. Like Rōyama, Ryū during college became interested in the rise of the proletariat, and like Miki, he created his own flexible interpretation of Marxism. During Ryū's senior year at Hitotsubashi, he established connections with the Social Thought Association, which Rōyama helped manage. Although one leader claims that Ryū was a member of the asssociation, other colleagues suggest that his contact with the group was less formal.[53] However loose Ryū's contact was, it indicated that he was already intrigued by the possibilities for a social democratic movement in Japan.

This interest in reform was evident in the progress of Ryū's graduation thesis.[54] It began as a study of the writings of Oswald Spengler, a project recommended by Ryū's mentor, Miura Shinshichi, who was a cultural historian trained in the Germanic idealist tradition. Ryū's essay, however, became critical of the utility of Spengler's theories for analyzing contemporary economic problems and evaluated Marxism favorably. Ryū's preoccupation with current issues was so great that he neglected the most sensational aspect of Spengler's work, its pessimism toward the fate of the West. Miura was displeased and delayed approval of the senior thesis.[55]

Ryū rejected Spengler's assertion that "the history of the world is the history of nations"[56] by arguing that Spengler had ignored completely the importance of class struggle in Europe. Because Spengler did not see the proletariat as a motive force in history, he attributed the appearance of an industrial proletariat and of an employer class to the advent of a machine culture, to a form of economic production in which both classes were slaves to the machine.[57] "This view," Ryū wrote, "is different from the current popular view of economic classes. For example, the bitter conflict between the proletariat and industrialists, which is the perspective of socialist thought and is becoming popular today, does not have great meaning [for Spengler]."[58]

Ryū's critique of Spengler did not explicitly affirm an acceptance of the Marxist viewpoint of the class struggle. Still, Ryū belittled Spengler's characterization of Prussian socialism as merely "something which symbolized German character," and he complained that Spengler neglected the problems of "the relations of production" and of the "relations of workers and industry."[59] From Spengler's viewpoint, Ryū judged, "one cannot grasp the fact that social relations definitely exist outside of the nation or that relations like those between capitalism and its agent, imperialism, exist not as just [theoretical] truth but as economic reality."[60]

Without challenging Spengler's prediction about the eventual triumph of some type of socialism in Europe, Ryū disagreed both with Spengler's contention that socialism was unrelated to the class struggle and his neglect of pressing economic dilemmas. "Thus Spengler's position can grasp a one dimensional aspect of phenomena as [cultural] ideals, but it cannot discern their external aspects. . . . This morphology of economic history attempts to view the basic trends of economic life and to show its ultimate destination; but it is far from the solution to present economic problems. Therefore we must resolutely recognize the need for an economic theory to attend to the responsibility of resolving basic economic problems." Finding this theory constituted Ryū's main intellectual task during his early career.

Ryū interpreted Marxism by comparing it to Spengler's basic theses. In so doing, he blended Miki Kiyoshi's "anthropological" analysis with the ideas of Kushida Tamizō, a prominent Marxist scholar at the Ohara Institute. Ryū used Spengler's specific criticisms of Marx as a vehicle to convey his own interpretation of Marxism. In *Prussianism and Socialism*, Spengler had assailed Marxism as a detached and lifeless rational system of historical explanation based on arbitrary speculation. According to Spengler, Marx had, "by means of a truly grotesque calculation" and "with the psychological naiveté of a scientifically trained mind of 1850," concocted a scheme in which the conflict between the English spirit of capitalism and the Prussian spirit of socialism was defined as class struggle between the bourgeoisie and the proletariat.[61] Marx, in Spengler's judgment, had betrayed the Hegelian tradition, which considered the state to be the main dynamic of history. Ryū saw both Marx and Spengler as indebted to Hegel.

Responding to Spengler's criticism of Marx, Ryū stressed the importance of Hegel's dialectical theory for Marx's own ideas.[62] De-emphasizing the objective and scientific truth of Marx's analytical approach, Ryū explicitly avoided the problem of what he called the "graphic" (*zushikiteki*) quality of Marxism: that is, its capability to predict the precise stages of social development.[63] Instead, he maintained that a basic "understanding of causality" in Marxism provided the key to grasping the principles that governed economic and historical development. Specifically, Ryū rejected Spengler's proposition that the Marxist analysis of causality was a detached and overly rational theory. He emphasized the centrality to Marxism of Hegelian theory, which he described as "the most important romantic model of trying to comprehend with a dialectical theory the movements of phenomena within themselves in a unitary manner."[64]

Ryū agreed with Spengler's contention that philosophical principles should not rely on detached speculation and that "they must penetrate a phenomenon." Marxism, in Ryū's opinion, had both qualities. It was not a theory of "stagnant relations simply discovered between objects" but "as a result of resolving the gaps between these objects, it is a principle of phenomena which have movement between themselves."[65] The central principle of Marxism was Marx's evaluation of Feuerbach—namely, "The greatest fault of all previous theories of materialism is that objects, in other words the character of reality and the senses, have [previously] been understood only in the form of an object or as conception and not subjectively as the practice or the sense activity of humans." Ryū suggested that the approaches of Marx and Spengler were basically similar in stressing "organic" historical development.[66]

Marx, Ryū said, sought principles of historical development "within developing phenomena themselves." In support of this position, Ryū argued that such fundamental Marxist concepts as the principle of value and the principle of economic reproductive relations should be seen as part of the flow of history, as principles which could "develop and change with the progress of history."[67] Marx himself had realized this when, in the postscript to the second printing of *Das Kapital*, he wrote, "What is this [method] other than the dialectical method?" As had Miki Kiyoshi, Ryū interpreted Marxism as a supple system of dialectical thought which could change and grow as part of historical development.

Although Ryū did not share Kushida Tamizō's literal faith in Marx's predictions, he shared Kushida's conviction that the theory of historical materialism provided a meaningful framework for analyzing social development. As a specific theory of social analysis, historical materialism, Kushida believed, had identified two central elements—that is, "the theory of the progress of social organization and the theory of class conflict." Both were dependent on changes in material production and relationships within the means of production.[68] The main contribution of historical materialism, Ryū wrote, was its emphasis on "how society is structured and how an economic structure forms the base for this social structure."[69] The major problem for historical materialism was the determination of whether or not economic developments really governed other social phenomena or whether economic phenomena simply interrelated with other events. Ryū, quoting Engels, favored a compromise solution: while all social phenomena interacted, "economic movements" were most important. "People make history, but in given conditions."[70]

Ryū's critique of Spengler presumed that history depended on the subjective actions of individuals and that economic conditions limited these actions. Because the dialectic of historical materialism included limitless possibility, Ryū denied that the theory could prophesy fixed results. Although he endorsed Marx's stress on the economic structure as the key to social progress, he, like Miki, did not view Marxism as a predictive theory to guide specific programs. Ryū ignored the popular debates about the proper strategy for the proletariat— whether it should be a revolutionary vanguard or ally with other social classes. In some respects, his assessment of Marxism was similar to that of the European writers Karl Korsch and Georg Lukács who, in the 1920s, de-emphasized Marxism as a set of specific scientific laws and presented Marx as a Hegelian philosopher who based his ideas on a general dialectical theory.[71]

During the 1920s, Rōyama, Ryū, and Miki each tried to formulate a comprehensive interpretation of developments in Japanese society. All three agreed that the rise of the industrial proletariat and the emergence of class conflict were crucial events. Rōyama saw occupational representation as one way to accommodate workers' demands and to preserve social peace. Miki and Ryū found the Marxist framework useful for analyzing the contemporary situation, although they did not support the strategy of violent class conflict. In this regard, these writers were not unique, because socialism and Marxism appealed to many Japanese intellectuals as the latest trend in thought imported from the West. Significantly, the basic analysis of society that each writer formed in his early career remained consistent throughout the interwar period; ten years later, Rōyama would still argue for functionalism, and Ryū and Miki would advocate the overcoming of capitalism.

Rōyama, Ryū, and Miki also became increasingly concerned about their political and social roles. This preoccupation was evident in Miki's review of Ryū's work on Spengler.[72] Ryū's careful exegesis of Spengler's works, Miki pointed out, was a valuable explication of the damaging "relativism" into which a demoralized German "intelligentsia" had fallen. In this way, it was, he said, a warning to the Japanese. Impressed by Ryū's analysis of Marxism, Miki implied that this ideology could rescue the Japanese intelligentsia by giving them a tool for analyzing social problems.

The Search for a Role

In searching for new activist social and political roles, Rōyama, Ryū, and Miki each tried to maintain his separate identity as an intellectual while attempting to relate to the incipient workers' movement. None of the three ever joined a proletarian party or a union or undertook political work. Instead, they chose to pursue academic research and to contribute indirectly to the labor movement. They wanted to guide this movement, but they refused to commit themselves to it. Such a commitment not only entailed increased risks of arrest and government harassment but also threatened their visions of their social status and roles.

Rōyama hoped for a strong social democratic party in Japan, as political developments abroad encouraged anticipation of political reform in the near future. Rōyama and his colleagues in the Social Thought Association regarded the British Labour party as their model. By 1923 it had evolved into a major political force and its leader, Ramsay MacDonald, had become prime minister.[73] The success of the Labour party raised the possibility of achieving a Japanese analogue in the Diet. Accordingly, Rōyama wrote that the "advance to a new society" required a parliamentary workers' movement.[74] He expected that a powerful and central party representing the working class could help correct the faults of what he called "bourgeois democracy" by fostering the "scientific and rational organization of the financial system and administration."[75]

Such a party, in Rōyama's conception, could also become an avenue for political influence for academics, although there was considerable opposition to this idea. Syndicalists and communists within the union movement, for example, wanted to eject academic theorists in order to create purely proletarian organizations, which would be more willing to use violence to gain power. Rōyama, however, argued that a strong party must "depend on the combination of the mass power of the workers' unions and of socialist groups, which include intellectual elements."[76] He preferred that the unions channel their energies into the creation of a moderate labor party in which intellectuals would provide the brains to guide the brawn of the workers' movement.

The imminent enactment of universal manhood suffrage, what Rōyama labeled the "new stage in our political situation," prompted his enthusiasm for this new party.[77] The impending entrance of the masses into politics was an epoch-making moment in modern Japanese political history because, "for the first time, the chance has come today for our labor movement to be not just a translation of foreign thought and policies but to be led by a judgment of reality born of its own experience and beliefs."[78] Rōyama rejected consideration of the established political parties, even those which had actively campaigned for electoral reform, as vehicles for political reform, but he was committed to changing the parliamentary system from within. Moreover, he denounced those Japanese socialists who criticized the formation of a parliamentary proletarian party and advocated a revolutionary course of action as isolated dogmatists whose insistence on the exclusive rule of the proletarian class was "nothing more than an example of [their] mistaking [their] own emotional agitation for the enthusiasm of the masses."[79] They were more concerned with "scream[ing] in their lecture meetings about profound theories of capital accumulation, surplus value, and noble theories of social progress and revolutionary movements," than with "everyday problems, such as workers' homes and city land."[80] Radicals' advocacy of a violent overthrow of the capitalist system and an advance to the dictatorship of the proletariat was, in Rōyama's view, unattainable. A more effective strategy would be for the workers to seize the historic opportunity presented by universal manhood suffrage and to join with the intellectuals in creating a parliamentary proletarian party.

Unlike some other members of the Social Thought Association, such as Miwa Jusō, Rōyama himself did not participate in the formation of a political party, because his academic career took precedence over his political aspirations. He left Japan in 1924, just before the passage of universal manhood suffrage, to study for three years in England, with occasional visits to Western Europe. Thus, Rōyama was not in Japan to experience the first days of the "new stage" in Japanese politics. This circumstance revealed both Rōyama's strong self-identity as an intellectual and his attitude toward politics. Although he wanted to consult on directions for political change, he did not want to organize a political movement. As a professor in the nation's most prestigious imperial university, he was content to keep his distance from activity at the grass-roots level.

During Rōyama's sojourn abroad the Japanese proletarian party movement encountered many difficulties.[81] The police disbanded the Farmer-Labor party (Nōmin rōdōtō) only thirty minutes after its formation on December 1, 1925. In March 1926, Miwa helped create the Labor-Farmer party (Rōnōtō). By October, however, he and other moderate socialists had bolted this party because they opposed the admission of communists. In December these defectors organized two new parties—the Social Democratic party (Shakai minshū tō) and the Japan Labor-Farmer party (Nihon rōnōtō). Afterward, government harassment and internal factionalization continued to impede the emergence of a strong social democratic movement, despite Rōyama's high expectations.

Ryū became involved in the social democratic movement through the Ohara Research Institute. After several years of graduate study in economics he joined the organization in 1928 as a research assistant. This appointment was a great honor, as the institute was the most prominent private center of social science research in Japan and its members were leading noncommunist intellectuals in the labor movement. The director, Takano, was a distinguished former professor, a pioneer in statistical studies concerning workers, a former adviser to the Friendly Society, and a staunch supporter of the Japan Labor-Farmer party.[82] Founded in 1919 with the backing of textile magnate Ohara Magosaburō, the Ohara Institute was unique in that it was financially secure, so that its members could devote their full time to research on social problems. Under Takano's guidance it became a haven for leftist academics who could not find regular university posts.

Ryū later commented that his experience at the Ohara Institute deepened his "interest in social problems."[83] He sharpened his skills in economic analysis by composing a study of the adverse effects of the Japanese tariff on rice imports for Takano's Ōsaka Free Trade Conference and translated several works by European socialists, including Karl Kautsky and George Plekhanov.[84] Ryū's most important task was serving as editor of the *Japan Labor*

Yearbook (*Nihon rōdō nenkan*), which the institute published annually to provide a wide range of information about labor conditions and workers' movements in Japan.

The closest contact Ryū had with union members was through his teaching in the Ōsaka Labor School (Ōsaka rōdō gakkō), funded initially by the Social Thought Association in 1922.[85] For three evenings a week, Ryū lectured the students, workers who were selected by their unions, on Marx's theory of currency and the theory of proletarian culture.[86]

Ryū's fascination with the rise of an industrial proletariat in Japan is undeniable. That his most intimate involvement in the labor movement was as a teacher in a "labor school" indicates the strength of his self-identity as an intellectual and scholar, especially because he chose to teach classes in abstract theory. While the notion of explaining Marxist concepts to factory workers who probably at best had completed only six years of elementary education seems idealistic and naive, there is no reason to doubt Ryū's sincerity. Scholars like Miki and Ryū felt that interpreting Marxist theory was also socially relevant because it appeared to be the most convincing and comprehensive explanation of the rise of the industrial proletariat. If scholars could find and propagate the correct interpretation of Marxist theory, then they could discover the solutions to contemporary social and economic problems.

Miki focused his activity on promoting scholarly research into Marxist theory. In 1928 he formed with Hani Gorō the journal *Under the Banner of New Science* (*Shinkō kagaku no moto ni*) to provide a platform for debate about Marxism, and later Miki helped establish the Proletarian Science Research Center (Puroretaria kagaku kenkyūjo). In this way, he played an important role in introducing Marxism to a broad intellectual audience. Some writers in the postwar period have argued that Miki's writings helped popularize Marxism among university graduates by analyzing it from a philosophical perspective.[87] At the time, many Japanese radicals roundly abused Miki's conviction that Marxism represented a form of anthropology—that is, one response to a particular basic experience—and that dialectical theory actually recognized the unpredictability of social change. Doctrinaire colleagues deprecated Miki's theories as bourgeois "revisionism."[88] This vehement reaction eventually forced Miki to resign from even the Proletarian Research Center.

These attacks resulted from Miki's unwillingness to commit himself to the doctrine of class struggle, not to mention his avoidance of political activity. He viewed Marxism as one theory that could be useful in analyzing social problems, but not as a blueprint for political action. Like Ryū and Rōyama, Miki wanted to analyze social issues and suggest solutions, but he was content to leave their implementation to others. While all three men wanted to be actively involved in social issues, they wanted to retain their identities as intellectuals who were concerned not just for the welfare of the proletariat but also of the whole society. As Rōyama wrote, a major concern was that the goals of one occupational group should not dominate. Their hope was that the moderate labor movement could be a force for reform that would respond to their guidance; their connection to the proletarian parties would be their avenue of political influence. This expectation rested on the assumption that the labor parties would quickly win popular favor with the expanded electorate. However, this goal proved much harder to achieve than the three men expected.

3. Perceptions of Crisis

The writings of Rōyama, Ryū, and Miki provide a clue to explaining the transition from the hopeful promise of Taishō democracy during the 1920s to the dark decade of the 1930s. On the surface, major political events of the two periods contrast sharply—the emergence of party cabinets in 1925 with their end in 1932 and Japan's participation in the Washington Conference with its abandonment of the League of Nations a decade later. Thus, the worldwide depression of 1929 and the actions of the military in Manchuria have often taken the blame for creating a national mood that was antagonistic toward parliamentary democracy, capitalism, and cooperation with the Western powers. The roots of this reaction, however, existed prior to 1930. The army's Imperial Reserve Association began in the Taishō period, as did legislation placing new limits on dissent. The rise of messianic "new religions" and the radical proposals of rural branches of the Youth Association suggested a popular revolt against the established political and economic order well before economic disaster and military expansionism dominated newspaper headlines.[1] Rōyama, Ryū, and Miki exemplified how even moderate intellectuals had become disaffected with that order.

These men were able to adjust to the issues of the 1930s without a significant sense of discontinuity, without altering their basic analyses of the ills of Japanese society. Their writings, however, did grow alarmist in asserting that Japan's politics, economics, and culture were all reaching a turning point. While the military ridiculed the political parties and fomented a crisis of national security to muster popular support for large budgets, Rōyama, Ryū, and Miki each defined a crisis in Japan as evidence for the inevitability of a "new society." In this way, their works contributed to undermining popular confidence in the political and economic system. For them, the dilemmas of the 1930s evolved from problems that were apparent years before.

The Manchurian Crisis

Japan's Manchurian policy posed challenges that Rōyama had anticipated as early as 1925, when he first examined the potential troubles of the newly formed League of Nations. Although Rōyama viewed the league as the beginning of "international politics" in the sense of establishing a world community, he foresaw serious difficulties for the organization. In particular, the development of "nationalism" and "nationalistic imperialism" worried him. Because the league could not regulate each nation's economic policies, it could not prevent the economic exploitation of small nations by more powerful ones. The main problem was how a strong nation could pursue its own interests and those of the larger international community.

Responding to this crucial question, Rōyama argued that it was the responsibility of scholarship, by which he presumably meant academics like himself, to devise a "new concept of sovereignty" to replace nationalism as a historical concept that was "born in the progress of history." Then perhaps nationalism could coexist with "internationalism."[2] Just as Rōyama desired a total reform of Japan's domestic politics, he envisioned a completely new system of international relations that would transcend the nation-state. At this point, he did not indicate what the new unit of international relations or what the new concept of sovereignty would be; clarifying these ideas would become one of his central tasks in the following decade.

The dilemma that Rōyama described pertained to Manchuria, where protecting Japan's national interests increasingly clashed with the policy of cooperation with China. During the 1920s the government had promoted Japanese investment and settlement in Manchuria and had used military force on several occasions to safeguard Japanese residents in China. These policies offended the growing Chinese nationalist movement that was led by Generalissimo Chiang Kai-shek's Kuomintang. Chiang aimed to unite the country politically and to demand an end to foreign privileges in China.

Rōyama's evaluation of this situation for the Japan Council of the Institute of Pacific Relations indicated the primacy of Japan's national interests.[3] He predicted that Japan's position in Manchuria could become a source of international tension because Japan was determined to maintain its rights. "No one can ignore the vital and still growing interests of Japan in Manchuria," he said. Moreover, he argued, Japan's investments there were mutually beneficial, with Manchuria providing important raw materials and Japan stimulating the Manchurian economy with investments. As long as China and the Western powers did not legally recognize Japan's de facto interests, however, the potential for friction and conflict remained. Rōyama thought his country's established interests should receive international approval, but that under present conditions they probably could not because of the ineffectiveness of the League of Nations. "Without what may be described as positive and reliable machinery for dealing with disputes that may arise between the countries bordering on the Pacific, so long will Japan view her relations with Manchuria of vital importance to her own strategy and imperial organization." He implied that only a special new organization of international relations in the Pacific area might permit a reasonable settlement of the Manchurian problem with "mutual understanding" and "international guarantees and security."

Only two years after Rōyama completed this pamphlet, troops of the Japanese Imperial Army swept across the plains of Manchuria. The bold initiatives of the Kwantung Army in the field received full support from home, as most Japanese responded enthusiastically to the news of Japan's smashing victories; within months the mass media were touting Manchuria as the "lifeline" of Japan.[4] In March 1932, the Japanese government sanctioned the creation of an independent government in Manchuria, defying the League of Nations, which had created the Lytton Commission to investigate the propriety of Japan's military actions. A confrontation between the league and Japan appeared imminent.

The possibility that strident Japanese nationalism would impede a proper international settlement of the Manchurian problem distressed Rōyama. He met with five colleagues, including Professor Yokota Kisaburō and the journalist Matsumoto Shigeharu, to discuss a solution to the crisis. In June 1932, this group issued for limited distribution a draft of several guidelines for future Japanese policy.[5] This document is significant, because it set a pattern for how Rōyama, and later Ryū and Miki, would justify Japan's expansion of influence in China.

This group of young writers and scholars, whom Rōyama dominated, lamented that the Japanese people had lost their "balance" in viewing the new situation in China. Fearing that blind nationalism would lead Japan into diplomatic isolation, they sought a more reasonable course based on four principles of Japanese policy in China. These were the restoration and guarantee of stability in Manchuria; the guarantee of international recognition of Japan's special relationship to Manchuria; the protection of friendly relations between China and Japan; and respect for the international peace structure and cooperation with it.[6] The enunciation of these four principles reflected a basic division within the group over the issue of national interests that had troubled Rōyama seven years before: Should Japan demand settlement of its claims to special rights in Manchuria or preserve cooperative relations with China and the West? Rōyama backed a plan that centered on the first two principles of the maintenance of stability and Japan's rights, while Professor Yokota championed the last two principles of international cooperation.[7] The group endorsed Rōyama's draft as "plan number one."

Although Rōyama and his colleagues warned against the dangers of nationalism, they agreed with the prevailing idea that the root of the Manchurian problem lay not in the recklessness of the Kwantung Army but in the "refusal of special relationships [with Japan] by Chinese authorities" and the faults of the international peace structure, that is, the League of Nations.[8] The report claimed that because the "present peace structure" was inadequate for protecting special interests, it made "national self-rescue measures" necessary.[9] International recognition of Japan's rights was a "basic condition" for peace, and only a reorganization of the entire structure of international relations in Asia could solve the Manchurian dilemma.

The aim of Rōyama's plan was to have Manchuria recognized as a self-governing state separate from China. If the West would not bestow international approval on this new entity, the group realized that its proposals would merely ratify the army's conquest.[10] The plan called for Japan to assist the residents of Manchuria in creating an effective political organization and maintaining internal stability through a special treaty.[11] In return, Japan would seek a settlement of tariff and foreign-trade problems relating to Manchuria through international consultations and would invite Western cooperation in economic development. Japan would uphold the Open Door Policy of the Nine Power Treaty.[12] Meanwhile, a "Far Eastern organ of the League [of Nations]" could locate in Tokyo to aid the creation of an independent Manchuria.[13]

Although Rōyama's colleagues argued that Manchuria was a special case, they realized that their proposals contradicted the American policy of cooperative diplomacy in China and of protection for China's territorial integrity. In January 1932, Secretary of State Henry L. Stimson affirmed this stance by announcing that the United States could not recognize territory seized in violation of the Kellogg-Briand Pact of 1928. Few Japanese, aside from Professor Yokota, were prepared to agree that their nation's actions in Manchuria were illegal under existing international law.[14] Rōyama's plan countered simply that the Kellogg-Briand Pact did not apply to the situation in Manchuria. The drafters of the plan admitted their proposals amounted to a seizure of Chinese territory and a "destruction" of the Nine Power Treaty.[15]

These writers viewed the Manchurian Incident as an opportunity for Japan to gain new influence in international diplomacy. In spite of the vocal, if impotent, Western criticism of the Manchurian war, Japan should continue to participate in the League of Nations because Japan could take a "leading position" and persuade other nations to its cause.[16] In contrast to its role in the Washington Conference of 1921–22, Japan could also aggressively sponsor international conferences that would deal with East Asian problems in the future. The Manchurian Incident had "world significance," Rōyama commented later, because it would be settled on the basis of "Oriental thought."[17]

The recommendations of Rōyama's group basically affirmed government policy because the group accepted the chauvinistic goal of preserving Japan's special interests in Manchuria. The plan challenged the government's insistence on Japan's right to recognize Manchukuo unilaterally,[18] but the draft fully supported the basic goal of Japanese policy during the spring of 1932—the creation of an independent Manchurian state under Japanese tutelage. The drafters just hoped that this goal could be achieved through negotiation rather than by unilateral fiat; to them, international cooperation meant Western agreement to Japan's paramount interests. There was, however, no assessment in the proposals of whether Britain or America would negotiate the Manchurian issue.

Rōyama's criticism of the League of Nations as a peace-keeping institution revealed a resentment against the West. He had voiced a general complaint in 1925 that the league could not control the great powers and the forces of imperialism; now, he voiced a specific complaint that the league could not protect Japan's special rights in China. Rōyama sensed correctly that Japan's actions in Manchuria posed a serious threat to the effectiveness of the league in maintaining world peace. His solution was a proposal for the establishment of a regional league, which Japan would presumably dominate as the major economic and military power in Asia. If the league would recognize Japan's leadership of Asia, then Japan could cooperate with the league.

To Rōyama, even more exciting opportunities awaited Japan. For example, he opposed the popular idea of devising an exclusive Japan-Manchuria bloc because he feared it would be too small to sustain Japan's economic growth.[19] A more promising alternative was "the forging of new economic relations with the Pacific." That region invited a "new adventure for Japan because of its advantageous geographical position." Japan must not seek an imperialistic economic advantage, Rōyama cautioned, but it must establish a new planned economy in the Pacific. If the Japanese displayed the same type of enthusiasm toward this goal as they did during the Manchurian crisis, they could become, in "thought" and "morality," the "champions" of the "Far East, the Pacific, and the world." These statements revealed Rōyama's growing conviction that Japan's security depended upon its leadership of both East Asia and the Pacific region.

Rōyama's stance on Manchuria was significant in two ways. First, his conviction that Japan's future lay in the dominance of Asia became an assumption of the entire Shōwa Research Association that he would form within two years. Rōyama's ideas set precedents for Miki Kiyoshi's later attempts to define a new philosophy to unite Asia and Ryū Shintarō's efforts to construct a regional economy. Second, Rōyama's proposals reflected his basic intellectual attitudes in their flexibility and their commitment to reform. His approach to crises during the 1930s, and that of Ryū and Miki, was not to oppose developments directly but to analyze them to discover their potential for creating a new Asia free from Western control and a "new society" at home. Influenced by the swell of popular support for the military, Rōyama eschewed criticism of Japan's military actions and envisioned how they could lead to a fundamental reform of international relations. One striking characteristic of Rōyama's writings was that, during the period which is known as the "dark valley," they remained optimistic that international and domestic trends were leading toward beneficial changes.

The Political Crisis

Rōyama, Ryū, and Miki had ample reason to be pessimistic about the domestic situation after 1930. Young military officers murdered Premier Inukai Tsuyoshi in May 1932 in the name of restoring the governance of the nation to the emperor and ending the parliamentary system, which they saw as corrupt. These officers were strongly influenced by the writings of Kita Ikki, Gondō Seikyō, and Tachibana Kōzaburō. Kita, whom the government would execute for his suspected role in the military mutiny of February 1936, advocated the elimination of large business combines and stricter state supervision of economic activity.[20] Gondō and Tachibana both questioned the benefits of the capitalist system in Japan and idealized rural self-government and communalism.[21] The youthful assassins of May chastised leaders of large enterprises for their greed and identified plutocrats as a major source of Japan's social ills.

The senior officers of the Imperial Army also took steps to challenge the market economy in Japan. The Kwantung Army implemented governmental controls over economic development and limited the activities of private Japanese companies in Manchuria;[22] in 1934 the Army Ministry published pamphlets calling for the end of the capitalist system in Japan and the institution of a centrally planned economy geared to military needs. The army presented itself as an agent of social and economic reform within Japan, and it pressed the government to follow its lead.

Meanwhile, unable to cope with either foreign or domestic crises, the political parties steadily lost popular support. The worldwide economic depression of 1929 hurt farmers by eliminating the export market for raw silk, an important side occupation in rural areas, and led to an industrial recession. The Minseitō, the party in power between 1929 and 1931, had little success in reviving industrial production. Nor could it muster a national consensus on foreign policy. Its participation in the London Naval Conference of 1930 and its agreement to limit naval construction only inspired vitriolic criticism from the navy and the rival party, the Seiyūkai, that national defense had been compromised. Protestors greeted the return of Japan's delegate with a dagger so that he could commit *hara-kiri*, and supporters of the London treaty within the navy were forced to resign.[23] After 1931 the army's actions in Manchuria defied efforts by both parties to control the situation.

At least three major problems confronted the political parties. First, the Meiji Constitution provided for the independence of the Supreme Command from the cabinet and thus placed the military outside their control. Second, the parties failed to develop a mass following because they relied upon "local influentials" (*meibōka*) in the countryside to deliver the vote.[24] Each party also projected an image of caring more for its own advancement than for the national welfare. For example, in 1934 the Seiyūkai refused to join a nonpartisan "united nation" cabinet headed by Admiral Okada Keisuke because the party hoped to force the formation of a cabinet under its exclusive control. The Seiyūkai gave the impression that it preferred a self-imposed exile from cabinet portfolios to cooperation with its rival party in the national interest.

In response to these dilemmas, Rōyama, Ryū, and Miki desired major changes in the economic and political structure through the gradual and peaceful evolution of social democracy. The failure of the proletarian movement, however, caused them to reconsider their tactics. The first election held under universal manhood suffrage in 1928 had yielded the victory of only eight candidates from the labor parties. Despite these meager results the government still tried to suppress the movement, and, even worse, the various labor parties continued to quarrel among themselves. Predictably, those parties fared poorly in the next election of 1930. By 1931, Rōyama's loss of faith in the parliamentary system was reflected in his criticism of the principles of democracy as well as those of Marxism.

Rōyama's *Citizen Politics* criticized the contemporary system of Japanese parliamentary democracy because it provided no effective means for citizens to affect politics. The rationale for democracy, Rōyama noted, rested on the belief that " 'the citizens' will' manifested in an election would be reflected afterwards in the political process."[25] In actuality, he wrote, even in a democracy ordinary people were too busy to care about politics. If citizens were actively concerned with political affairs, they probably could not understand the complexity of Diet proceedings. "Modern politics has come to deal with all social and economic problems technologically and professionally. The items of debate are created by large administrative offices and separate research and consultative committees of the cabinet. To understand these items,

I think, is impossible with the energy and knowledge of ordinary citizens."[26] The implication that the bureaucracy of the national government, and not the Diet, was becoming the innovative force in Japanese politics is striking, as is Rōyama's judgment that the typical Japanese citizen was incapable of understanding or evaluating contemporary issues.

Rōyama argued that the basic concept of democracy—that the citizen was a "political animal" who would always act rationally on his own behalf for his own interests—was outdated. Major issues and the operation of modern politics had become too complex for such a simplistic principle to work. He also doubted whether elected representatives of the political parties understood important issues any better than the voters did. Debates in the Diet, he suspected, were fueled mostly by the pursuit of individual and narrow interests. The ordinary citizen had good reasons to be estranged from politics.

The apathy of the electorate had doomed the proletarian party movement and all hopes for better government. Rōyama despaired that although there was general disaffection with the established parties, the "opinion of the governed [would] not arise" because citizens were "generally politically passive." "It is a great mistake to think that if general elections become more comprehensive, the proletarian parties will grow naturally. If the leaders of the proletarian parties have such thoughts, they unfortunately could not be more mistaken."[27] The fears of those who had worried about the revolutionary danger of universal manhood suffrage were ludicrous because "the results of the general elections seem to have benefited the strength of the established parties."[28] Universal manhood suffrage, as its proponents had contended, had become a stabilizing force in politics, not a prologue to drastic change. Rōyama would not, however, concede that the general elections under universal manhood suffrage represented an expression of the true popular will in Japan.

Although Rōyama denied that general elections would bring reform, he did not ascribe to the belief that only an inevitable revolution could solve Japan's political problems. In particular, he raised two theoretical objections to dialectical materialism as a political ideology. Dialectical materialism overemphasized economic developments, such as the growth of contradictions within capitalism and the dictatorship of the proletariat, and it neglected immediate political strategy and the importance of the power of the state. Echoing his earlier equation of politics and administration, Rōyama argued that the "goal of politics is to improve social relationships by using the power of the state."[29] Socialists thought differently. Because they believed that "there was no direct relation between grasping and administering power and improving society," they erred in thinking that socialism would triumph as a natural social development. Moderate socialists could not expect to celebrate victory at the polls, and the communists were unrealistic in their apocalyptic expectations.[30]

Rōyama was not an economic determinist. Indeed, he argued that the concept of class struggle could not be applied to Japanese society. It was too simple to see a struggle between workers and capitalists as the determinant of Japanese politics. The economic crisis, for example, had revealed deep differences of opinion about solutions between the conservative Minseitō and the free-spending Seiyūkai, and even among businessmen. The proletariat was split too, with skilled workers in the more prosperous and well-paid munitions industries much less prone to strikes and radical activity than workers in smaller and less prosperous industries.[31] The structure of Japanese society, Rōyama observed, was too varied to be analyzed merely through the concept of class struggle.

Although Rōyama's prediction about the slim possibilities for violent revolution in Japan were correct, his critique of socialist theory was not convincing. Contrary to his contention that faith in dialectical materialism induced political inactivity, socialists and communists, in Japan and elsewhere, concentrated on political strategy and the "seizure of power." Moreover, the fragmentation of Japanese society that Rōyama detected could, in a Marxist interpretation, be taken as evidence of the growing contradictions of capitalism. Rōyama's rejection of radical socialism was probably related more to his previously stated preference for peaceful and gradual political change than to the faults he perceived in socialist theory.

In this respect, it is worth noting that both Miki and Ryū were hostile to the Japan Communist party. Miki became isolated from radical Marxists, as they severely criticized his works. Ryū opposed the communists, even suggesting that their mass arrest in 1928 might actually help to unify the rest of the proletarian movement by "driving the radical left wing movement underground."[32] Later, Ryū blamed the communists for the failure of the proletarian parties because the "expansion of the leftist underground movement, which attacked the legal parties, limited the support of the masses for these legal [proletarian] movements."[33] Ryū hoped for the success of the moderate socialist movement in Japan. When that stalled, the problem for him, as well as for Rōyama and Miki, was finding a new means of effecting reforms.

If the problems of the proletarian parties destroyed Rōyama's faith in parliamentary democracy, his analysis of the basic ills of Japanese society remained remarkably intact. According to Rōyama, the basic trend in Japan was still the fragmentation of the nation into occupational interest groups. The development of a "machine civilization" through industrialization had created a class distinction between the owners of fixed capital and workers and a clash in life-styles between rural and urban laborers.³⁴ Each individual had become part of an occupational group and his attitudes were determined either by the type of enterprise he owned—a farm, mine, railroad, factory, or bank—or by the place where he worked, or by the nature of his profession.³⁵ Danger existed because the welfare of the group would soon supersede the welfare of both the individual and the society as a whole. The individual was losing both his autonomy and his awareness of being a citizen of the society; instead, he was becoming interested only in the immediate goals of his economic group or class. This prompted Rōyama's fear that the "individual and the nation will only operate as abstract concepts, and not as reality."³⁶

Rōyama returned to a problem he had raised before. If, as he had advocated, functional groups became dominant social units, the problem remained whether such groups could conduct the politics of society as a "whole that transcends these groups" and their interests. The solution rested in a special kind of education that would impart to the average Japanese citizen a broad national perspective on issues and liberate individuals from subjugation to an economic interest group. Through education, a "new state" would emerge.

In *Citizen Politics*, Rōyama envisioned a vague socialist solution to Japan's political problems and affirmed the need for a "socialization of the means of production" and the "equalization of income."³⁷ Through the power of the state and education, the nation should also become the focus of individual loyalty in Japan. Unlike nationalists who shared the same idea and cited Japanese classics to buttress the idealization of the state, Rōyama turned predictably to a Western source, Greek philosophy: "Plato said that the state is the guide for our good life, the realization of the highest good; if this is so, there is meaning to submitting to the power of the state. Thus, I think, the expression of individuality can progress smoothly."³⁸ The state must stand above class and group interest and allow equal political representation for all professions and all economic groups.³⁹ The state should also educate the individual to be free from his narrow allegiance to an economic group or class.

Citing Plato's belief that the "condition of politics is the product of education," Rōyama argued that education was an effective means of political reform; he proposed to inculcate a new social ethic through what he called a "citizens' education" that would de-emphasize vocational courses in favor of creating "citizens who can adjust to the goals of communal society."⁴⁰ The main goal of "citizens' education" was to induce increased social and national consciousness and to suppress class or group consciousness. "There will be no distinction between politicians and the masses, between laborers and capitalists. They will all be educated as constituent members of a citizens' society."⁴¹

Rōyama's proposals were ambivalent toward the possible conflict between individual liberty and state power. On the one hand, he deplored the government's suppression of radical thought and, comparing this policy to that of the tsarist regime in Russia, argued that suppression would only create a dangerous underground movement. He pointed out that England had achieved political stability through allowing freedom of speech and that a "citizens' education," while it should be offered as a "system of the state," should not constitute indoctrination. His aim was a "politics of popular opinion" based on freedom of expression. On the other hand, Rōyama believed that for the politics of popular opinion to run smoothly, the "masses must have eyes" provided by an education which would impart critical ability and the power of judgment necessary to assess different ideologies.[42] One specific goal of citizens' education was to replace the economic group or class allegiances of Japanese individuals with a national awareness. Education would be a process of indoctrination in which the individual would learn to sublimate his interests to the greater welfare of the nation. Rōyama was torn between a desire for more freedom of thought in Japan and a belief in the need for greater citizen awareness of the nation and its welfare. Gradually, he decided the latter concern was more important.

The overt emphasis on the state was a new feature in Rōyama's writings, but it was a natural development in light of his background and recent events in Japan. The growing nationalistic mood in Japan, which Rōyama noted during the Manchurian Incident, facilitated glorification of the nation. Because of his academic training in administrative theory, Rōyama also found it convenient to think of the state bureaucracy as a means of social reform. He had proposed, for example, in 1927 that in order to eliminate widespread tenancy in Japan, the state should purchase all agricultural land and place it under the control of prefectural governors, who were officials of the Home Ministry.[43] Then, he argued, "self-governing organs" composed of both government appointees and local farmers could handle routine affairs. Although Rōyama called this a democratic and cooperative method of reform, it was basically a bureaucratic solution and demonstrated Rōyama's interest in using the power of the state as an instrument of change. *Citizen Politics* revealed that this interest had acquired a new dimension in that Rōyama now viewed the state as a moral force—a "guide" for the "realization of the highest good"—as well as a bureaucratic one. This perception of the dual roles of the state would persist in Rōyama's political writings and later in the proposals of the Shōwa Research Association.

As the moderate proletarian movement floundered, the power of the state, to Rōyama, seemed like the only available agent of reform that could halt the fragmentation of society. This reaction was not unique to Japanese intellectuals. During the early 1920s, disappointment with workers' movements and disillusionment with parliamentary democracy in Italy led many neosyndicalists there to a new emphasis on state power to solve social problems and eventually to a position as ideologues of the Italian Fascist party. Those intellectuals, like Sergio Panunzio, began advocating the political education of the masses by the nation and the need for "a more tangible state by diffusing state attributes into the organizations constituting society."[44] Only in this way, Panunzio thought, could the individual gain a sense of participation in the government. Rōyama's perception was similar, and it led him also to the vision of a corporate state.

Prolonged Economic Crisis

Ryū too worried about the fate of the proletarian movement, but he was even more concerned about the general condition of Japan's economy. While Rōyama criticized parliamentary democracy for depending on individualistic principles, Ryū indicted the operation of the market economy. Like Rōyama, Ryū wrote for an increasingly popular audience, first in reformist journals, such as *Warera*, and then in mass-circulation magazines, such as *Chūō kōron*.[45] He achieved stature as an economic commentator because he discussed the crucial economic issues facing Japan. He assumed that these issues could not be resolved without the complete collapse of the Japanese economy.

Impressed by the writings of contemporary European socialists, Ryū took a Marxist approach in analyzing contemporary economic problems. His perspective became apparent during the banking crisis of 1927, which developed when the semiofficial Bank of Taiwan experienced a shortage of cash due to large loans made to the overextended Suzuki Corporation. The Bank of Japan refused to make an emergency loan to the Bank of Taiwan without a guarantee from the Japanese government; when this guarantee was delayed, a general panic ensued. Depositors swamped banks all over Japan with a demand for cash. Despite an immediate doubling of currency by the Bank of Japan and a three-week moratorium on cash withdrawals, many Japanese banks went bankrupt or had to merge.[46]

Ryū's "Background of the Bank Panic" avoided specific policy recommendations and concentrated on the underlying causes of the emergency.[47] Borrowing from the writings of the prominent German social democrat Rudolf Hilferding, Ryū predicated his analysis of the financial crisis on the assumption that it revealed "changes in the relations of production." Rather than blame the specific policies of the banks and government, Ryū singled out the concentration of capital in manufacturing concerns, what he called the "dominance of industrial capital over finance capital." More specifically, Ryū underlined the importance of three structural features of the Japanese economy: namely, (1) most bank loans were tied up in large manufacturing concerns; (2) these loans were not easily recoverable; and (3) large manufacturing corporations had not sufficiently reduced and rationalized their operations following the exposure of their wartime overexpansion with the recession of 1920. Following the present crisis, Ryū predicted, the "unification of bank capital" would accelerate and large concerns would cooperate more with finance capital as they pursued their rationalization program by forming trusts and cartels.[48] This process would eventually lead to the dominance of finance capital over the economy. The masses of consumers, especially the workers, would, in turn, suffer from the artificially high prices supported by the trusts and cartels, and class conflict between the capitalist and working classes would intensify.

Ryū believed that Japanese capitalism was entering a stage of dominance by monopoly finance capital and of the establishment of trusts and cartels as preludes to the collapse of the capitalist system. His pessimistic prognosis about the fate of the capitalist system in Japan did not, however, include any specific recommendations for coping pragmatically with the bank crisis. Instead, Ryū denounced those economists who sought expedient solutions to specific problems because, "absorbed in dreams of yesteryear," they did not comprehend as "warriors of liberalism" the inevitable "deepening of class conflict."[49]

After Japan's recovery from the crisis of 1927, several developments seemed to confirm Ryū's analysis of Japan's financial situation. Ryū's prediction of a concentration of bank capital, for example, proved correct. The number of banks in Japan decreased after 1927, and the average net worth of the remaining banks increased. In 1926 the so-called "Big Five" banks—Yamada, Mitsubishi, Mitsui, Sumitomo, and Daiichi—held 19.5 percent of national loans and 24.3 percent of private deposits. By 1931 their shares had increased to 30.5 percent and 40.0 percent, respectively.[50] Ryū's forecast of the dominance of bank capital in the formation of economic policy was essentially correct. During 1928 and 1929, as economic growth remained sluggish, the leaders of the Japanese financial world, led by the president of the Bank of Japan, Inoue Junnosuke, pressed successfully for a return to the gold standard.

The proponents of reinstituting the gold standard claimed that this measure would facilitate economic growth because the stabilization of the international money market would simplify international trade and transactions for overseas investments.[51] The director of the giant Mitsubishi Bank, Yamamuro Sōbun, reasoned that a stable exchange market would allow presently idle capital in Japan to be used for the purchase of foreign bonds, until the resultant shortage in domestic currency would raise interest rates in Japan and improve investment opportunities within Japan. "The unstable exchange market," Yamamuro wrote confidently, "was a large reason for the sluggishness of business in Japan. If this cause is removed, business will pick up, and trade will prosper. If we do not lift the gold embargo, we cannot hope for the recovery of the financial world."[52] Yamamuro also hoped the measure would increase economic cooperation between the Western powers and Japan.[53] This goal complemented the general platform of the Minseitō, which favored disarmament and increased diplomatic cooperation with the West, as well as financial retrenchment. In July 1929, Hamaguchi Osaichi, the party's leader, formed a new cabinet. Embarking on a policy of budgetary and currency contraction, Finance Minister Inoue Junnosuke soon lifted the gold embargo.

In 1928, Ryū had anticipated future economic crises and more pressure on the middle class of small capitalists and salaried workers, but he in no way foresaw the economic catastrophe that accompanied the return to the gold standard in connection with the onset of the Great Depression.[54] The deflationary policy of the Hamaguchi cabinet initially succeeded in lowering domestic prices and in strengthening the value of the yen. The collapse of the world economy that was precipitated by the Wall Street crash of 1929, however, soon depressed foreign markets for Japanese goods, especially for raw silk, a crucial export commodity. Nevertheless, Finance Minister Inoue viewed the American stock market crash as a temporary phenomenon, and he continued his deflationary policy.

Although prices within Japan had dropped after the return to the gold standard, they still lagged far behind the decline in world prices, with disastrous results.[55] As Japanese exports became less competitive because of their comparatively high price, Japan's trade situation worsened. Japanese exports declined 53 percent and imports 55 percent between 1929 and 1931. Thus, many financial leaders concluded that Japan could no longer afford the gold standard, and in anticipation of the future devaluation of the yen, they used gold to purchase foreign currencies. The capital and credit market within Japan consequently shrank still further, exacerbating the economic crisis. The popular press depicted the purchase of foreign currencies by the Japanese banks as symbolic of the selfish greed of Japanese capitalists.[56] Partly for this reason, the party in power, the Minseitō, was badly beaten in the general election of 1932 because it was viewed as an ally of the banks.

Japan's villages suffered most because of the depression. Even before 1929 agricultural production had stagnated for a decade, and the standard of living for farmers had hardly improved at all.⁵⁷ In the early 1930s conditions for the farmers deteriorated even more owing to falling prices for agricultural products and poor harvests. The contraction of the agricultural consumer market—47 percent of the total work force in Japan—had a depressing effect on manufacturing industries. As industrial unemployment rose, many of the unemployed returned to their home villages and thus added to the economic burden of the countryside.⁵⁸

Despite the industrial and agricultural depression in Japan, the Hamaguchi cabinet adhered to its deflationary policies and sought to correct Japan's international balance of payments by encouraging exports. Through the creation of the Bureau for Temporary Industrial Rationalization in June 1930 and the passage of the Law for the Control of Important Industries in April 1931, the government facilitated the unification and rationalization of medium-sized enterprises in Japan in order to increase their competitiveness. The Industrial Rationalization Bureau of the Commerce Ministry invited closer links between large banks and businesses. Unused funds, though, accumulated in Japanese banks because of the lack of sound investment opportunities in the poor economy.⁵⁹ When Great Britain abandoned the gold standard in September 1931, many economists and businessmen demanded the reimposition of the gold embargo. The gold standard became the central economic and political issue of 1931, a development which had dire political consequences for the Minseitō.

Ryū Shintarō approached the question of whether Japan should abandon the gold standard in the same way that he had assessed the 1927 banking crisis. He was less concerned with specific recommendations for a better monetary system than he was with ascertaining the general historical meaning of the controversy over the gold standard.⁶⁰ Accepting the argument of European Marxist Eugen Varga that postwar capitalism throughout the world had entered a "third stage" of decline, Ryū interpreted the world depression as the entry of capitalism into its final phase of demise.⁶¹ Even Ryū, however, was surprised by what he believed was the rapid slide of capitalism, "like the setting sun," into its "third stage."⁶²

Following his earlier arguments, Ryū focused on the struggle for power between finance and industrial capital. Accordingly, he wrote that the demand for removing the gold standard and instituting a new foreign exchange rate was "only the sad cry of weak and small industrial capital," against the control of finance capital. Industrial capital, Ryū reasoned, favored the reimposition of the embargo on gold because it would make Japanese exports more competitive by lowering the value of the yen, thus aiding Japanese manufacturers. Ryū, though, would not endorse a new embargo on gold as a means of stimulating Japanese industry, because Japanese workers would probably not share in the new prosperity. Ordinary workers would not gain any advantage from an economic policy that depended on mere currency manipulations, because their wages would be repressed in order to maintain corporate profits.[63]

The plan to abandon the gold standard was, Ryū argued, "basically a self-destructive act of capital."[64] A new embargo on gold and the complete abandonment of the gold standard would shatter the capitalist monetary system because currency, unsupported by gold, would be worthless. Even if the gold standard were retained at the new parity rate set for the yen, gold would still lose its character as a standard of fixed value and would eventually cease to function as a support for currencies.

Ryū thought capitalism in Japan could not survive. Many Japanese economists, including those writing for the prestigious *Far Eastern Economic Review* (*Tōyō keizai shinpōshi*), argued that a temporary gold embargo and a lower parity for the yen in relation to gold could revive Japan's foreign trade. Ryū also accepted a reembargo on gold, but not for its predicted salutary effects on the economy.[65] He favored moving off the gold standard because he accepted Marx's argument that a currency based on gold was essential to a capitalist society. Although he was aware of the new monetary theory developed in Europe by John Maynard Keynes and others, Ryū believed that the economy could not change from a gold standard to a "paper standard" without imposing great hardship on the national economy.[66] Ryū's refusal to support the gold standard, in other words, was prompted by his conviction that its abandonment would cause severe problems in Japan's economy.

Ryū held that the value of all currency in capitalist systems ultimately depended on gold. In his view, even bank notes and promissory notes, which were examples of "credit currency," had value only because they could ultimately be exchanged for gold. Judging as worthless any currency not backed by gold, Ryū sounded like a conservative financier in disparaging economists who equated the value of a currency with a nation's economic strength. "To give a theoretical base to a paper currency standard is actually to grasp a general basis for sanctioning a policy of inflation."[67] Inflation, in turn, constituted the "boldest and greatest means of plundering from the hands of the masses through the value of currency."[68] The demand for inconvertible paper currency represented a sign of desperation by the bourgeoisie during an acute crisis "that lays bare the remarkable decline of the whole capitalist productive structure and the extreme bankruptcy of national finances."[69]

Ryū's analysis of the economic problems induced by lifting the gold embargo avoided positive policy alternatives. He concluded that the Japanese economy would crumble, no matter what policies were implemented. Ryū did not suggest how the economy could be rebuilt or how, in an ideal situation, the problems of material resources, international trade, and monetary structure could be solved. He also did not comment on the attempts of the Minseitō cabinet to reduce military spending by agreeing to limitations on naval construction at the London Naval Conference in 1930 or to increase economic cooperation with the Western powers. Instead, his analysis of the gold standard assumed that Japanese capitalism was in a hopeless position. Although abandoning the gold standard was supposed to aid Japan's trade, this act would, Ryū reasoned, cause a damaging inflation and hasten the destruction of the Japanese capitalist system.

Ryū's opinions reveal that he was as alienated from Japan's economic establishment as Rōyama was from the political establishment. Ryū believed that capitalism exploited workers for the benefit of the leaders of finance capital, by which he seemed to mean the directors of large Japanese banks. This was a common theme in Japan during the early 1930s. In 1931, two prominent financial leaders—Inoue Junnosuke and Takuma Dan—were assassinated by right-wing fanatics who viewed Japan's plutocrats as the main cause of social injustice. Large *zaibatsu* like Mitsui became so concerned about popular antipathy that they sold public stock and made large donations to charities in order to improve their public image.[70] Ryū's economic writings in widely read journals and magazines reflected and reinforced this growing mood of anticapitalism in Japan.

When the Seiyūkai came to power under Premier Inukai in December 1931, it abolished the gold standard immediately. The devaluation of the yen stimulated the recovery of Japanese exports, and Finance Minister Takahashi Korekiyo's fiscal and monetary expansion policies spurred a recovery of industrial production. Although the textile industry yielded only a moderate growth rate, the new industrial sectors of chemical, machine, and metal manufacturing expanded rapidly. Between 1930 and 1936, for example, the metal manufacturing sector expanded 434 percent, raising its share of the economy from 8.5 to 18.9 percent.[71] By 1936 these industries comprised approximately 50 percent of Japan's industrial output, and governmental policy encouraged the organization of cartels in these sectors. The growth in these areas had been sustained, in part, by ad hoc deficit financing that underwrote military expenditures after the Manchurian Incident.[72]

The inception of Takahashi's policies caused Ryū to reiterate his gloomy prediction that rapid inflation would mean more acute problems. Ryū censured the policy of issuing government bonds in order to finance expansion of military operations on the mainland: "If a real increase of the goods in circulation would cause this increase in paper currency, there would be, of course, no inflation of paper money. However, paper money, which has now expanded for procuring munitions, will still remain as a surplus beyond the goods in circulation after these munitions have disappeared into smoke on the fields of Manchuria and in the skies over Shanghai. Paper money newly printed to correct a [budget] deficit shares the same fate."[73] Although severe inflation had yet to materialize, Ryū argued that it was inevitable.

Grim references to postwar Europe reinforced Ryū's bleak outlook, as he wrote that Japan in 1932 faced the danger of hyperinflation comparable to that which Weimar Germany had experienced in the early 1920s. While granting that Germany had had special problems, particularly the burden of war reparations payments, Ryū argued that its postwar inflation was related "ultimately to the fact that Germany, under the political and economic fetters which she was forced to bear as a nation defeated in war, had lost its power to struggle against the imperialistic Western nations. . . . Such a situation does not exist in present-day Japan, but, instead, [even] worse than this, there is a deep worldwide depression based on a narrowing world market and [growing] colonial [market] areas. Japan is being given a place as a weak wing of the [Western] capitalist countries which are joining hands in this panic."[74] The pitiful condition of the German economy in 1922 had forced German industrialists to seek private capital from foreign currency markets. "Thus occurred the denationalization of Germany's means of production, the Dutch possession of German land, and the dollar domination of German industry. Finance capital and German industry have progressively come under the umbrella of international finance capital."[75] Although Ryū realized that the German economy had revived subsequently, he brooded that financial collapse awaited Japan if its government continued to pursue an inflationary policy that benefited finance capital. This collapse was necessary, though, for the rise of a new and more just economic system.

The Crisis in Thought

Miki Kiyoshi best summed up the mood of intellectuals like Rōyama and Ryū when he defined this era as being one of "anguish and crisis." In 1928, as the government conducted its first mass roundup of radical dissenters, Miki became preoccupied with the theme of crisis in Japan. By 1929 he was arguing boldly that the crisis in "thought" mirrored a conflict between economic "classes."[76] Miki believed that intellectual change was normal for any society and that a political crisis usually occurred when a new doctrine was stubbornly resisted by a ruling class that identified dissent as "dangerous thought" to be eliminated. Through these general comments Miki blamed the Japanese bourgeoisie for the suppression of the proletarian movement and indicated his feeling that this struggle was central to Japan's future. He revealed his own sympathies by stating that only an "emerging class" could understand such a crisis in a proper "dialectical framework" and create a truly new type of thought. Still, the growing divisions of Japanese society disturbed him. Miki's analysis of Japan's problems was similar to that of Rōyama and Ryū in that it complained about the fragmentation of Japanese society during the process of industrialization. Rōyama bemoaned the rise of occupational groups, while Ryū and Miki focused on the splits between economic classes. All three men lamented that narrow partisan interests, rather than a concern for the welfare of the whole society, determined governmental policies. Rōyama placed his hopes for an end to these divisions in the effects of "citizens' education," Ryū thought the collapse of capitalism might somehow yield beneficial changes, and Miki discussed the need for a new "thought" championed by a "new class." At this stage each writer was obviously still groping for a program of reform.

Unlike Rōyama or Ryū, Miki was a direct victim of the government's harsh policies of suppression. In May 1930 the police arrested him on the charge that he had contributed money to the Japan Communist party through an intermediary.[77] Miki was freed soon, but then he was tried in July and imprisoned until November. Shocked by this incident, Miki resigned all of his academic positions after his release. He avoided university affiliations and supported himself through his writings in popular monthlies; by 1935 he had begun to compose a weekly column for the *Yomiuri*, a newspaper with a large national circulation.

The arrest and the Manchurian Incident focused Miki's attention on the growing nationalistic mood in Japan and its effect on intellectual activity. Like Rōyama, Miki feared that intellectuals, as well as the masses, might lose their "balance" and abandon their role as the leaders of society. In 1933 his article "The Thought of Anguish and Overcoming It" queried: "Thus since last year has not a fairly remarkable change occurred in the spiritual condition of the intelligentsia within Japan?"[78] Miki's answer was affirmative in suggesting that "because of influences after the [Manchurian] incident, the spiritual mood that has emerged among the intelligentsia is nothing other than 'anguish.'" Miki did not give a specific example of an "anguished" Japanese intellectual, but he implied that Japanese intellectuals were becoming confused about their social and political roles. He feared that the nationalistic mood of Japan after the seizure of Manchuria would deter Japanese scholars from analyses of Japan's social problems and involvement in social issues. The Manchurian Incident raised serious issues not only of foreign policy and politics but also of class conflict, because government harassment of the proletarian movement promised to increase under the banner of national mobilization. Under this pressure, it would be too easy for Japanese intellectuals to retreat from the real problems facing their nation.

Miki drew a direct parallel between the current mood in Japan and the intellectual scene in Europe during the turbulent post-World War I era. This period was distinguished by the "literature of anguish" in France and the "philosophy of anguish" in Germany. In the philosophy of anguish, Miki explained, emotion dominated rationality: "Trust in things related to *logos* generally—intellect and reason—is lost, and it is believed that the affective life is the basis of man."[79] Sigmund Freud's stress on the *libido* as the dominant factor in man's behavior was one example of this alleged overemphasis on emotional forces that had dominated European thought during the previous decade. Miki admonished against a similar loss of rationality in Japanese thought: that is, a de-emphasis on objective analyses of social problems as embodied in Marxism.

A major fault of the philosophy of anguish, to Miki, was that as a product of introspection and isolation from the concerns of "objective society," it led to a paralysis of constructive activity for intellectuals.[80] Now less insistent on the importance of class conflict in causing crises in thought, Miki wrote that Japanese intellectuals should concentrate on solving the problem of their "anguish." Whereas he maintained that intellectual anguish was related to social anguish, he specifically rejected a Marxian strategy of revolution, asking, "Why should I sacrifice myself and act for a social revolution?"[81] Instead, Miki proposed that "philosophy should clearly, correctly, and pragmatically define a type of new human being." Japan's intellectuals should concentrate on "giving a new philosophical definition to sense or speculation, to feeling or will, or the body, or society; thus [they] must recreate and define man thoroughly in the light of philosophy."[82] That task deserved a "dialectical" solution that would stress the equal interaction of both rationality and emotion, "*logos* and *pathos*." This constituted an admission that the rational analysis of Marxism would not suffice as an ideology to solve Japan's problems. Like Rōyama, Miki was beginning to recognize the need to appeal to the emotions and loyalties of Japanese in order to influence them.

This essay revealed that Miki himself was anguished and that his own thought was changing. He explicitly renounced revolutionary Marxist strategy, but he insisted that Japanese intellectuals should remain concerned with social issues. Moreover, Miki's assertion that intellectuals could help solve social problems by creating a new philosophy and a new type of man represented a shift in his thinking because Miki no longer emphasized the need for a resolution of class conflict. This stand was probably a partial concession by Miki to increasingly strict censorship, which discouraged discussion of class struggle. Still, a desire to outline a new philosophy for Japan motivated many of Miki's writings during the next seven years. He would soon contend that only a new philosophy transcending Marxism and liberalism could help guide the government toward constructive political and economic reforms, as well as define a new role for Japan in Asia.

Rōyama agreed with Miki. Upset by government attempts to limit freedom of expression by arresting dissenters, including even moderate liberals like Professor Takigawa Yukitoki at the University of Kyōto, Rōyama contended that a confused "thought of anguish and crisis" was permeating Japan.[83] Believing that "conquering" this thought was the greatest problem for Japan, Rōyama also called for a new national ideology. Significantly, the perception of crisis in Japan inspired neither Miki nor Rōyama to overt political activity or support for a particular political party. By defining the solution to Japan's problems as the creation of a new type of education or ideology, these writers reinforced their own pride in their status as elite intellectuals because they felt they alone had both the training and impartiality to undertake this important task.

Several characteristics in the thought of Rōyama, Ryū, and Miki stand out. One is their continued fascination with Western thought and trends. Rōyama identified Japan's ills as common to all industrialized societies and used Plato to justify his new concept of the state. Relying upon the analyses of the European economy by Hilferding and Varga for his conceptual framework, Ryū compared economic trends in Japan with those in Germany. Miki defined Japan's intellectual mood through trends that he perceived in Europe.

The combination of continuity and flexibility in the ideas of these men is also striking. Rōyama's, Ryū's, and Miki's basic analyses of the strains in Japanese society remained constant from the 1920s into the 1930s, but their views of possible solutions began to change. Ryū's attitudes changed least. The debate over the gold standard and Takahashi's deficit spending drew Ryū's attention to the importance of the government's economic policies, and this interest presaged an increasing preoccupation with the economic role of the state. Still, Ryū believed in the social democratic movement.

Rōyama was more impatient, asserting, "It is natural for democracy . . . continually to adapt to the appearances and developments of an era." Observing the energetic activity of "right-wing" and "left-wing" groups, he complained that "democratic theorists" were not creating new national policies and had earned the label of "old-fashioned liberals."[84] He called for a general revival of liberalism, by which he meant its redefinition from something negative to something more positive. Liberalism could no longer focus on just the defense of individual rights: "Freedom means control, and the individual must experience a developmental change on the basis of thought that does not contradict the state."[85]

The statement that freedom means control gave the impression that Rōyama was speaking in paradoxes. This perception of freedom, though, fit a pattern that was common to fascist ideologues in Europe, who redefined freedom as existing "within the collectivity." Mussolini, for example, declared that fascism alone valued the higher spiritual and creative needs of the individual citizen who, under bourgeois liberalism, stood "by himself, self-centered, subject to natural law which instinctively urges him toward a life of selfish momentary pleasure." Il Duce explained that individualistic freedom created "abstract dummies," whereas fascism represented the "only liberty worth having, the liberty of the State and the individual within the State."[86] Rōyama was advocating a similar kind of liberty—a release from material desires and economic competition and a joy in cooperative effort on behalf of the national community. This redefinition of freedom laid the foundation for future arguments to increase state control over economic and political affairs, as well as over education.

Miki's desire to create a new type of human being revealed his lack of confidence in the gradual triumph of the proletariat. His drift away from Marxism had been evident for at least a year, ever since he had published *A Philosophy of History* (*Rekishi tetsugaku*), in which he sought to create an "anthropology of history."[87] The book disturbed Miki's former admirers because of its neglect of dialectical materialism and Miki's new fascination with the "basic experience of history" as a "reality" (*jijitsu*) that determined an individual's "historical consciousness" and thus history itself as "existence."[88] Miki now argued that historical development was a dialectical interaction between this new reality and history as existence, that man could create history while it influenced him. To many readers, Miki's new efforts had become religious in a quest for a reality separate from existence. Some critics charged that after 1930 Miki had "apostatized" his former Marxist convictions and had changed his philosophical perspective entirely. Even postwar Japanese biographers of Miki have concurred with this criticism.[89]

At the time, however, Miki vigorously rebutted charges of apostasy. His critics, he replied, had not read his works carefully. First of all, Miki insisted that his concepts of "basic experience," "anthropology," and "ideology" had remained unchanged since 1928. His definition of the basic experience of history as reality was merely a natural elaboration of his former basic concepts and "one dialectical development" in his thought.[90] Responding specifically to one of his critics, Miki affirmed his belief in the dynamic quality of thought: "If this [my philosophy of history] is apostasy, from now on, whether Mr. Honda likes it or not, I will often commit apostasy and will certainly not be ashamed." Although Miki perceived a broad continuity in his own writings, he assumed that his ideas would develop, because any system of ideas should progress dialectically by creating its own self-criticism and response. "My thought is in a process of growth. . . . The basic concepts of my thought will be redefined from now on and supplemented by new ones."[91] Miki clearly did not view previous changes in his ideas as extraordinary, and he accurately anticipated more changes in the future.

4. A Turn to the State

Responding to trends in both Japan and Europe, Rōyama, Ryū, and Miki gradually turned to the state as an agent of reform.[1] Rōyama suggested an explanation for this change when he described Ryū during the 1930s as a "great nationalist" and wrote that their generation had been deeply affected by an "emotional nationalism," despite the "influence of . . . democracy, socialism, and liberalism." Between 1931 and 1932 both Rōyama and Miki had adjusted to what they saw as an increasing nationalistic sentiment in Japan. By 1935 there were over three hundred right-wing organizations complaining about the advance of parliamentary democracy and other Western doctrines. Nationalistic groups had also scored a major victory by forcing the resignation of the distinguished law professor Minobe Tatsukichi from the University of Tokyo and the House of Peers. Minobe's crime had been arguing that the emperor of Japan was merely the highest "organ" of government instead of emphasizing the monarch's divine origins. Ignoring the emperor's own approval of Minobe's long-accepted constitutional theories, these groups forced the government to reject Minobe's views in issuing a formal statement, entitled a "Clarification of the National Polity."[2] In the mid-1930s, when the growth of nationalism seemed inevitable, intellectuals like Rōyama, Ryū, and Miki must have felt that taking advantage of this force could only increase their influence.

The growing authority of the Japanese state was also evident during the early 1930s. In response to the economic depression the state intervened more actively in the economy. The government formed cooperative associations in many villages, and it passed legislation to encourage mergers for industrial rationalization and to regulate foreign exchange transactions. The Army Ministry had completed a national network of reservist associations for young men between the ages of twenty and forty. In every hamlet these groups promoted values of patriotism and communal cooperation, while the Youth Association continued to expand its local branches with the support and guidance of the Education and Home ministries. Perhaps the most chilling example of the increased power of the state was the thought-control system. Using the authority of the Peace Preservation Law of 1925, the special police of the Home Ministry arrested thousands of radicals as "thought criminals," who were then handed over to the Justice Ministry for prosecution. The government's strategy was to induce those prisoners to recant their extremist beliefs through a carefully planned application of coercion and persuasion and to reintegrate the deviants into their communities. This program proved very effective.[3]

Nationalism as a Force for Reform

Not surprisingly, in this atmosphere many Japanese intellectuals, including Rōyama, Ryū, and Miki, began to identify the increased power of the state and of nationalistic sentiment as crucial developments. Rōyama was intrigued by the doctrines of Italian fascism because they touted the state as a force for economic and political reform. The rise to power of Mussolini and Hitler made fascism a popular topic of political commentary, as Japanese writers offered interpretations of the causes of fascism and predictions of its emergence within Japan. A comparison of Rōyama's views with those of Sassa Hiroo, a respected political critic and a former colleague in the Social Thought Association, will illustrate how positive Rōyama's approach to fascism was in a time when many intellectuals were still skeptical about it.

Sassa was then a staunch opponent of fascism because he adhered to a conventional Marxist interpretation. He regarded fascism in Japan as an attempt by monopoly capital to impose a dictatorial government for protection against impending collapse. Mussolini's Italy provided a prime example of this process. Fascism had grown in Italy, according to Sassa, because of the inability of parliamentary government to deal with social and economic problems after World War I: that is, a wave of strikes and large deficits in the government's budget. Although the fascists had first tried to appeal to workers by advocating a forty-eight-hour work week and higher corporate taxes, they had found success in 1922 only by opposing the workers' demands and playing to the fears of the capitalist middle class.

Sassa argued that in an economic crisis the middle class was the most affected "because, in an economically weak society, where social imbalance cannot be corrected, the middle class can face being shut out [of power] along with the elite of the proletariat." "This middle class, except for a few who are close to the proletariat, tend towards fascism. Italy is a good example. Fascist demagogy gathers unusual popularity, especially in a situation where mass poverty develops quickly in a deep depression."[4] Sassa warned, however, that fascist demagogy was not sincere, that fascism eventually worked to protect the interests of wealthy capitalists by controlling social reform movements.

Fascism, Sassa maintained, did not represent a scientific or valid theory of historical or social development. It was not "something supported by an objective truth or a theory born from historical experience."[5] Fascism was just an ideological fabrication to rationalize dictatorial government. Although he considered the formation of workers' organizations (the *syndicati*) as a special characteristic of Italian fascism, Sassa noted that they had no "class character" and were merely extensions of state administration. Fascism offered a "view of the nation which contained spiritualism void of content."

Sassa's appraisal of Italian fascism was more persuasive than his assertion in 1931 that fascist movements were prevalent in every nation except the Soviet Union. Even in England, the leader of the Labour party, Ramsay MacDonald, had cooperated with conservative parties in organizing a "national cabinet." Thus, the Labour party, which a decade before had inspired members of the Social Thought Association, "had come to play a reactionary role as a so-called bourgeois labor party" because MacDonald had demanded a "free hand" in national policy during the election of 1931. This demand was the "first step toward a fascist dictatorship."[6] While Sassa's fears concerning the British Labour party were misplaced, his views were fully in accord with those of the Comintern, which then regarded all parliamentary social democratic movements as fascist.

Sassa worried about the menace of Japanese fascism. "The year 1931–32 was an epoch-making period in our political history. In 1930 unprecedented financial scandals shocked public opinion. This was, however, only a prelude to the political development of fascism, which has surfaced in every aspect of the political situation in 1931."[7] The police slaughter of suspected dissenters in 1923 after the devastating Tokyo earthquake had been the first sign of Japanese fascism. The Tanaka cabinet of 1927–29 had furthered the development of fascism by brutally suppressing ideological dissent. Recent government policies were also fascist, because they aided the "rationalization of capitalism" in Japan through implementing a balanced budget and returning to the gold standard.[8]

In 1931, Sassa noted, Japanese liberal democracy had faced a grave crisis when the Hamaguchi cabinet was pressed by the conflicting demands of capitalists for fiscal retrenchment and the need for social welfare programs to aid farmers and workers. The inability of the government to enact a labor union bill that would extend legal recognition to nonpolitical activities of unions represented the failure of Japanese parliamentary democracy to reconcile the struggle between capital and labor.[9] Soon, Sassa believed, Japanese political parties would dissolve and a "transcendental dictatorial government" would arise to repress that struggle.[10]

Rōyama challenged Sassa's analysis,[11] asserting that his former classmate had not sufficiently recognized the importance of nationalism in fascism and wondering how fascism could be regarded as an international phenomenon if nationalism was a central element. Rōyama also denied the relationship between fascism and the so-called last stage of capitalism by observing that in the last ten years "fascism that developed first came from countries in which capitalism was comparatively young."[12] If mature capitalism produced fascism, it should have developed first in England. Furthermore, Rōyama pointed out, fascist Italy did not support the gold standard, the prime symbol of international capitalism, and had adopted tariffs without hesitation. "Is not the policy of fascism to cut itself off from world cooperation and to complete and protect a regional economic bloc?"[13]

In Rōyama's view, fascism was propelled by nationalism. He asserted that one of the first acts of the Italian fascist government was to expel foreign capital and that Hitler's main goal was the liberation of Germany from foreign economic oppression, from the "finance capital of the Jews."[14] The underlying purpose of fascism was to establish a "national economy" (*kokumin keizai*) free from foreign influence and to create a state as a comprehensive political unit that could not be divided into class interests.[15]

Like Sassa, Rōyama realized that fascist nationalism contained "spiritual and irrational elements." Still, this was a less grievous defect than that of communism, whose emphasis on the economic causes of fascism did "not recognize such qualitative elements from a rationalistic position."[16] The essential meaning of fascism for Rōyama was that nationalism, as an emotional force, now constituted an important factor in contemporary politics.

Because the Comintern shaped Sassa's interpretation of fascism, he criticized that doctrine and could not establish a dialogue with Rōyama. In response to Rōyama's question concerning the links between the last stage of capitalism and the rise of fascism, for example, Sassa answered that fascism had occurred in nations where capitalism was weakest primarily because capitalism needed the most protection in those countries. Even if fascist governments did not protect institutions of international finance, they did try to preserve capitalism in their countries.[17] Although Sassa repeatedly warned Rōyama about the demagogic tactics of fascism, Rōyama became increasingly enamored of the policies and ideology of Italian fascism.

By 1934, Rōyama's perception that world trends were opposing both democracy and the social democratic movement had encouraged his interest in fascism. To him, the parliamentary system had outlived its useful historical role in advancing the broad welfare of various societies throughout the world. Democracy had become the tool of class interest: "When previously the capitalist class stressed economic freedom and liberty as citizens, the human reason that supported that class opposed the authoritarian politics of the nobility and monarchical dictatorship. Now, capitalists have reached a position of protecting their profits and privileges through the parliamentary system." In Japan the ineptitude of the Diet had spawned the popularity of nationalist and communist ideologues and had fundamentally damaged "belief in the democratic system which is based on liberalism." Finally, the rise of economic nationalism as manifested in the enactment of import tariffs and the creation of regional bloc economies had revealed the weakness of social democrats by mocking their efforts to establish an international proletarian movement and to encourage world cooperation.[18] Rōyama had previously "deeply hoped and believed that the key to solving Japan's future social, economic, and political problems lay in democratic thought." Now he wrote that "not only in Japan, but generally, policies and systems based on the political ideas of democracy are in a state of crisis and almost in a condition of stalemate. . . . Thus, I cannot help investigating the parliamentary system once again and reconsidering democracy."[19]

Disturbed about his changing ideas, Rōyama blamed youthful enthusiasm for his earlier attraction to democratic socialism and dismissed charges of fickleness. His interest in socialism had not been "simple imitative thought, foreign thought, or a fad," but his fascination was part of a deep yearning for reform that most university students had shared after World War I. "It was as if people of the North, who have been shut in for a long while by ice and snow, suddenly feel the warm wind and rain, see the green grass sprouting in the earth freed of snow, and feel the inexpressible goodness of mankind. Our feelings were the same as if these people, wanting to see at once the plum, cherry, and peach blossoms come out together, did not notice the flowers' lack of delicacy, because there was no time to appreciate in detail their characteristics or elegance one by one."[20] Rōyama implied that his desire for change remained, but in the future ideas and strategies of reform would have to be more realistic.

Rejecting both liberalism and communism, Rōyama saw "nationalism" in the form of fascism as a promising ideology of reform. Unlike liberalism, which assumed that man was rational in always acting in his own self-interest, fascism, Rōyama thought, made effective use of human emotions. "Powerful social thought now . . . has adopted measures and policies adaptable to circumstances by using obedience to authority, customs, and traditions which lie in people's feelings and by supporting a new social order."[21] New ideologies of social reform would have to appeal to an individual's sense of loyalty to the nation, as well as outline a new social structure. Nationalistic doctrines, Rōyama claimed, had great potential, and fascism in Italy was the "most obvious example" of a "nationalistic ideology" that posed an alternative to social democracy.[22]

Rōyama's understanding of fascism as mobilizing nationalistic feelings derived from the writings of European ideologues like Italian Minister of Justice Alfredo Rocco. Rocco believed that the core of fascism as a "thought" or "theory" was the organic view of the nation as a historical and unified "social group" with a "life which is really its own."[23] He stressed the emotional ties that created a nation: "the unity of language, of culture, of religion, of tradition, of customs, and in general of feeling and of volition."

Rocco's writings also convinced Rōyama that fascism was innovative in stressing the welfare of the nation, as opposed to "atomistic" liberalism and socialism, which centered on the welfare of individuals. Rocco declared that fascism depended not on the principle of "society for the individual" but of "the individual for society." "For Fascism, society is the end, individuals the means, and its whole life consists in using individuals as instruments for its social ends." Thus the state had to intervene in the economy to ensure "justice among the classes." In Italy, strikes and lockouts were illegal, and special courts arbitrated disputes between management and labor. While allowing labor syndicates, the government required both workers and capitalists in every province to organize together into associations under state guidance to promote technology and efficiency and to elect political representatives to local or national assemblies. Because these bodies were called corporations, Rocco termed Italy's fascist system the "corporate state," whose goal was to create more wealth and to distribute it more evenly to improve the living standards of the working class.

Uncritically citing Mussolini's and Rocco's explications of fascist ideology, Rōyama perceived two distinct elements in Italian fascism. One was nationalism (*minzokushugi*)—the emphasis on the nation as a unit; the other was syndicalism—the organization of workers and capitalists by industry into groups controlled by the state. Syndicalism, according to Rōyama, provided fascism with its potential as a reformist ideology. "For fascism to be a dogma appropriate to modern society the real problem is by what methods can the nation—as an organic and historical concept—actually organize individuals and all social groups. Otherwise fascism will end up restorationism—a simple reactionary nationalism."[24]

Rōyama reinforced this point by reference to the assassination of Premier Inukai. The young officers who had led the attempted coup d'état on May 15, 1932, were not fascists, from Rōyama's standpoint, because they had advocated the restoration of imperial rule and had not formulated long-term plans for coping with concrete political and economic problems caused by industrialization. The young officers represented nationalism without a coherent ideology; they were restorationist, not reformist. "Therefore, if this restorationist thought is to progress to the reform of present political administrative bodies and economic structures, it must realize the union of new social elements, such as organs of finance capital, organs of big, medium, and small businesses and industries, of industrial workers' unions, and farmers' cooperative unions—all of which capitalism has produced. In particular, it must solve the difficult question of how the spirit of restoration can grasp the complicated mechanisms of transportation, distribution, and the structure of production, which is based on modern science and technology."[25] Referring to the Meiji Restoration as an example of progressive social change toward the development of capitalism under a nationalistic rubric, Rōyama anticipated a similar momentous change beyond capitalism through a "Shōwa renovation" (*Shōwa kōshin*).[26]

Yet some aspects of Rōyama's views on economic reform remained basically consistent with his previous writings. He still argued for a socialistic and functional economic structure to replace capitalism, and he openly advocated authoritarian government. "Now there is one thing that party politics have lacked until today—the quality of resolution and strength in political activity," and one of the most flagrant examples of this fault was the inability of the government to control the aggression of the Kwantung Army in Manchuria.[27]

Japan could no longer afford the bickering and shortsighted tactics of party politics. "Public opinion is united on one point, namely the necessity for a strong government." Comparing the coalition cabinet in Britain headed by Ramsay MacDonald and the nonpartisan cabinet of Saitō Makoto in Japan, Rōyama reflected that "there has emerged the idea that rather than worship the special nature of party politics, [leaders] must satisfy the general demands of politics."[28] He did not feel that Japan had yet reached the desperate stage where it needed an overtly dictatorial "one-party" fascist system. Still, he speculated that the "transcendental cabinet" of Admiral Saitō was a "transitional and provisional" stage in political development. Toward what, Rōyama neglected to say, but he hoped for a reform-oriented and strong government.

Three factors conditioned Rōyama's generally sympathetic treatment of Italian fascist doctrines: his desire to accomplish basic reforms in Japan, his willingness to adapt to new trends, and his attraction to the use of state power. Despite Sassa Hiroo's admonishments about his being duped by fascist propaganda, Rōyama was impressed by the potency of nationalism as a political force and by fascism's rejection of parliamentary parties and of an unfettered free-market economy. Sassa attempted to expose nationalistic sentiment as a weapon of the capitalist class; Rōyama was more opportunistic, seeking to harness the force of nationalism to work for basic political reforms. He advocated using state power to achieve reforms and argued that the state should educate a new "citizen" and that the state should become the focus of an individual's loyalties. Soon, Rōyama began to outline what specific political reforms the state could achieve.

Rōyama defined his political position as "social progressivism" (*shakai shimpōshugi*). He advocated gradual reforms to adjust "political forms" to new social conditions with the aim of "not denying the basic principles which the parliamentary system implies, but to reform the faults, distortions, and nondevelopment of these principles."[29] Fearing a bitter conflict between the fervent advocates of nationalism and the left-wing supporters of "proletarian universalism," Rōyama sought a compromise between the two political camps.[30]

This difficult task was eased by Rōyama's reliance on the concept of *form*, which had been set forth by Miki Kiyoshi in his discussion of dialectical materialism. Rōyama could therefore describe liberalism as a "historical form" that had arisen in the nineteenth-century era of laissez-faire capitalism, but was now obsolete because the economic system was changing.[31] "Fascism" too became a type of form, a "special form of the 'corporate state' " made up of the "merger of syndicalism and nationalism."[32] Form gave greater flexibility to Rōyama's thought by permitting him to argue that certain forms of political and economic ideologies were appropriate to certain eras or circumstances without attempting to ascribe ultimate values to any one ideology.

In Rōyama's analysis of modern social thought, fascism and liberalism, as well as Marxism, were merely varieties of form which responded to the needs of certain eras and circumstances. He evaluated the Italian system of syndicates and corporations in a comparative survey of national "economic councils" in industrialized nations and argued that the structure of fascism in Italy was adjusting to the need for economic planning in industrial societies. Even in democratic countries, consultative economic councils that included representatives of industry and labor had formed because "parliamentary systems in democratic countries have revealed their faults due to the development of modern industry."[33] In contrast to the economic councils in parliamentary systems, in Italy the Central Council of Corporations had assumed after 1930 the task of discussing comprehensive plans for the economic development of the nation. The central council was aided in this function by the provincial councils of corporative economy, but did not have the authority to enforce economic plans, as did Gosplan in the Soviet Union. Approving of the progress that the fascists had made toward a planned economy, Rōyama wrote that fascist Italy stood "between socialism and democracy."[34]

Rōyama thought that the Japanese government should also establish an economic council to represent new economic interest groups. He pointed out, as he had in 1921, that capitalist organizations and trade unions were developing and deserved recognition. The growth of these economic bodies now constituted the most important problem for the political parties.[35] The creation of an economic council as a vital advisory body to the Japanese cabinet would aid in restoring the latter's authority because the council could provide extraparliamentary support from both unions and business groups. He also believed that an independent body unconnected with the parties should supervise the government's economic policies.[36] The adoption of comprehensive economic planning was inevitable.

Many of Rōyama's specific proposals for feasible and immediate reforms aimed at reducing piecemeal the power of the established political parties, what he called "authoritarianism" because of the parties' interference in governmental administration and their control over individual Diet members.[37] Explicitly rejecting Yoshino Sakuzō's advocacy of party cabinets, Rōyama viewed the "irresponsible dictatorial trend" of party cabinets as the Diet's major weakness. The banes of party politics were pointless rivalry and corruption. To lessen conflict between the two main parties, he recommended that the speaker of the lower house be an independent and have more authority to mediate party disputes. The speaker should chair a stronger "discipline committee," which could punish Diet members harshly for "misconduct": that is, electoral corruption caused by the "increasing severity of party struggles." Anticipating party penetration of the conservative House of Peers, Rōyama suggested allowing some members of that body to be elected on the basis of occupational representation.[38]

The Diet's failure to grasp more administrative authority must have disappointed him because a decade earlier he had observed that in Europe a powerful elected assembly could spur the process of governmental centralization and functionalization. He favored reforms to spur similar developments in Japan by making the Diet more efficient and influential.[39] Diet sessions should extend beyond the current three-month standard; special standing committees should deal with increasingly complex matters of policy; and the Diet should have more power, including the power to ratify foreign treaties—then the responsibility of the Privy Council. Nonetheless, Rōyama began to wonder whether the state bureaucracy might have to seize the initiative regardless of the Diet's situation.

Rōyama did not expect the Diet to produce a strong movement for reform, despite the existence of "reform-minded parties." He remarked that in the bureaucracy the "functions of administrative offices which are being established with large organizations and budgets are more important" and hinted that the executive branch should initiate change: "As for the self-awareness [of officials], if they are relatively serious men, both the tumult of the times and the confusion of thought will be an inspiration and a spur to progress."[40] As Rōyama's interest in economic planning revealed, he viewed the central government as an ally in the movement for economic and political reform in Japanese society. This conviction and a new view of the role of intellectuals in politics soon led him to try to influence national policies directly.

While Rōyama pondered directions and strategies of political reform, he wondered what role Japanese intellectuals could play. Previously, he had emphasized the contribution of intellectuals allied to a proletarian party movement. Now, he argued, the greatest political strength of intellectuals stemmed from their detachment from the concerns of ordinary life and specifically from a commitment to economic interest groups. The masses tended toward extremism and prejudice, but the intellectuals "had no reason or impetus to introduce directly into politics the life activity relating to their profession."[41] Therefore, only intellectuals could act as impartial "observers" (bōkanjin) over national politics.

Rōyama did not explain how he developed this perception of the role of intellectuals or how they would gain political influence. Significantly, his ideas fit Alfredo Rocco's preference for government by an elite, by persons who could persistently rise above self-interest and consider national interests because of the "intuitiveness of rare great minds, their traditionalism and their inherited qualities."[42] In order to influence national policies, however, Rōyama, like Ryū and Miki, a detached intellectual without a power base, would have no choice but to accommodate his ideas to the main thrust of government policies implemented by those whom he wished to impress.

The Quest for a New National Ideology

As Rōyama struggled to combine the emotions of nationalism with ideas of reform, Miki Kiyoshi continued his efforts to create a new philosophy to solve Japan's "crisis." During the spring of 1935 he called for a "new liberalism" in Japan. The vilification of Minobe Tatsukichi's "organ theory" of the Meiji Constitution prompted Miki's plea. He noted that because of the incident, a "reexamination of liberalism has been occurring," and he reflected "that liberalism is powerless and must decline seems to be the general opinion."[43]

Miki strongly defended intellectual freedom and stipulated that because the masses showed fascistic tendencies, a new liberalism must be the product of an intellectual class that would be defined not by its economic position but by its intellectual activity. Complete critical freedom for this class was essential. "Freedom must be recognized for promoting fully the function of human cultural and intellectual activity; this is necessary for the development of history and the realization of its meaning."[44] Like Rōyama, Miki saw disinterested intellectuals playing a crucial role in guiding the future of Japanese politics.

Miki's strong dedication to freedom for the intellectual class, rather than for the masses, did not lead to a defense of the parliamentary system in Japan. He stated clearly that a new liberalism should replace the old "liberalism of the bourgeoisie" and become completely different from any previous political or social ideology. Nor did Miki rally to the defense of the principle of individual freedom. The new liberals would be "humanists," but unlike Western humanists, they would be "opposed to the rationalism, the individualism, even the human-centered-ism of previous humanists."[45] The new humanism would focus not on the activity and welfare of the individual but on that of society as a whole. Accordingly, he specified that the new liberalism would not be bound by "social definition"—the interests of one economic class, such as the bourgeoisie or the proletariat. The new liberalism would transcend economic classes, and unlike Marxism, the new ideology would be free to "negate itself," to change freely. Miki thus hoped that a new ideology could avoid class conflict and mused that as left-wing thought and right-wing thought clashed and negated the old liberalism of parliamentary democracy, the new liberalism would emerge as a "negation of a negation."[46] Miki was clearly heading toward a redefinition of liberalism and freedom similar to that already advocated by Rōyama—a freedom based on the primacy of the welfare of the whole society.

These views represented some important developments in Miki's thought. He started to fulfill his own injunction that academic intellectuals should become involved in controversial issues by commenting on contemporary political problems. Miki had also reached a position where he was ready to make the nation a focus of his new philosophy for Japan because he asserted that neither the individual nor an economic class could serve that purpose. Only the society as a whole could stand above the competing interests of economic classes. Like Rōyama, Miki tried to merge the sentiment of loyalty to the nation with rational plans for social and political reforms. This effort would culminate four years later in his philosophy of cooperativism.

Miki's concern for the Japanese nation first appeared in his discussion of Japan's policies in China.[47] In 1935, as the Kwantung Army set up puppet governments in North China, Miki wrote that recent incidents there worried him. Japan could not rely on force alone in China, because constant military expansion would cause Japan to become "oppressed by her own burden" of maintaining troops. In view of the need for a Sino-Japanese cooperative defense against Soviet infiltration, he presented another tactic: The only way to prevent the revival of reactionary Confucianism or the spread of revolutionary Marxism was to create a new inspiring ideology. "Now," Miki asked, "with what [new] powerful thought can Japan help China and unite with her for defense against communism?" The feeling of a unique Japanese spirit had little meaning for the Chinese people and was inadequate as a principle for achieving "coexistence and prosperity"; only a new universal ideology could inspire the Chinese in place of Marxism. As Rōyama had suggested several years before, Miki now believed that Japan should create an "Oriental thought" to guide the future of Asia.

Acknowledging Spengler's argument that the West was declining, Miki cautioned that the Soviet Union was a new power and that there was little proof, at least as reflected in ideology, that the East was "rising" in place of the West. "If [the term] 'Japanese' is to become a word revealing one new age in the history of world culture," Miki queried, "what will be an appropriate universal idea in Japanese culture? If we do not present such a universal idea, we cannot extend a dominance of thought over China." The basic struggle in China was one of ideas and culture. He believed if Japanese intellectuals could point the way to a new dawn in world history arising in a united Orient, the bloodshed in China would end, and Japan and China would live in coprosperity. In 1939, in the middle of a protracted war in China, he stated that the conflict was a test of Japanese culture. In order to win, Japan had to triumph in the "battle of cultures." Miki then revealed his view of Asian cultural unity in asserting that although the cultures of Japan and China had to "join hands," one culture had to lead the other.[48]

In 1935, Miki's ideas blended smoothly with the newly professed goals of the Imperial Army on the continent. Concerned with the Soviet Union's armament program and with rising anti-Japanese sentiment in China, the military began to emphasize the need for increased control there, both in the occupation of more territory and in increased cultural and economic influence. Officers of both the China Expeditionary Force and the Kwantung Army declared the need to add the five provinces of North China to the "Japan-Manchuria Bloc." The Army Ministry concluded: "We cannot permit China to transcend Japan's sphere of influence morally or economically; we ourselves must progress to the cooperation of Japan, Manchuria, and China."[49] Miki did not deny the concept of an Asian cooperative bloc, but he preferred to achieve it through intellectual ingenuity rather than military force.

The State and Economic Reform

Just as Rōyama and Miki promoted the establishment of a new political ideology, Ryū Shintarō cautiously began to envision the state as a potentially powerful agent of economic reform. The poor showing of the proletarian parties convinced him that the state was the only force capable of challenging the capitalist system, and the increasingly frequent attempts of the state to regulate the economy indicated that the government would become more powerful. Ryū opposed current policies of the government because he thought they benefited the capitalist class, but this analysis led him to a tentative awareness that stricter state controls could modify Japanese capitalism on behalf of the national welfare.

By 1933, Ryū's critique of the established economic order had made him a respected commentator on contemporary economic issues. He sharply criticized the most popular and eminent economists who wrote for the widely read "opinion magazines" like *Chūō kōron* and *Kaizō*, he berated non-Marxist economists of the classical or Keynesian persuasion, and he put forward anticapitalist views and a sense of national crisis that were very much in accord with the views being cultivated by the military during the early 1930s. Indeed, persistent warnings about the impending self-destruction of Japanese capitalism were part of the popular polemic against capitalism set forth by the armed forces and many nationalistic organizations. This polemic did not abate, despite the impressive results of the government's inflationary economic policy.

The sharp increase in industrial production and the growth in Japan's export trade that occurred under the leadership of Finance Minister Takahashi Korekiyo finally gained Ryū's attention in 1934. Now Ryū insisted that the economy would improve with even more state control. As before, he claimed that the recent increase in production was a temporary phenomenon that had not eliminated the ominous features of the Japanese economy. The formation of cartels and trusts represented a "concentration of monopoly capital in the continuing process of the depression," and the merging of large companies into trusts symbolized the development of "national monopoly capitalism" and the "fusion of national power and finance capital."[50] The Japanese government, Ryū conceded, had encouraged the formation of cartels through the 1931 Industrial Control Law, which had the noble intent of promoting cooperation among firms in each industry in order to control production and stabilize consumer prices. The increased profits of companies in cartels, however, only revealed the inability of the cartels to curb the selfish greed of the member companies. In other words, Ryū reasoned, these companies were using cartels to inflate prices and stricter forms of governmental control were necessary to limit the power of monopoly capital.

Monopoly capital remained the basic source of all economic evils in Japan because it sought to escape from the economic depression by a needless expansion of production. "Monopoly capital lost hope of overcoming the endless and enormous difficulties of the world depression and chronic overproduction by using its best tool, namely, limitation of production. Here, monopoly capital made a great change in policy for escaping the depression. This was expansion of production."[51] This decision to expand production, according to Ryū, had caused two dangerous developments—export dumping and inflation.

Citing Marx, Ryū argued that the cycle of economic reproduction demanded that commodities at the end of the production cycle in the capitalist system be transformed into money, which could then be used as investment in a new production process.[52] Because of the devaluation of the yen, Japanese exports were being sold so cheaply that they were earning no foreign exchange and were disrupting the capitalist reproduction cycle. "When the free portion [the discount on goods] reaches the amount of surplus value of these [export] goods, their production will contribute nothing to the expansion of the reproductive process in this country. When the discount exceeds the surplus value, its effect will be negative."[53]

Ryū derived no comfort from Japan's increased exports. He also belittled the prosperity and profits of the domestic munitions industries, which he attributed to the infusion of inconvertible paper currency into the economy by the issuing of government bonds to fund military expenditures. Ryū criticized both the printing of paper money not backed by gold and its use in stimulating the production of munitions that would not generate new capital. Because money used for armaments did not enter into the economic reproductive process, it was "annulled in value,"[54] worthless currency that would only stimulate inflation. Pessimistic about other aspects of the Japanese economy, he interpreted the growth of bank deposits in 1933 as indicating the lack of demand for funds in the private sector and saw only one outlet for finance capital in Japan—continued investment in government bonds and expansion of munitions industries.

Ryū was certain that Japanese business would capitalize on the international tensions that encouraged rearmament. "The plan of finance capitalism . . . is clear. The capitalists who control credit did not ignite the spark of inflation just because of events like the dollar-buying incident. They wanted to direct inflation towards their own goals. Was not great inflation in munitions and heavy industry the most direct means for stimulating the industrial sectors under their dominance?"[55] The question was rhetorical. Monopoly capital had destroyed the "self-control of the reproductive cycle" by promoting munitions production. This policy, in turn, had implanted the seeds of a dangerous inflation.

The mild inflation of the early 1930s worried Ryū because of its long-term effects.[56] Although the recovery of Japanese industry had substantially increased employment for Japanese workers, inflation would chip away at the real value of their wages, and additional inflation would erode the value of fixed capital investments. Finance capitalists would then attempt belatedly to curb inflation in order to protect their investments, even if this action meant limits on government bonds and armaments production. Inflation, however, would be so serious that "putting on the brakes" would not work.[57] Japan would suffer an economic collapse comparable to that which Germany had experienced during the early 1920s, and the only way to ward off this calamity was to stop inflation.

Ryū was convinced that the government's monetary and credit policies would not resolve the menace of inflation. His critique rested on a refusal to concede any credibility to Japanese advocates of Keynesian economics, who argued that the country's economic problems could be resolved by a form of state intervention in the economy that neither challenged the principle of private property nor limited private profits. Encouraged by the new Foreign Exchange Law of 1933, these economists were calling for a "managed economy" (*tōsei keizai*) in which the central government would actively use monetary and fiscal policies, such as regulating currency exchange rates and deficit financing, to stimulate economic growth. Ishibashi Tanzan, the editor of the *Far Eastern Economic Review*, was especially optimistic about the chances for economic recovery through the adoption of such policies.[58]

The concept of a managed economy was quite distinct from the socialist concept of a planned economy, in which the state formulates comprehensive economic plans concerning the distribution of raw materials, sets the goals for production in various industrial sectors, and controls the prices of all goods. Ryū found the Keynesian notion of a managed economy deficient in two respects: It did not contain basic reforms of the capitalist structure of the Japanese economy, and it did not devise a means to control monopoly capital. "In short, the present journalistic meaning of a 'managed economy' is an attempt to view the bright future of capital and the revival and development of capital without noticing the crisis of capital and capitalism, which are in the throes of a world depression."[59] He criticized the idea of a managed economy based on the regulation of foreign exchange and domestic currency in three ways.

First, a managed currency divorced from the gold standard would only create rampant inflation. Because the Japanese and British experiences provided little support for this position, Ryū used as proof of this contention the inability of currency controls in the American economy to overcome the effects of the depression. Japan would emulate the American experience because Japanese capitalism was hampered by "special weaknesses"—an agricultural depression, a lack of natural resources, an unfavorable balance of payments, a narrow domestic market, and a heavy burden of military expenditures.[60]

Second, Ryū assumed that the special weaknesses of the Japanese economy required drastic solutions. The Bank of Japan had legal control over important fiscal and monetary policies through the "open market operation" in which the Bank of Japan bought government bonds and then sold them to private banks. In theory, the Bank of Japan could control the amount of currency available to private banks for investment purposes. In reality, finance or monopoly capital controlled the Bank of Japan because monopoly capital wanted to buy government bonds in order to use up its surplus capital. As evidence, Ryū offered the increasingly short repayment periods for national bonds. Short terms were advantageous to finance capital because they guaranteed frequent renewals of bonds.[61] Only a basic alteration in Japan's economic structure could, in Ryū's estimation, produce a system of economic control that could effectively curb the power of monopoly capitalism.

Third, exchange and currency regulations would damage international trade. Exchange regulation could stabilize the international exchange rate of the yen only if strict controls were imposed on foreign imports and the export of capital from Japan. Unilateral import restrictions would prove contagious, and the consequent multilateral trade restrictions would soon cause a further contraction of world trade and deepen the depression. Exchange controls would lead to economic ruin, invite more state control over foreign trade, and eventually lead to the creation of a bloc economy in East Asia. It was inevitable that finance capital would "with fascistic boldness" support the implementation of exchange controls and demand new markets and a self-sufficient regional economy.[62]

Ryū's critique of a managed currency rested on two axioms. He accepted Marx's theory of the reproductive cycle and regarded any policy that did not propose a basic structural reform of Japanese capitalism as a palliative that would fail. He also assumed that "monopoly capitalism," not the Japanese military, was responsible for the expansion of armaments production. His analysis of the policies of credit and currency control, which regarded finance capital as the leader and representative of the capitalist system in Japan, ignored the Japanese army.

In 1931, Ryū saw Japanese capitalism as the "weak wing" of Western capitalism, and he pointed to the inflation experienced by Weimar Germany as an example of the fate awaiting Japan. Ryū repeated these admonitions in 1934, again declaring that monopoly capitalism had already initiated a policy of expansion of production that would produce a ruinous inflation. At this time, Ryū neglected the innovative economic policies of Nazi Germany as an alternative frame of reference to Weimar Germany. His writings, however, mirrored a growing interest in the role of the state, especially its potential to harness and control monopoly capital. His dislike of the managed economy rested on its ineffectiveness, not on an a priori aversion to a state-managed economy.

Ryū's accent on the possibility of state control paralleled his disenchantment with the proletarian party movement in Japan, as seen in his forewords to the *Japan Labor Yearbook*. He bemoaned the plague of factionalism in the labor movement, pronounced his dismay over the rise of the Japanese National Socialist party (Kokka shakaitō), and equated the "rise of nationalism" (*kokkashugi no taitō*) with the development of fascism in Japan. In particular, he traced the trend toward national socialism to developments within the proletarian movement and to a general reaction against the *zaibatsu* spurred by the agricultural crisis. In not applying the standard Marxist definition, which regarded fascism as a defensive reaction of monopoly capitalism against its inevitable collapse, he evaluated Japanese fascism as a proletarian and agrarian movement opposed to monopoly capitalism. His definition of fascism did not include consideration of the army or the growth of radicalism within the military.[63]

Ryū's definition of proletarian nationalist movements as fascist rested on his unwillingness to identify the Japanese state completely with monopoly capitalism. In his opinion, the government had been extremely successful in promoting a "feeling of crisis" (*hijōji ishiki*) and a "patriotic atmosphere" among the Japanese people. Because Japanese workers, too, were now enthusiastic about the idea of "national service," new possibilities appeared for the Japanese "to grasp the special character of this country and this era." In restructuring his own perception of Japan's political and economic situation, Ryū hinted at a basic change in his own attitudes toward the challenges facing Japan. "One must finally recognize that the progress of [national] crises not only has brought about aggressive attacks by the dominating classes against the workers, but it has also opened gaps in the political domain of the national control of the dominant classes. Thus, the complete dominance of capitalists over the weak workers and farmers has itself brought about a situation that cannot escape criticism. Japan's labor and agricultural problems are now connected to considerations of the structure of the nation [*kokka kikō*] beyond the conflict of pure capital and labor, and have opened up complex and multifaceted possibilities."[64]

Like Rōyama, Ryū respected the power of nationalistic feelings in Japan and regarded the "structure of the nation"—the policies of the national bureaucracy—as a more important issue than the struggle between labor and capital. No longer identifying the state with monopoly capitalism, he suggested that the state could act as a force for reform in Japan. The problem was how to use the power of the state to bring about political and economic reforms that would solve the dilemmas of Japanese capitalism.

His disenchantment with the social democratic movement in Japan dovetailed with a gloomy assessment of the social democratic movement in Europe. For example, the British Labour party in 1932 had rejected a resolution to conduct a general strike automatically if a European war erupted. This was sufficient evidence to prove that the British Labour party itself doubted whether other European social democratic parties would cooperate in a general strike against war. Ryū was also disheartened by the Soviet Union. It had dampened the activities of the Comintern in the present world crisis; it had joined the League of Nations; and it had "joined hands" with America and France to oppose Germany. In Ryū's perspective, the Soviet Union had abandoned the goal of leading a world revolution and was concentrating on the lesser goal of "one-nation socialism."[65]

Ryū complained that communist and social democratic parties in the European nations were forsaking international socialism for domestic struggles against nationalistic fascist movements. Although he depicted the reactions of European socialists and communists to the rise of Nazi Germany as a betrayal of the international social democratic movement, he did not assess the meaning or significance of German and Italian fascism. He merely concluded that 1934 "was a year in which the world, which had recovered from the economic depression, tried to change course into a 'political' depression."

Events in his own country supported Ryū's conviction that Japan's social democratic movement had also crossed the new threshold of a "political depression." In October 1934 the Army Ministry published "The Basic Principles of National Defense and Proposals to Strengthen It." This pamphlet urged national mobilization to prepare for a war in the future, and it denounced the "ideas of liberalism, individualism, and internationalism, which neglect the nation." The pamphlet called for a "basic reconstruction in public finances, the economy, foreign relations, political strategy, and the education of the people, to organize and control the great potential spiritual and physical energy of the imperial nation for the sake of national defense and to administer it in a unified manner."[66] The army's national defense program was less surprising than the reaction of the largest proletarian party in Japan, the Social Mass party, led by Kamei Kanichirō and Aso Hisashi, which endorsed the army's goals. Ryū thought that the pamphlet and the reaction it provoked were the "most important signs for divining social trends in Japan."[67]

Ryū interpreted the beginning of the "united front" strategy in Europe, which later became official Comintern policy in the summer of 1935, as the end of international cooperation among socialist parties on behalf of world peace. Similarly, he interpreted the decision of leading Japanese socialists to cooperate with the military as allying the social democratic movement with a force considered fascist by European socialists and as altering the movement in a basic way. He explained this crucial change:

> The Social Mass party now seems to stand above the contradictions [of espousing both peace and national defense]. This is a [tactical] "necessity" and it is not an earth-shaking change for Japanese social democracy. We will not argue whether [this condition] depends on the special historical and economic character of the Japanese army or on the special nature of Japanese social democracy. We cannot, however, ignore the fact that a distinct social force has been newly formed. This is very different from the attitudes that European social democratic parties have taken in their antifascist movements. We will not discuss here which historical and social conditions are causing these special Japanese developments. Also, we cannot judge whether these trends will lead to fascist control or social control [by the masses]. (Moreover, all problems center on this point. Regretfully, I cannot agree with Mr. Kamei's extreme optimism as leader of the Social Mass party on this important "issue.") At any rate, the form and shape of the "international" character of the labor movement within Japan has disappeared.[68]

By 1935, Ryū was stressing what many Japanese socialists had already realized: The Japanese military was a new political force and the authority of the state would become increasingly important in economic affairs. The important question was whether the state and the army would be able to impose a radical restructuring of Japanese capitalism.

The social fragmentation and strife caused by the process of industrialization in Japan continued to motivate Rōyama's, Ryū's and Miki's desires for political and economic reforms. Meanwhile, governmental policies revealed the growing power of the state, as popular enthusiasm for the seizure of Manchuria and the popular indifference toward the fate of Professor Minobe indicated the spread of nationalist sentiment. The nondoctrinaire quality of the thought of Rōyama, Ryū, and Miki gave them the flexibility to adjust to these new circumstances, and their tendency to stress the needs of the whole society over the principle of individual rights enabled them to accept the subjugation of the individual to the state for the purpose of promoting the general welfare.

The growing political and economic influence of the military troubled them less than the structural problems of Japan's politics and economics. Far from being alarmed by the assassination of Premier Inukai, Rōyama chided the rebels for not having a rational program of reform. Ryū thought that finance capital was responsible for Japan's military buildup. All three writers focused on the unfolding of a new historical era in which the entire political and economic structure would change. The demise of social democracy and the rise of fascism in Europe indicated the course of future developments.

Rōyama, Ryū, and Miki saw a corporatist state, which could recognize and reconcile the interests of diverse economic interests,[69] as inevitable in Japan. They could wait no longer for a gradual evolution of this state because they believed finance capital dominated the Diet and would not permit any challenges to its authority from mass political movements. They would come to believe that the intervention of an impartial state bureaucracy would hasten the creation of a governmental structure to provide equal representation to all major economic groups. The strategy of Rōyama, Ryū, and Miki for the rest of the decade would be to direct the power of the state and the force of nationalism toward their long-term goal of building a new Japan.

At the same time, Rōyama's argument that intellectuals alone could improve Japanese politics and Miki's statement that only a "class" of intellectuals could create a new ideology for Japan reflected these writers' growing belief in their special mission, as well as their aspirations for influence. Their new tactic was to avoid an alliance with one economic class, such as the proletariat. Instead, they would stand above partisan interests and formulate national policy for the welfare of all citizens. During the next five years, Rōyama, Ryū and Miki would strive to fulfill that expectation.

5. Confronting Fascism and Nationalism

As fascism grew stronger in Europe, the policies of Hitler and Mussolini attracted the attention of many Japanese writers. Within Japan, the rise of nationalistic sentiment was obvious in the controversy surrounding Professor Minobe's "organ theory." In 1936 fifteen hundred troops from the army's First Division in Tokyo mutinied against the government and seized the center of the city. Inspired by the writings of Kita Ikki, these rebels sought an end to parliamentary government and the institution of unimpeded imperial rule. They assassinated Finance Minister Takahashi and former premier Saitō; Admiral Okada, the current premier, barely managed to escape. Although the coup d'état failed, the political influence of the army increased substantially in the months that followed. In this setting, Rōyama, Ryū, and Miki attempted to define the rise of fascism and nationalism as portents of a radical restructuring of Japan's economic and political systems.

The drama of major political events has focused the attention of many Japanese and American historians on reactionary Japanese nationalists who, during the 1930s, advocated the reform of Japanese capitalism and the end of parliamentary democracy as part of a return to traditional values and to a mythical period of direct imperial rule. Rōyama, Ryū, and Miki charted a new course that would utilize the force of nationalism to accomplish economic planning, occupational representation, and a new "totalitarianism."

Toward a Planned Economy

After 1935, in a major shift in his career, Ryū became increasingly involved in making recommendations for national economic policy. At the request of editor in chief Ogata Taketora, Ryū abandoned his promising scholarly career at the Ohara Institute to join the editorial staff of the *Asahi* newspaper in Tokyo, a plunge into what he called the "real world" where he could "try some concrete activity."[1]

The concrete activity was influencing national policy. Although some Marxist scholars, like Tosaka Jun, severely criticized large modern newspaper companies as "weapons of the bourgeoisie," Ryū was attracted to the prestige of the *Asahi* and to its large audience of perhaps three million readers.[2] Many writers recognized the influence of newspapers with a national circulation; Rōyama believed "an important national policy cannot be pursued if there is no support or approval from popular opinion. This, however, relies mostly on propaganda that journalism creates and guides."[3] Although Ryū would later discount many aspects of his journalistic writings with the observation that police pressure had inhibited his freedom of expression,[4] this constraint was already evident when he entered the *Asahi*. Joining the paper provided an opportunity to mobilize popular opinion in favor of national policies to restructure the economic system.

Ryū's writings before 1935 had made frequent comparisons between Weimar Germany and Japan. After that time, Ryū, along with many Japanese intellectuals, demonstrated an increased attraction to the economic policies of Nazi Germany. Many of the problems experienced by that government in instituting a state-directed economy were not apparent to Ryū, but the rapid increases in Germany's industrial output and employment were obvious.[5]

Ryū's views also meshed with the new trends of Japanese politics following the 1936 rebellion. Once the mutiny had ended, Hirota Kōki's cabinet actively pursued a "renovationist" policy that tried to wrest political power from the Diet and to introduce economic reforms to increase state control over the economy. In August the cabinet formulated an ambitious national defense policy that entailed building an enlarged navy for further expansion into the Pacific and an enlarged army for the consolidation of Japan's position in Manchuria and North China. Ultimately, Hirota's program envisioned the removal of the Western preserve in China and the realization of the "principle of coprosperity" in East Asia.[6] The cabinet agreed that more state economic planning was necessary for Japan to achieve those goals. In accordance with those policies, Finance Minister Baba Eiichi prepared an expanded budget for 1937 predicated upon a huge increase in military expenditures, which was to be financed through the issuance of government bonds.

When the cabinet of General Hayashi Senjurō assumed office in January 1937, it chose to continue the basic policies set by the Hirota cabinet through the spring of 1937. After the Diet had balked at passing the Baba budget in full, Hayashi's finance minister, Yūki Toyotarō, reduced it to an acceptable size by slashing expenditures for public welfare.[7] As part of the mobilization of the economy for war, the Hayashi cabinet also created the Cabinet Planning Bureau (Kikakuchō), which was charged with designing comprehensive plans for the development of the national economy. For the next year the Army Ministry's five-year economic plan, which promoted ambitious increases in industrial expansion and extensive government supervision of new investments, became a central issue in discussions of economic policy.

At this juncture, Ryū published a critique of current government policies, *The Quasi-Wartime Controlled Economy*. This was Ryū's first effort to explain his ideas in book form to a mass audience.[8] It also reflected his efforts to assess the significance of Nazi economic measures and to devise a strategy for coping with the growing political power of the army and its demands for new economic policies. The main arguments of Ryū's book were divided into two categories. One reflected the basic tenets of Ryū's earlier economic analyses —primarily the danger of ruinous inflation exacerbated by deficit spending for munitions and the evils of the economic control by monopoly capitalism. The other was a discussion of specific issues—the policies of finance ministers Baba and Yūki, the economic role of the army, the proposed electric power control law, and the need for a planned economy.

In Ryū's opinion, the advent of the Konoe cabinet in June 1937 presented an opportunity for reflection on the government's economic policies.[9] As before, this insistence on the need to "stop and reflect" implied the need for radical changes in the economic structure. Finance ministers Baba and Yūki had not been able to solve Japan's basic economic problems of inflation and low productivity.

Acknowledging that both men had mouthed the slogans of national control and planning for economic renovation, Ryū doubted whether Baba and Yūki had significantly changed Japan's economic policies.[10] Baba, he asserted, had merely bowed to the desires of the military by proposing an increased budget. Moreover, although the government would assume the administration of railroads and arsenals under Baba's vision of "national control," the government would not attempt to break the power of monopoly capital in Japanese industry as a whole.[11] Yūki's policies reflected the desires of Japan's financial leaders, such as Ikeda Seihin (the director of the Mitsui combine and the president of the Bank of Japan in 1937), to extend their control over munitions industries. Touting the "expansion of productive power" through increased investment, Yūki had tried to revise the bylaws of the Bank of Japan to allow direct loans to industries. Although this attempt had failed, Ryū noted that the bank was now supporting credit issued by the government's Industrial Bank. Yūki wanted to reduce deficit spending and the issuance of government bonds in order to lessen the danger of inflation within Japan, while stimulating the economy with investment credits offered directly by the government.[12]

Because Yūki proposed to substitute the use of credit for paper money, still without the backing of gold, Ryū maintained that Yūki's policies would not reduce the potential for inflation. They would, though, allow the Bank of Japan, as an institution of monopoly capital, to control investment in munitions industries more carefully and to identify its interests more directly with those of the army. This constituted a challenge to the state as a rival of monopoly capital: "Instead of the will of the state that seems to conflict partially with the wishes of monopoly capital . . . trying to place some limits on its development, monopoly capital is attempting to represent the desires of the state. This is the nub of the new policy to encompass the wishes of the military that is said to be the driving force in politics."[13] The central question was whether Japanese financial leaders would merge their interests completely with those of the military, or whether the plans of the army for a controlled economy could begin a radical restructuring of the economy by the state.

The bitter debate in the Diet over an electric power control law intrigued Ryū, who supported the eventual nationalization of the electrical power industry as both economically desirable and historically inevitable.[14] Electrical power was a unifying force in modern economies, because, unlike steam power, which each factory produced, electricity could be generated at a central location and then distributed to many factories over a large area. From a broad historical perspective, the development of electrical power constituted a "third industrial revolution." Although private companies had created the electrical energy industry, national management was essential because electricity had become vital to the economy.[15]

The proper economic policy was comprehensive national planning designed to assure the efficient production and reliable distribution of electrical power. The large utility companies in Japan would not voluntarily cooperate to achieve these goals because of intercompany rivalries and the need to protect profits. "The necessity of the development of electrical industry has confronted the anarchy of [capitalist] production [*seisan no museifu*] and has taken as its mission the demand for a planned economy."[16]

In view of this so-called historical necessity, Ryū endorsed the army's demand for an electrical power control law even though the army's program called only for national management of the electrical power industry, not for nationalization. The "plan for national management of electrical power contains the idea of suppressing monopoly [capital] through the power of the state."[17] The army's goal of national control, furthermore, was to increase the production of electrical energy and to ensure its even distribution and low cost. "In this way by emphasizing productive power and the value of the use [of electricity], the viewpoint of the military is closer to the viewpoint of benefit for all capital [*zen shihon*]."[18]

Ryū was moving away from his focus on the workers' movement, although his complaint that Japan's economic growth had depended on reduced real wages and longer working hours for laborers showed his continuing sympathy for the proletariat.[19] Following his realization in 1935 that Japan's economic problems transcended the simple conflict between capital and labor, he argued that the "position of all capital," by which he meant the benefits accruing to industrial capital, such as manufacturing firms, as well as finance capital, should determine national policies. The position of all capital was progressive because it valued the "development of productive power" and the "socialization of production" rather than an increase in profits for monopoly capital.[20]

Ryū regarded state management of the electrical industry as sponsored by the army as one step toward increasing the productivity and efficiency of the industry through national planning. The national orientation of the military was better than that of finance capitalists who cared only for their profits, but Ryū criticized the army for its narrow concept of the means and goals of increased state economic control. There was a danger that under the bureaucratic supervision proposed by the army "wide groups of citizens will not have special safeguards. The powers representing the views of all capital, in other words, will not in any form change into new representatives of the people."[21] The army naturally wanted to use electrical energy primarily to increase munitions production without any consideration for widening Japan's domestic market by raising the workers' standard of living. When the army no longer needed electrical energy for munitions production, Ryū predicted, Japan would face an economic crisis, because there would be a surfeit of electrical energy that workers could not afford to buy. There would be, in effect, a "contradiction between productive power and productive relations." "Only when the reality of the wartime economy had disappeared, must the surplus of productive power seek another key to resolve [this dilemma]."[22] Presumably, the key would be a radical restructuring of the entire Japanese economy. Ryū advised the masses that their "duty" was to "present forcefully the demands of the people regarding how the results of technological development must be used."[23]

Ryū's contention that the demands of the military could serve as a basis for future economic reform in Japan contradicted his earlier rebuke of the Social Mass party and Kamei Kanichirō for endorsing the army's national defense program. Although Ryū had treated this stance as part of Japan's "political depression" of 1934, he was emulating Kamei's strategy with a vengeance in 1937. He lamented that the army's policy for a "broad national defense" had become in fact a "narrow national defense." Nevertheless, he contended that the electric power control law sponsored by the army would advance reforms of the Japanese economy.

Ryū knew that the leaders of private business had opposed the law by calling it a form of national socialism. He conceded this point, but replied that the "real enemy of monopoly capital" was the "dynamic force of electricity" as "the material power that wishes to clear up completely the anarchistic form of capitalism."[24] The long-term goal of reducing the power of monopoly capital justified the new measure, even if it smacked of national socialism. The extension of government control in general over Japan's economy alarmed some journalists, and one prominent political critic even called the electric power control law the clearest example in Japan of "dyed-in-the-wool fascism."[25] To Ryū, the law revealed the future pattern of national regulation of other industries.[26]

Ryū's attitude toward the military was at least as ambivalent and opportunistic as that of the leaders of the Social Mass party. After the war, Ryū would claim that direct criticism of the army's policies was impossible during the 1930s and that he had criticized the expansionary fiscal policies of Baba and Yūki as a means of indirectly questioning army policies.[27] There is some validity to this position. Ryū, in his new book, did recount the determined resistance of Finance Minister Takahashi to the army's demand in 1935 for increased deficit financing for enlarged military expenditures. Ryū argued that during World War I munitions production had not brought substantial economic gains to Western nations and reiterated his belief that current military spending by the government only fanned Japan's inflation. He observed that Japan's military expansion in China sometimes conflicted with the growth of peaceful and profitable trade with China. At the same time, Ryū rationalized the army's role through his interpretation of recent Japanese economic history.

Ryū believed that after the Meiji Restoration of 1868, Japan had become a "premature" imperialist power.[28] A lack of natural resources and of a large domestic market compelled Japan to search for overseas markets and supplies of raw materials for developing modern industries. Japan had followed "two paths" of imperialism consisting of peaceful foreign trade and military expansion on the continent. The earlier wars with China (1894–95) and Russia (1904–5) had proven economically profitable in increased access to markets and raw materials, just as the Opium War had brought the British great gains at little cost. The age of simple imperialism, however, had passed.

Wars, in Ryū's estimation, were now being fought among the imperialist powers over the redistribution of colonial lands. More significantly, although Ryū constantly stated that Japan had entered the stage of "monopoly capital," he did not draw the concomitant Marxist conclusion that Japanese expansion on the mainland constituted a desperate attempt of monopoly capital to overcome the growing contradictions of Japanese capitalism. Despite the Japanese army's occupation of Manchuria and the army's presence in North China, Ryū did not explicitly discuss this aspect of Japanese imperialism; nor, obviously, did he relate China specifically to his contention that modern wars were a struggle for the redistribution of colonial lands.

The realities of the mainland could not be ignored; Ryū, in fact, described the heavy military burden that Japan had assumed with the Manchurian Incident, the withdrawal from the League of Nations, and the abrogation of the London Naval Treaty.[29] Because Japan's economy was faltering under the burden of the nation's international position, Ryū asserted, "there is no choice other than to progress beyond the productive power of Japanese capitalism."[30] Ryū, in short, affirmed the reality of the international crises confronting the nation and, with the army, demanded that Japan must become industrially powerful. This challenge could only be met through a restructuring of the Japanese economy by the state.

Ryū's critique of the military assumed the distorted guise of disapproving the evolution of the "broad defense" policy of the Hirota cabinet into a "narrow defense" policy that neglected the "life of the people" and centered solely on the development of defense industries.[31] He favored a truly broad defense economic policy that would foster total economic strength for the country. The Soviet Union's five-year plans and self-sufficiency in munitions were admirable: "The rapid expansion of munitions by the Soviet planned economy naturally cannot help forming a great desire for planning in the national economy of Japan."[32] Even before the China Incident of July 1937, Ryū advocated a planned national economy based on a comprehensive view of national defense. This perspective represented his new strategy for publicizing his favorite themes of the weakness of Japanese capitalism and the necessity for national economic planning.

Although the Soviet Union offered a general example for planning, Ryū turned to Italian and German policies for the concrete models that Japan should emulate. Arguing for tighter state control over industrial cartels to eliminate the adverse effects of competition among participating companies, he declared that the "laws of Germany and Italy seem to point the way for the future Japan."[33] Germany had enacted major new economic legislation in the mid-1930s.[34] The government assumed the authority to enforce participation in cartels, set maximum prices, and modify cartel agreements. The director of the new Economics Ministry could organize occupational and geographic associations for the purpose of encouraging productivity and cooperation with government policies. The minister could appoint the associations' directors and compel participation by companies.

The problems that the Nazis faced in attempting simultaneously to increase munitions production, reduce unemployment, balance a chronic trade deficit, and limit inflation were similar to Japan's dilemmas. In Germany, Hjalmar Schacht's "New Plan" of 1934 monitored imports carefully, and Schacht attacked inflation by imposing a ceiling of 6 percent on stock dividends, with excess profits transferred to a government bank for the purchase of government bonds. The government could also revoke a bank's license if its investment policies "violate[d] important general interests." The creation of an office to supervise price formation in Germany particularly impressed Ryū, although he realized that the demands of rearmament and trade difficulties inevitably caused inflation because of shortages of civilian goods. Despite reservations about the Nazis' lack of commitment to raising the standard of living of the German populace, Ryū admired Schacht's frank recognition of the threat of inflation and the relative success of his policies: "Thus one can say that price control in German inflation has shown its contradictions in the oppression of the people's livelihood and the problem of raw materials, but, within these limits, price controls have seen some success in some areas. Of course, prices are rising—food prices are especially remarkable—but, in other sectors they are not great compared to the scale of the mobilization of industry for rearmament. . . . Japan more than Germany is extending the problem of inflation into the future and is, by all odds, making it worse."[35] Economic planning and forceful intervention by the state was essential.

Ryū's acceptance of the need for a wartime national defense economy in Japan and his advocacy of state economic planning fit the general goals proposed by the Army Ministry in the Hirota cabinet. He regarded some of the economic legislation as important attempts to control the abuses of monopoly capital, and he wanted to use the trend toward more state economic regulation in the name of national defense to modify Japanese capitalism and to introduce national economic planning.[36]

Balanced economic planning for the national welfare was his goal. The state would have to guide the economy firmly. "All Japanese industry—no, the whole economy—has begun to suffer from a 'lack of planning' which is the ailment with which it was born. It seems that the lack of 'planning' and 'control' is presently Japan's greatest problem."[37] He approved of the army's insistence on increasing the nation's military might, but he warned against a policy that would sacrifice "peace industries," especially textiles, for the temporary benefit of munitions production. He criticized capitalists who sought to increase production by exploiting workers and not raising their standard of living, but warned that wage increases would spur inflation to the detriment of everyone.[38]

In affirming Japan's foreign policies, Ryū took for granted Japan's diplomatic isolation, the abrogation of the naval limitation treaties, and expansion on the mainland. He neither explicitly denounced Japanese imperialism nor did he interpret it as a product of fascism or as an agent of monopoly capital. Although Ryū wrote that the growing political power of "capital," as manifested in Yūki's policies, had "to a certain extent formulated the special character of Japan's political structure in the same direction as the forms of fascism in Western Europe,"[39] he did not specify what he meant by fascism in Japan or Europe. Although Ryū criticized specific economic policies of the government and the military, he stressed current progressive trends, namely, the development of a quasi-wartime economy which could help the evolution of a planned economy in Japan.

Fascism and Politics

Like Japan's leaders of private business, party politicians experienced new challenges to their authority. The assassination of Premier Inukai Tsuyoshi and the appointment of Admiral Saitō Makoto as his successor had weakened the political parties. The Minseitō and the Seiyūkai dominated the Diet, but the emperor's adviser, the *genro* Saionji, did not dare return to the rule of party cabinets. Unhappy with the resulting "national unity" cabinets, the parties strove to regain their lost authority. Some of their actions, especially those of the Seiyūkai, only served to confirm popular criticisms of the corruption and selfish rivalry of party politics. The financial scandal concerning the Teijin Company in 1934 caused not only the resignation of the Saitō cabinet but also the exposure of unsightly corruption on the part of important party leaders.[40] Frustrated in its attempts to regain power, the Seiyūkai refused to support the next cabinet of Admiral Okada and expelled members who accepted portfolios. In the Diet, this party vociferously criticized Professor Minobe's liberal constitutional interpretations in a futile attempt to embarrass and bring down the cabinet. The election of February 1936 rewarded the Minseitō's loyalty to Premier Okada and to Dr. Minobe with a smashing victory and even yielded eighteen seats to the Social Mass party; but the military rebellion, barely a week afterward, nullified the effect of the party's triumph as a sign of popular support for parliamentary democracy.

After the mutiny was suppressed, the army and the Diet clashed head-on, as the demands of the military became more ambitious. Besides trying to limit the number of party members with portfolios in the new cabinet and requesting a huge increase in expenditures, the service ministers desired radical reforms of the central bureaucracy to increase administrative efficiency for the sake of national defense.[41] The army's reform program received severe bipartisan criticism in the Diet. Hamada Kunimatsu of the Seiyūkai reprimanded Army Minister Terauchi Hisaichi for the military's increasing arrogance.[42] The Minseitō's Saitō Takao openly criticized the rise of military influence in domestic politics since 1931.[43] This criticism helped block the immediate adoption of the military's reform program, but the parties were still far from regaining authority over the cabinet.

Rōyama Masamichi interpreted these developments as part of a gradual trend toward meaningful political reform in Japan. By 1935, Rōyama had endorsed using the power of the state as a weapon against the established political parties by enthusiastically supporting the government's Election Purification Movement (Senkyo shukusei undō) as the only means to eradicate the corruption of party politics. Under the direction of the Home Ministry, and with the aid of its police, the movement aimed at rooting out corruption in political campaigns and elections. Rōyama was sensitive to criticism of the movement as a bureaucratic program, but he defended it as a national movement of great significance. If it spread throughout the country, the movement could establish "provincial political groups" to endorse candidates, make them self-supporting, and eliminate the need for party endorsements of Diet candidates.[44] Then, perhaps the Diet could implement occupational representation; this remained Rōyama's ideal because he remained convinced that occupational groups, and not individuals, were the basic units of society. If direct occupational representation was not feasible, Rōyama suggested that at least the government should permit the nomination of candidates from workers' unions.[45]

Concerned with the increasing political dominance of the military and the civilian bureaucracy, Rōyama argued that the Diet should be more efficient in considering legislation to influence policy decisions more effectively. This could emerge through a "different form" of two-party competition. If the Minseitō and the Seiyūkai united, as some party members suggested, then a "new mass party," based on the proletarian parties, could arise as a potent rival. A two-party system was necessary because the "Japanese political character" would not tolerate a "communistic" or "fascistic" rule by a single party.[46] At this point, Rōyama did not describe what policies the new party would champion and he did not explain why his proposed two-party system would be more stable and efficient than the current competition between the Minseitō and the Seiyūkai.

The army's political demands after the 1936 mutiny dashed Rōyama's expectations for the rapid development of a new two-party system and the reassertion of parliamentary authority. Rōyama stressed the "complicated character" of contemporary political developments and could only speculate that the electoral success of both the Minseitō and the Social Mass party in 1936 was a fragment of a gradual sweeping process of change in Japan and that the rebellion itself did not signal a new political era.[47] Although the "moralistic" emphasis of Premier Hirota's promise to effect an overall reform of politics was commendable, his cabinet would not drastically alter the structure of Japanese politics. The February 26 Incident was only "one frame" of a process of continuous political change.[48] Instead of criticizing the reactionary goals of the rebellion, Rōyama concentrated on the sources of the rebels' discontent.

Rōyama interpreted this latest mutiny, which a few junior officers plotted, as a sign of broad popular dissatisfaction with contemporary politics, and he castigated the political parties in the Diet for failing to provide strong political leadership.[49] Although abhorring the violent tactics of "fascistic" nationalist groups and of the young military rebels in Japan, he assigned a positive role to these "fascist movements" in exposing the impotence of the political parties. The rise of nationalistic thought was compared to the growth of the National Learning School (*kokugaku ha*), which in the eighteenth and nineteenth centuries had helped create the ideological seeds of the Meiji Restoration movement. Contemporary fascist movements, which appealed to nationalistic emotions, were similarly "trying to restore the people's confidence to do away with the present situation."[50] Obviously, change was needed, and the most important intellectual task facing Japan was to merge nationalistic thought with a program for future social and political reform.

Having observed the policies of Nazi Germany as well as fascist Italy, Rōyama reaffirmed his belief that fascism in Europe had successfully linked nationalistic ideology with policies of reform. Both nations were altering capitalism and introducing "the concept of a planned society with social and technological elements." Moreover, Rōyama approved "Schacht's proposal for a reorganization of the world economy."[51] Later, Rōyama would cite Germany's quest for a new order in Europe as a model for Japan's foreign policies.

Rōyama's *banzais* for the progressive force of fascism in Europe led him to an intriguing analysis of the composition of Japanese fascism. He concluded that private nationalistic and terrorist groups in Japan did not make up a powerful movement because they had no single leader and no unified ideology, and he denied that the political parties and big business represented Japanese fascism as the last-ditch effort of monopoly capitalism to save itself. In fact, they resisted the real Japanese fascists: that is, the civilian and military bureaucrats who attempted to impose state control over the economy through the "structure of the nation."[52] Significantly, Rōyama and Ryū were both increasingly attracted by the power of the structure of the nation as an agent for economic or political reform.

Endorsing the ideal of centralized economic control, Rōyama argued that a "social progressive type" of planned economy, which would develop "piecemeal within the structure of the bourgeois state," was the most plausible path for Japan.[53] The economic controls already proposed for increasing production within Japan were steps toward the control of prices, investments, and profits and would win the support of a broad social coalition: "elements of the proletariat which belong to social democratic unions and the proletarian parties"; the "backbone of the agricultural class," which was attempting to escape from the economic depression; the "general intellectual class and the class of technicians"; and a few "progressive capitalists." Thus, just as Ryū Shintarō backed economic measures to benefit "all capital," Rōyama proposed that the state gain the support of enlightened members of all sectors of the society by implementing fascist bureaucratic controls over the free-market economy.

Rōyama's specific proposals agreed on many points with administrative reforms favored by the army. The army's proposal for a superministerial planning agency would threaten the Diet's authority, but an "investigation committee" composed of representatives from "cultural" groups, presumably to allow for the participation of intellectuals, as well as "occupational" organizations, would introduce economic planning effectively. A "permanent investigation committee covering the whole of personnel administration in each ministry" would reorganize the government to promote unity and efficiency.[54]

Despite his fascination with the administrative power of the state, Rōyama remained committed to the principle of popular participation in government. The success of the Social Mass party in capturing eighteen seats in the Diet election of 1936 rekindled his hopes for implementing occupational representation, and he attributed the party's popularity to votes from skilled workers and the "intellectual class"—teachers, "company men," civil servants, and so forth—who felt threatened by political and economic unrest.

The party's previous support for the creation of Manchukuo and its leaders' endorsement of economic mobilization for war in 1934 were not discussed. Although both right-wing groups and the Social Mass party rejected liberalism, which was equated with the "present situation and a lack of control," the two political camps had different goals:[55] the former desired to "overcome liberalism by a fascistic totalitarianism," while the latter desired a "conquest of liberalism" through a "reform of the Diet system centered on functionalism." The mission of the Social Mass party with its new base of support was to replace the doctrine of "atomistic individualism [based on the principle of] one man, one vote" with the doctrine of "groupism [based on] the organized management of agriculture, organized technology, organized labor, and organized capital."[56] If Rōyama opposed "right-wing" fascism, he still wanted to transform the Diet into a deliberative assembly for representatives of occupational organizations similar to the corporations and syndicates in Italy.

A basic alteration of the Diet and its system of representation involved changes in the Meiji Constitution, toward which Rōyama had a distinctly ambivalent attitude. "Constitutionalism," the recognition of the present constitution, should be a common basis of all political activity. Every political group should respect the constitution and work within it; groups that tried to effect political change through the use of violence should be stopped. The basic character of the constitution must be an "organic system which has an ethical meaning. . . . It is a system that is above class [interest] before which all ideologies must swear loyalty; one can see that the moral ideal of the nation is first realized in a nation with a constitution." Subservience to a constitution signified a "common moral responsibility to the existence of the nation as members of the nation."[57] The strength of the Meiji Constitution, which supported the existence of the Diet, could even prevent the rise of a fascist dictatorship.

However, "when the creation of a new political structure and system is necessary," a belief in constitutionalism "should not necessarily view the individual regulations of the constitution as fixed and stable."[58] They should change according to the demands of the era. The workers' movement should "establish a constitutional order following the principles of fairness and justice and eliminating the irrationality present in [Japan's] social organization and industrial structure." The content of a real "Shōwa restoration" had to include a "real economic constitutional government in place of a legalistic and formalistic constitutional government."[59] If the government desired national unity, Rōyama argued, then this type of reform was the most effective means to guarantee the loyalty of the people. Although Rōyama realized the "legalistic" Meiji Constitution was a barrier to fascism, he was willing to revise it to facilitate political and economic reform.

Fascism and Japanese Tradition

For Miki Kiyoshi, the definition of Japanese tradition became an important topic after 1935. His interest was more than academic because the proliferation of nationalistic groups and the Minobe affair had focused the attention of many politicians, officials, and writers on the nature of Japanese tradition as a political issue. Critics of Western liberalism often stressed its alien nature by asserting that the *kokutai*, the sacred relationship between the divine emperor and his subjects, was the distinctive feature of Japanese history. In 1937 the Education Ministry joined this chorus by issuing the pamphlet *The Fundamental Principles of the National Polity* for national distribution in the schools.

This publication condemned the doctrine of individualism and the Western ideologies of liberalism, socialism, and communism as causes of social strife. It promoted the unique Japanese polity that depended on reverence for the emperor as the father of the national family. A basic premise was that Japanese culture was unified throughout history by special bonds of loyalty, such as the "great spirit of founding the nation" (*chōkoku no taiseishin*) and the "spirit of harmony" (*wa no seishin*).[60] The unbroken line of Japanese emperors embodied the former spirit, while all aspects of Japanese life reflected the conviction that social harmony was more important than individual competition. Even the motives of Japan's industrial entrepreneurs, the authors contended, had been tempered by a sense of duty and a concern for public welfare.[61] In adapting Western thought, Japanese scholars had to "purify" it so that the natural bonds of loyalty and harmony in the national polity were not destroyed. Continuing to learn from the West was crucial if the Japanese were to build a "new culture" in their inherently "creative" manner.[62]

Miki Kiyoshi sought to create a new culture by conceiving a new Japanese philosophy with world impact. The task of examining Japan's culture and developing a new Japanese thought had immediate political import for Miki in helping to prevent the emergence of what he considered fascism in Japan, and he defined Japanese tradition to suit this purpose. Explicating Japan's past was the most crucial issue facing Japanese intellectuals.[63]

Miki construed fascism as "irrationality." When Martin Heidegger joined the German Nazi party in 1933, Miki rebuked his German tutor for succumbing to the emotional forces of fascist nationalism.[64] The Minobe affair and the attempted military coup d'état of 1936 prompted Miki's concern with Japanese variants of fascism. He bemoaned the growing strength of "Japanists" who wanted to reject modern Japan as too Western.[65] The shrill cries of these ideologues urging Japanese to return to traditional values were "unscientific" and misguided because they neglected the real "process of historical development" in Japan. They sought to reject the accomplishments of modern Japan and to return to a period of benevolent imperial rule and social harmony that probably never existed. Unscientific "Japanism" represented "fascism."

Miki considered the present infatuation of many Japanese writers with an imaginary pure tradition as an escape from contemporary problems, a "retreat from the struggles of the intellect," and attacked the influential romantic school (roman ha) of authors and literary critics who sought a genuine Japanese spirit similar to that manifested in works of ancient literature. Although the members of the romantic school saw themselves as uncovering the true Japanese spirit, Miki found them to be crude imitators of the Western philosopher Friedrich Nietzsche in fabricating a national "genealogy" of "heroic romanticism."[66] Creating a myth of the past was paramount to adopting a Western perspective on Japan's tradition.

Japan had not a rigid tradition but a succession of different cultures.[67] Japanese character was dominated by "pure emotion" and was "formless form, ununified unity, . . . where opposite things suddenly become in agreement."[68] The flexibility of Japanese character—its "world spirit"—had proven advantageous during the early Meiji period, when Japan had been receptive to Western influence.[69] Consequently, Japan had become a powerful nation. Now, in the 1930s this inquisitive spirit was weakening. Although Miki thought that the emotionalism and the tolerance of the Japanese made them vulnerable to irrational fascist ideology, he still hoped that the eclecticism of their culture could prevent the excesses of a fascist dictatorship instituted under the guise of shielding Japan from the contamination of foreign thought.

The important task was to maintain the dynamism of Japanese culture so that Japan could remain a world power. Absorption of Western thought had become the source of Japan's superiority over the other nations of East Asia. Emulating the importation of Buddhism centuries ago, the Japanese had to continue to simplify Western thought and adapt it to Japanese life.[70] Modern Japanese had to imitate their "ancestors'" ingestion of Chinese and Indian cultures. "Our responsibility is to actualize Western culture which has the feeling of borrowed clothes." "A new type of Japanese must be born, and [we] must create a new type of culture." Miki understood the implications of Japan's new national power. He reminded his readers that "for the first time," Japan had entered the "stage of world history," and that it should "seek the world character of Japanese things."[71] Unlike the nation during the splendid isolation of the Tokugawa era, modern Japan could not cut itself off from the world in which it had an important role to play.

Recognizing the threat of reactionary nationalistic movements to the freedom of inquiry and expression in Japan, Miki admitted that "cultural liberals, too, are pressed for political decisions," but did not defend the parliamentary system or the Meiji Constitution as established elements of Japan's tradition.[72] He demeaned party politicians by claiming that they lacked both the technical expertise and the broad perspective to deal with complex social problems, but failed to address the problem of fascism evolving through bureaucratic controls over the economy and parliamentary system.[73] Ambivalent toward the bureaucracy, he criticized both the typical Japanese attitude of "respect the official and despise the people" (*kanson minpi*) and its growing power. Bureaucratic controls would not lead to a true "national unity" (*kyokoku itchi*). Nevertheless, because the technical expertise of civil servants was essential to a modern state, their role would become more important, especially if they would pursue broad social reforms.[74]

Miki carefully distinguished his belief in "rationality" from a commitment to "liberalism" that championed the rights of the individual against the demands of society.[75] Criticizing the lack of individual "respect for one's own personality and [of] a consciousness of respect for the personalities of others" in feudal Japanese society, he insisted that "man was born from society" and was inextricably linked to it. "The concept of personality is certainly not individualistic. On the contrary, a personality is a personality [only] in relation to others."[76] Lauding the emotional unity of Japanese culture, its flexibility, and its openness, Miki rejected the ideologies of liberalism, fascism, and Marxism, but did not indicate what the new form of Japanese culture or politics would be.

The "totalitarian" doctrines of European fascism both repelled and stimulated him. Worship for the nation as an unchanging "totality" could too easily degenerate into a rationale for preserving the status quo and suppressing liberty. There was, however, the possibility for a more rational definition of a national totality as in the process of "dialectical" evolution—an entity that bound its members while being shaped by their creative efforts.[77] Such a society would reject the obsolete values of the primacy of individual freedom, but would somehow allow for the expression of individual creativity. Miki's main task was now to adapt new Western ideas to the Japanese situation by defining a new "totalitarianism."

By 1937, Rōyama, Ryū, and Miki were each beginning to envision a new form for Japan. They had each rejected the strategy of violent Marxist revolution and even the peaceful social democratic movement. Similarly, they criticized liberalism, which they, like many Japanese, associated with the current free-market economy and party politics in Japan, and they criticized the principle of individual freedom. They assumed, and hoped, that the age of individual political and economic liberty linked with the rise of liberal democracy in the West was passing. Rōyama, Ryū, and Miki wanted an alternative to both socialism and liberalism.[78]

In Europe intellectuals faced with a similar dilemma often turned to fascism as a "third force."[79] Rōyama and Ryū advocated state intervention in the economy and changes in the political system based on European fascist models. Despite his warnings that a "rational" and repressive fascism could arise by "conforming to the social structure in Japan," Miki urged a more active role for public officials in solving problems.[80] Although these writers were aware of the dangers of bureaucratic dictatorship in Japan, they supported the imposition of more state controls, a development that would only increase the opportunities for the exercise of arbitrary authority.

All three writers desired a strong Japan because of its growing international significance and an ideology and program of reform that would allow the state to curb partisan interests and to promote the welfare of the entire nation. Ideally, the government and the masses would unite in a less fractious and corrupt society free of divisive competition between individuals and organizations, such as political parties and private companies, that appeared to dominate industrial societies. To the extent that the corporate state in Europe appeared to achieve these goals in a rational way, fascism would present an increasingly attractive Western model of reform.

In Japan, the struggle of the political parties to defend the Diet's constitutional authority against the demands of the military for more political power did not excite much interest from Rōyama, Ryū, and Miki. Nor did the resistance of Japanese business to economic controls. These prominent intellectuals expected the destruction of the old order to yield new political and economic systems and a new culture. Within a year, they began to cooperate with each other in the Shōwa Research Association for the specific purpose of outlining and implementing policies for a new Japan.

6. The Early Years of the Shōwa Research Association

The Shōwa Research Association (Shōwa kenkyūkai) represented a novel effort of Japanese intellectuals to gain national influence by providing an opportunity for journalists and academics to discuss issues regularly with government officials. Rōyama helped form the association in 1933, and Ryū and Miki joined five years later. The involvement of these writers in the association paralleled their increasing fascination with employing the power of the state and the force of nationalism to effect political and economic reforms.[1] Contact with government officials and other prominent private citizens who advocated enhanced political efficiency, more state control over the economy, increased national unity, mass mobilization for a potential major war, and Japan's leadership of Asia encouraged Rōyama, Ryū, and Miki to consider fascist models to achieve these goals in Japan.

The Origins of the Association

Many of the most active participants among the charter members had cooperated before in three different organizations: the Youth Association, the Alliance for a New Japan (Shinnihon no dōmei), and the Education Study Group (Kyōiku kenkyūkai). These groups affected the mood and the goals of the Shōwa Research Association because of their members' belief, from a non-Marxist perspective, that basic reforms were necessary to increase the effectiveness of the political system and economic justice. The alliance's quest for a new party as an alternative to the established parties and to socialism came to dominate the political strategy of the Shōwa Research Association. The theme of inculcating an ethic of national service, the crux of many of the association's proposals, was already developed and refined in the Youth Association and the Education Study Group.[2]

Gotō Ryūnosuke was a member of those three groups and the person most responsible for creating the Shōwa Research Association. Although he had attended the prestigious First Higher School and had formed a close friendship with the headmaster, the eminent Nitobe Inazō, a prolific writer on Western affairs, he was an unlikely candidate for the task of molding the most talented intellectuals and officials in the nation into an advisory group. He was notably lacking in academic prowess and was best remembered by his classmates for taking six years to complete the three-year program and for his skill in judo. Still, Gotō considered himself a man of action and impressed others with his concern for the nation, his strong will, and his dynamism.[3]

At the University of Kyōto, Gotō became close friends with his higher school classmate Konoe Fumimaro, the scion of the ancient Fujiwara family. In 1923 he secured a position in the Youth Association, while Prince Konoe served as chief director (*rijichō*) of the Japan Youth Hall (Nihon seinenkan) in Tokyo. The central purpose of the Youth Association, which was under the direction of the Education Ministry, was to organize rural youths in each village in order to promote good works, cooperative spirit, and individual morality. After Gotō joined the Youth Association, his career became closely entwined with that of Prince Konoe. During the 1930s, Gotō was known as a close and devoted companion of Konoe and as a man who harbored no personal political ambitions.[4]

Just after the assassination of Premier Inukai in May 1932, Gotō departed on a year-long voyage which included visits to America, Germany, and Russia. As Gotō recounts, "During that time, Japan's domestic situation changed greatly. Moreover, as for the world situation, the rise of men like Hitler was causing great changes in the world."[5] Observing the rise of Hitler and the end of party cabinets in Japan, Gotō decided that Japan's political parties and domestic politics needed change. He turned to Nitobe Inazō for advice: "Japanese party politics must be reformed, and I want to do it. What do you think?" Nitobe, according to Gotō, replied with uncharacteristic fervor, "Do it. In Japan there is a misconception of democracy. Democracy must always renew itself."[6] Receiving this encouragement, Gotō conferred with Prince Konoe, and they agreed to establish a study group that would chart new national policies to rejuvenate Japan through the reform of its social, political, and economic systems. These new policies would form the basis for a new cabinet headed by Konoe.

Belief in the inevitability of drastic political and economic changes was widespread in Japan. As Gotō and Konoe were creating their study group, for example, Yatsugi Kazuo, a former member of the Harmonization Society (Kyōchōkai), began to confer regularly with army officers to discuss new national policies. The plans that Yatsugi's group formulated, he claims, provided the basis for the Army Ministry's notorious 1934 pamphlets on national defense. In December 1933, Yatsugi founded the National Policy Research Association (Kokusaku kenkyūkai) to examine a broad range of policy issues.[7] In operation until the early 1940s, this association enlisted the aid of scholars, civil servants, politicians, and military officers. There was no formal relationship between Yatsugi's group and the one created by Gotō and Konoe, but several prominent Japanese participated in both organizations. The National Policy Association and the Shōwa Research Association were founded within a few months of each other because of the fear of economic and political difficulties in Japan.

The first administrative problem for Gotō and Konoe was the leadership of their new group. "Everyone knows," Gotō recalls, "that I am not very bright. Therefore, although I wanted to create the group, I did not have the ability."[8] There were, however, impressive reports about Rōyama Masamichi, who had recently been working with Nitobe on an agricultural problems study group sponsored by the Japan Youth Hall. Gotō decided that Rōyama had the prestige and ability to develop and direct the research program of the new study group.

The Shōwa Research Association began meeting in October 1933, and fifteen charter members were appointed in December.[9] From academia came two political scientists—Rōyama and Kawai Eijirō—and three professors of agriculture—Tōhata Seiichi, Nasu Hiroshi, and Satō Kanji. The *Asahi* was represented by Sekiguchi Tai and Maeda Tamon, the Social Mass party by Kawakami Jotarō and Matsuoka Komakichi. Three participants were bankers —Araki Eiichi, Tanabe Katamaru, and Tajima Michiji. The most prominent members of the original group included Tazawa Yoshiharu, the originator of the modern Youth Association and the director of the Japan Youth Hall, and Count Arima Yoriyasu, a friend and colleague of Prince Konoe in the House of Peers; Arima would later serve as minister of agriculture in the first Konoe cabinet. Among the charter members there were no delegates from the Minseitō or the Seiyūkai.

Although the Shōwa Research Association had strong connections with the Social Mass party, as evidenced by the presence of Kawakami and Matsuoka in the founding committee and by the early participation of Asō Hisashi and Kamei Kanichirō in study groups, the links with the Youth Association were more important. Tazawa Yoshiharu, for example, headed the Youth Association; Prince Konoe and Gotō Ryūnosuke were top administrative officers; and professors Rōyama, Tōhata, and Nasu Hiroshi had all participated in its study groups.[10] Moreover, Shiga Naokata, a former general, a friend of the Konoe family, and a director of the Youth Association, initially funded the organization. Later, more officials from the Youth Association joined, but no members of the socialist party remained as leaders by 1936.

The Youth Association had first emerged as a national movement in 1915 as a sub-division of the Hōtokukai, an auxiliary rural organization supervised by the Home Ministry. The Youth Association was incorporated as an autonomous organization with the establishment of the Japan Youth Hall in 1921, and by the 1930s had a branch in every village. The Japan League of Youth Associations (Dainihon rengō seinendan), which Tazawa created in 1922, was self-consciously "impartial" in political affairs. The association was, he insisted, above the narrow partisan strategies of the existing political parties and the social divisiveness caused by radical nationalist or revolutionary movements. The association should conduct "political education" for the masses in order to instill "the responsibility of serving the nation . . . under constitutional politics."[11] Tazawa deplored the current Japanese parliamentary system as a "struggle of party factions" conducted by base men who were motivated by a "greed for power." "Political education," therefore, was not a "defense of the present battles of political parties which have many evils." Under Tazawa's direction, "political education" aimed at improving the morality of politics, and the Youth Association maintained a position of political neutrality which rejected the major political parties in Japan.

"Service to the nation" was basic to Tazawa's conception of the role of the Youth Association. "In a word, the association is like a nursery. Splendid saplings [youths], which have been nurtured in the nursery of the Youth Association, have strong bodies and healthy spirits; they have developed a cheerful nature and superior skills; and they can be transplanted to the mountains of either the conservative, liberal, or labor parties. They can be transplanted to the fields of capitalist landlords or those of tenant workers. The national mission of the Youth Association is that all parties, classes, and professions should be composed of a healthy populace, because this nursery supplies healthy saplings. We will always supply a healthy citizenry to every area of the nation."[12] Association members were to dedicate their lives to the nation. In fostering such a spirit, Tazawa believed that his organization could also "protect human nature" against the dehumanizing effects of "machine civilization," which valued the individual only for his specialized skills. Like Rōyama, Tazawa thought loyalty to the nation could soothe the disruption and alienation caused by the process of industrialization.

Soon after the Shōwa Research Association formed, Gotō and Tazawa created a national Young Adult Association (Sōnendan) for males over the age of twenty-five. This organization was to be very active politically, as the branches of the new organization were to be potential "central forces" (*chūshin no chikara*) in local politics, and the ultimate goal was mustering popular support for a national new party to challenge the Minseitō and the Seiyūkai. Gotō and Tazawa hoped such groups could foster popular enthusiasm for reforms of the political system. In 1938, Gotō would use the facilities of both the Youth and Young Adult associations to create a national movement with the help of the Shōwa Research Association.[13]

With the help of two Home Ministry officials active in the Youth Association, Gotō Fumio and Maruyama Tsurukichi, Tazawa had first tried to implement his ideals politically through founding the Alliance for a New Japan in March 1925.[14] This forty-man elitist group included Ogata Taketora and Prince Konoe and counted civil servants, Diet members, local politicians, and journalists among its members. Facing the imminent passage of the Universal Manhood Suffrage Act, the alliance aspired primarily to design a political program that would absorb the masses into the Japanese political system, prevent revolution, and promote reform of the corrupt political parties through "political education."

Unfortunately for Tazawa, the alliance floundered in its attempts to create a new political movement. Tazawa believed that Japan needed a "liberal party" as an alternative to the socialists and conservatives. Conservative parties received support from "capitalists, landlords, military men, and bureaucrats" and the socialist parties appealed to workers. A liberal party, he predicted, would attract the "middle class, professionals, and a group of intellectual workers."[15] Hammering out an attractive political program proved difficult; Tazawa could suggest only the vague slogans of "democratic liberalism," "social reformism," and "international cooperation." Another challenge was building a political organization to gain electoral support. Tazawa and his colleagues considered supporting candidates in the general election of 1928 who would form a neutral "liberal party," but they were unable to carry out their plan. A well-known Diet member, Tsurumi Yūsuke, helped the alliance create a neutral block of representatives in the lower house. Even the venerable champion of Taishō democracy Ozaki Yukio joined, but this group, the Clear Politics Association (Meiseikai), soon disbanded. Gotō Ryūnosuke subsequently characterized the alliance as ineffectual.[16]

Some members hoped that Prince Konoe would lead such a new party movement and that his prestige would ensure political success. But, the alliance did not have the resources to research national issues systematically and to draw up comprehensive new policies. Nor did the members have the ability or patience to carry out the tedious political organizing necessary to win seats in the Diet. The failure to create a new party movement may well have discouraged Tazawa, Konoe, and Gotō from further attempts to effect reforms through the established electoral process.

If Tazawa, Gotō, and Konoe were frustrated by the difficulties of creating a new political force, they retained an active interest in educational reform, as shown by their participation in the Education Study Group. This group included one other founding member of the Shōwa Research Association, Nasu Hiroshi, and prominent officials such as Gotō Fumio and Abe Shigetaka. The main organizer was Abe, an official of the Education Ministry and a professor at the University of Tokyo.[17] The purpose of the group was to assess Japan's educational system and to recommend changes.

Although the direct impact of the group's recommendations is unclear, its 1931 report anticipated by four years several important changes in Japan's educational policy. The aim of the report was to eliminate social inequities and to promote the ethic of national service. The members espoused several measures, such as the extension of compulsory education through the middle school (grades seven through eleven) and scholarships, to enable students from poor families to stay in school.[18] For those students who still could not afford to enter or to complete a regular middle school, there would be special national youth schools (*kokumin seinen gakkō*) to serve part-time students. The report criticized elitism by complaining of a "bias toward intellectual training" in the present school system and glorified vocational instruction and ethical indoctrination. Middle school curricula should "foster morality and knowledge relating to the life of society and the nation" and should emphasize "business education to make work enjoyable and to sharpen skills and knowledge necessary for a life of work." The disdain of the group for Japanese academia was evident in proposals to eliminate higher schools and universities. On the premise that education should be more than an escalator for social status, the members suggested the "abolition of all degrees and privileges that come with graduation from schools" and the transformation of graduate schools into technological and industrial research centers open to all students. The Education Study Group wanted to reform Japan's educational system to eradicate privilege, extend educational opportunity, and reaffirm the importance of working for the nation. There was no stress in the report on fostering the values of parliamentary democracy or individualism.

Aside from the curious proposal to eradicate institutions of higher learning, most of the main themes of the 1931 draft of the Education Study Group echoed the plans advanced by the Education Ministry and the Army Ministry for the purposes of national mobilization. The national system of vocational schools in Japan had expanded after World War I; in 1925 the Education Ministry had, with the prompting of the army, established youth training centers to provide more education and military drill for working youths. The Education Study Group conceived of its proposed national youth schools as enlarged versions of the youth training centers with compulsory attendance and a program that included "assigning military drill and exercises." In 1935 the Education Ministry would merge the training centers with technical schools to create youth schools, which were compulsory for youths not in middle school and were increasingly used by the army for military instruction.[19]

Without reference to socialist theory, the alliance, the Youth Association, and the study group expounded many of the ideals developed by Rōyama, Ryū, and Miki. These groups' espousal of the need to end social divisions and economic inequality and to instill a patriotic spirit among the masses demonstrated how widespread those ideas were becoming in Japan. Agreement on these goals would serve as the basis for cooperation in the Shōwa Research Association among intellectuals and officials of varying intellectual and professional backgrounds.

The Role of Prince Konoe

Still, a commitment to national service alone was not sufficient to attract members. The status of the Shōwa Research Association as a brain trust for Prince Konoe was probably the most powerful lure for recruiting members.[20] In 1933 thoughtful Japanese were already beginning to view the aloof aristocrat as an influential political figure and as a potential premier. New members of the association wanted to gain direct access to Konoe. Sassa Hiroo, for example, observed that he had attended a "gathering sponsored by Gotō Ryūnosuke"—the Shōwa Research Association—expecting to meet the prince. Sassa observed that Konoe's unique appeal was his noble lineage and lack of identification with a particular interest group.[21] Konoe's antipathy toward the established parties and desire for a "new deal" in Asia helped determine the mood of the association.

During the early 1930s, Konoe, as president of the House of Peers, had become increasingly active in politics as a critic of the major parties. After the attempted coup d'état of May 1932, the assassination of Premier Inukai, and the resultant end of party cabinets, Konoe had reevaluated the political situation. Saionji, the last surviving *genro* and Konoe's original protector, began to worry about his protégé's growing connections with nationalistic groups and the army. Konoe professed his sympathy with criticism from the army and nationalistic groups directed against the parties. Indeed, he advised Saionji at one point that the parties could not lead unless they recognized a "new direction of fate" for the nation and seized the initiative from the army. Presumably, Konoe meant that in order to rule, the parties had to prepare the nation for a major war in Asia. More specifically, Konoe proposed that Saionji nominate as premier either Baron Hiranuma Kiichirō, the president of the reactionary National Essence Society (Kokuhonsha), or General Araki Sadao, an avid believer in the imperial way and the expansion of military power. Saionji flatly rejected Konoe's advice and designated the moderate Admiral Saitō Makoto.[22]

Meanwhile, Konoe became increasingly dissatisfied with Western attempts to limit Japanese influence in Asia. This was evident during a trip with Rōyama in 1934 to America, where Konoe met with political and business leaders. The American desire to protect the principle of the Open Door Policy in China and to induce Japanese cooperation in giving economic aid to the Nationalist government upset both men. Because Americans did not comprehend the principle of the recent Amau Declaration, that only Japan was responsible for maintaining peace in Asia, a fundamental difference in American and Japanese aims in China existed. "It is necessary," Rōyama concluded, "to make them [Americans] understand thoroughly Japan's view of China."[23]

In November 1935, Konoe went one step further by demanding new recognition for Japan's power in Asia. Basing his argument on a recent article by Colonel E. M. House, Konoe discussed the basic problems of international peace. He reasserted House's division of nations into two categories—the "haves," who possessed plentiful natural resources, and the "have-nots." The present structure of international peace embodied in the League of Nations favored the Western nations that possessed or controlled most of the world's resources. Because the Japanese had previously erred in accepting this international order, they were now justified in seeking, along with Italy and Germany, a redistribution of the world's wealth, an international "new deal."[24]

Konoe's call for basic political reforms and for a new deal in Asia helped set the fundamental goals of the Shōwa Research Association. No leading member of the group ever dissented from the basic aim of redressing the distribution of resources in the world. Moreover, the association enthusiastically pursued Konoe's dictum to seize the initiative from the army by promoting an aggressive foreign policy.

Konoe's direct personal relationship to the organization, though, is unclear. Despite encouraging Gotō Ryūnosuke to arrange the group, Konoe quickly ceased attending meetings, partly because he wished to end speculation that he was preparing to form a cabinet soon. He insisted, however, on receiving summaries of the association's discussions.[25] Many of the original participants were his personal acquaintances, but as the association expanded, many of the newer members had no personal connection with Konoe. Still, Gotō and Rōyama remained his close friends and advisers; and throughout the association's existence participants considered themselves an advisory body of the prince. The lack of harassment from the thought-control police, in spite of the presence of suspected leftists, also suggests that the group enjoyed the protection afforded to a relative of the imperial family. This security permitted the association to develop into a large and active organization.

Early Organization and Goals

During its first years, the Shōwa Research Association remained an informal organization, a *"sukiyaki* society."[26] Members usually met in Gotō's office in the Aoyama district of Tokyo and even paid a small fee to cover some of the expenses. Three main study groups formed: one on agricultural problems, another on educational reform, and one on comprehensive national policies. Initially, only the latter group was called the Shōwa Research Association. Ad hoc committees assembled to debate specific issues, and as the association's membership and activities grew, the structure became more formal.

The Shōwa Research Association became a distinct entity in 1935 when it moved to its own headquarters in the central Marunouchi business district of Tokyo.[27] The members defined their goals in research loosely: "(1) reform within the framework of the constitution, (2) rejection of the existing political parties, and (3) [to decide] from an anti-fascist viewpoint (a) where to place the emphasis of economic policy and (b) how to reform the political structure of Japan."[28] Although the association sponsored numerous discussion groups in its early years, there are no records of specific policy recommendations. The few surviving records of group discussions during 1935 reveal a strong interest among members in bureaucratic solutions to Japan's political and economic problems.

Plans for a new national policymaking body first drew the attention of members. By 1934, in response to the wishes of the army, major policy decisions were made by an "inner cabinet" composed of the premier and the army, navy, foreign, and finance ministers. Because party politicians were no longer appointed to these crucial posts, a small group of bureaucrats was beginning to determine policies. To counter this trend, Tokonami Takejirō, whom the Seiyūkai had expelled for joining the Okada cabinet, and Machida Chūji of the Minseitō proposed the creation of a national policy council.[29] They wanted an organ similar to the former Foreign Policy Deliberation Council (Gaikō chōsakai) established during World War I to involve party and business leaders with cabinet ministers in defining basic national policies.

The creation of a national policy council became an important topic of discussion within the Shōwa Research Association. Gotō Ryūnosuke, for example, approved the envisioned body on the condition that it be able to make national policies and carry them out.[30] He suspected, though, that the new council might infringe upon the constitutional responsibility of both the Diet and the cabinet for policy decisions. The prospect of political reform of any kind thrilled Sassa Hiroo. When economist Takahashi Kamekichi asked Sassa if he could really place great trust in the council, Sassa replied that he was happy that such an institution would "test new trends in the structure of national politics."[31]

Sassa's views were typical because he believed that the council would spur political reform, as a "force to stimulate the Diet, to make the parties sincere in establishing policies, and, furthermore, to encourage the awakening of the parties and the revival of party politics."[32] He also hoped that the council would produce plans "on a scientific basis." The proposed body would provide an opportunity for wider participation in policymaking by citizens outside the Diet and bureaucracy by "centering on an investigation bureau." His lament that "men of intellect are becoming indifferent to politics" indicated a preference for a staff of intellectuals.[33]

In May 1935, Premier Okada's establishment of the Cabinet Consultative Council (Naikaku shingikai) must have pleased members of the Shōwa Research Association. Pressure from the service ministries forced the premier to eliminate questions of national defense and foreign policy from the council's purview. Still, Okada opened the possibility for major policy initiatives by defining the council's mandate in broad terms as "setting national policy and planning the reform of the political situation."[34] The membership consisted of party and business leaders along with representatives from the House of Peers. The Cabinet Investigation Bureau was formed to administer the council's work and to conduct research into national issues. The bureau delegated research on specific topics to special committees that utilized the talents of young, reform-minded officials from all ministries, as well as prominent academics and journalists. Many of these men were connected with the Shōwa Research Association. Among its original members, Satō Kanji, Kawakami Jotarō, Tōhata Seiichi, and Maeda Tamon were active in the Cabinet Investigation Bureau, and Abe Shigetaka, the organizer of the Education Study Group, served as a specialist consultant in the bureau. Other members who later participated in the Shōwa Research Association included Yoshida Shigeru, Matsui Haruo, Nakajima Kenzō, Ōkochi Masatoshi, Ōkura Kinmochi, Takahashi Kamekichi, Okuyama Teijirō, Masaki Chifuyu, and Katsumata Seiichi.[35] Yoshida Shigeru, the first director of the Cabinet Investigation Bureau, and Matsui Haruo, the director of the Resources Bureau in 1936, were widely known as leading "new bureaucrats"—that is, fervent advocates of political and economic reform.[36] By 1936 they had also become leaders of the Shōwa Research Association.

Although they differed on the extent of reform needed in Japan, most members of the Shōwa Research Association assumed that changes in Japan's political and economic structures would occur through the employment of state power. Matsui Haruo championed the need for comprehensive national economic policies.[37] Kamei Kanichirō argued that state-affiliated groups, such as branches of the Imperial Reserve Association and the Industrial Association (Sangyō kumiai), would become the "forces of the future" in bringing political change to Japan.[38] Indeed, he grandiosely compared the possible alliance of such bureaucratic groups against the parliamentary system to the coalition of rebellious domains against the Tokugawa regime in the mid-nineteenth century. Sassa Hiroo regarded many of the new bureaucrats as opportunists, but he felt that some of them shared a conviction with all concerned Japanese that the political system required basic change. Noting that even Professor Minobe Tatsukichi had censured the selfish tactics of the political parties and had supported plans for the Cabinet Consultative Council, Sassa summed up the contemporary mood by remarking that Minobe's stand was "not conservative liberalism centered on capitalists but progressive liberalism centered on the people. This progressive trend has a basis in the thought shared generally among the people, whether they are intellectuals, young bureaucrats or military men."[39]

Accordingly, Sassa, along with most members of the Shōwa Research Association, endorsed the Election Purification Movement that the Home Ministry was then implementing.[40] Tazawa Yoshiharu began the Election Purification League in 1929. Requirements for members were simple: a pledge to vote according to their convictions, a contribution of forty *sen* to the candidate of their choice, and a letter to their candidate stating their personal confidence in him.[41] Tazawa's movement had minimal results until Gotō Fumio, Home Minister in the Okada cabinet and, in Sassa's judgment, a leader of the new bureaucrats, proposed a comprehensive national election purification campaign devised to end corruption committed by the political parties in elections. The election laws were revised in 1934 to grant prefectural governors, as Home Ministry officials, more control over the management of elections, and in May 1935 the cabinet announced the official inception of the government's Election Purification Movement. Tazawa became executive director, and Rōyama Masamichi served as a director.[42]

Many discussants at Shōwa Research Association meetings sympathized with using state power to enforce the "purification" of elections. Gotō Ryūnosuke wanted to insure that "national men" who could rise above local concerns would be elected to the Diet. Takahashi Kamekichi urged the mobilization of all existing groups, including even reservists, to clean up elections.[43] Sassa called for the public supervision of elections and favorably assessed the purification movement, despite the increased interference of the state in politics. "The purification movement creates a premise for the cleansing of the political world and for the reconstruction of the political parties. The constraints of the revised election laws and the bureaucratic coloring of the act of purification bring some evils; but one must recognize the chance for the rebirth of the political parties and for the readjustment of the political scene."[44] The state would be an ally of the people against the corruption of the established political parties.

One striking indication of the members' attitude toward the role of the state was Sassa's new view of the Okada "national unity" cabinet. Although Sassa had predicted in 1931 that the institution of a nonparty cabinet in Japan would lead to fascism, he now refused to identify the Okada cabinet as fascist. He defended the cabinet and argued that radical fascism could not occur in Japan, because the Japanese economic situation was healthy. Furthermore, he did not think that the controversy over Minobe's organ theory of the Meiji Constitution signaled the start of a fascist or militarist movement. Criticizing the attempts of the Seiyūkai to overthrow the present cabinet, he supported a "united nation cabinet" as more feasible than a party cabinet and better than rule by the army; he hoped that a new political party would emerge to support a nonpartisan cabinet.[45]

Sassa's fears and hopes were similar to those of many members of the Shōwa Research Association. They worried about the efficacy of Japanese politics and hoped for the emergence of a new political force to unite the nation. Soon, the association began systematic research into specific proposals for political reform to bind the government and the masses. This task would involve the formalization and expansion of the group's activity.

Reorganization and Expansion

The organization and the activity of the Shōwa Research Association grew considerably by the end of 1936. Its financial support became more diffuse, as Shiga Naokata cut off funding. Although records do not remain to pinpoint exactly when or why the elderly general withdrew his backing from the group, the participation of men with socialist backgrounds was one source of friction, according to Gotō. Gotō also claims to have severed relations with Shiga because of his insistence that the association conduct research for retired colonel Kobayashi Junichirō, the founder of a well-known nationalistic society, the Thirty-six Club. Afterward, the association obtained funds from the large *zaibatsu*—Mitsui, Mitsubishi, and Sumitomo—in recognition of its concern for important national issues.[46]

After the military rebellion of 1936 had signaled a forceful rejection of a cabinet supported by a political party and had brought a new assertion of military influence in domestic politics, the association rationalized its structure and enlarged its program.[47] The leaders hoped to take advantage of what promised to be a period of rapid change as an opportunity to influence national policies. The formal Executive Board of the Shōwa Research Association (Shōwa kenkyūkai jōnin iinkai) of ten members (later expanded to fifteen) evolved to define general goals and policies, the special committee (Shōwa kenkyūkai iinkai) of twenty men provided a pool of consultants, and the administrative bureau (Shōwa kenkyūkai jimukyoku) handled organizational and publishing matters. These groups constituted the permanent members of the association, which arranged year-long study groups on diplomatic, political, economic, agricultural, and educational affairs.

Each year, the executive board defined the general research goals of the association as a whole and the specific topics for its subsections. The board chose the members of the individual study groups and drew up the budget. One member from the administrative bureau and one from the special consultative committee were assigned to each study group and served as consultants and channels of liaison. The executive board also established a special study group to evaluate the results and conclusions of the other groups. The records of discussions remained secret, but the administrative bureau was responsible for publishing the conclusions of the general research in the name of the entire Shōwa Research Association.

This organizational structure had several advantages. It maintained a constant leadership core in the executive board and in the consultative committee, while allowing the involvement of a larger and more diverse circle of participants in the study groups. In one year, for example, the association had some 130 participants listed on its membership rolls.[48] Individual members in the study groups were given an unusual opportunity to present their ideas to an audience of prominent academics, journalists, politicians, and government officials. Influential members of the executive board could then pass on the results of research to top levels of the government. Moreover, the Shōwa Research Association could also arrange for the publication of its members' collective recommendations for national policies without exposing individuals to police pressure.

Along with the bureaucratization of the structure of the Shōwa Research Association, young new bureaucrats became prominent in its leadership.⁴⁹ Gotō Fumio and Matsui Haruo, for instance, became members of the executive board, as did Karazawa Toshiki, the head of the Home Ministry's Police Training School. Kaya Okinori, who would serve as Finance Minister in Konoe's first cabinet, joined the consultative committee in 1936, and by 1939 he served on the executive board. Five of the original founders remained on the executive board: namely, Rōyama Masamichi, Gotō Ryūnosuke, Tazawa Yoshiharu, Nasu Hiroshi, and Tajima Michiji. Takahashi Kamekichi and Sassa Hiroo also joined the board. No members of the Social Mass party continued as formal leaders of the association.⁵⁰

The consultative committee in 1936 included prominent bureaucrats, too, such as Yoshida Shigeru (head of the Cabinet Investigation Bureau), Yoshino Shinji (vice-minister of the Ministry of Commerce and Industry), Arita Hachirō (foreign minister in the Hirota cabinet), and Aoki Kazuo and Taki Masao, who would later serve as directors of the Cabinet Planning Board. The committee also encompassed well-known intellectuals, including Professor Ōkochi Masatoshi, Professor Taniguchi Toshihiko, and economist Miura Tetsutarō, as well as the journalist and politician Kazami Akira, who would be chief cabinet secretary in Konoe's first cabinet.⁵¹

The executive board held a series of meetings in the fall and winter of 1936 to interpret recent developments in domestic and foreign affairs and to determine the basic research approach of the association. These meetings marked the first attempt to chart guidelines for a comprehensive foreign and domestic policy.⁵² In many ways, the leaders of the executive board were seeking to seize the initiative from the army by formulating very ambitious goals for Japan's foreign policy.

In the controversy over Japan's foreign policy that followed the signing of the Anti-Comintern Pact with Germany, the executive board concurred that "all the unrest in our country stems from problems of foreign affairs."⁵³ Indeed, some Japanese criticized both the secrecy of the negotiations that preceded the signing of the pact and the alliance itself with Nazi Germany. There were fears that America and Britain would view Japan as part of the "fascist bloc."⁵⁴ Reiterating Konoe's public views, the board asserted that the central problem of world peace was not fascism but the struggle of the "poor" nations and affirmed that the "voices of the world are saying that there can be no real peace as long as the great powers [the United States and Britain] do not compromise."⁵⁵

Sweeping aside fears of an alliance with the "fascist bloc," the board judged that the Anti-Comintern Pact had instead irrevocably linked Japan with the "poor" nations (Germany and Italy) against the "rich country bloc" (Great Britain, the United States, and the Soviet Union).[56] The significance of the pact was less the containment of international communism than the polarization of the world into two competing groups—the poor nations and the rich. Because the pact strengthened Japan's position to challenge Britain's power in the Far East, the Anti-Comintern Pact represented a diplomatic defeat for Britain in East Asia, "whether she realized it or not." Significantly, the board ignored China as a poor nation. Its members, though, agreed that a lasting settlement of the China problem could be accomplished only through a redistribution of world economic resources through an international conference that recognized the grievances of the poor nations.[57]

The executive board was convinced that the only way to gain influence over the army was to "take the army by the hand" through outlining ambitious goals for foreign policy. "It was recognized again," the records state, "that a positive and constructive plan was necessary . . . to accomplish this goal."[58] Cooperation with the army's general policies was necessary. "Regarding criticism against the actions of the army, former unkind criticism from a position of liberalism or from an antimilitary standpoint will not do at all. All agreed with the opinion that it was necessary [to have] a method of argument to persuade the army by abandoning a hostile position, following the direction of the Manchurian Incident, and [arguing] that to accomplish its anticipated goals, these [policies] are necessary."[59]

This strategy to "seize the initiative" seemed the most propitious way to cope with the military during the fall of 1936. The executive board as a whole thus adopted an approach for changing government policies similar to that of Rōyama, Ryū, and Miki. The board chose not to confront major trends but to guide them toward utopian goals; thus, the ultimate aim of military action in China should be peaceful cooperation with Japan's Asian neighbors.

Because the cooperation of the Chinese people was essential if Japan was to contain Soviet expansionism and pursue the "hundred-year policy of southern advance," the board proposed a program to establish Japan's leadership of the continent. Japan should liberate China by opposing the domination of the Western powers and forsaking any "territorial ambitions."[60] Japan's political ambitions to dominate China, however, would be clear. "Japan will not recognize the Nanking government but it will recognize independent provincial governments." Japan would "greatly help governments that declare[d] a will to cooperate with Japan," and it would "completely harass governments that [were] opposed to Japan, no matter whether they [were] central governments or provincial governments."

The executive board had merely ratified the "divide and conquer" strategy that the army had pursued in North China since 1933. Japan should establish "pro-Japanese governments in the five provinces of North China but it should not interfere boldly south of this area," and it should give the Chinese people economic aid to "cooperate greatly for the enlargement of the buying power of the people and for industrial development." Relying on the "spirit of mutual aid between different peoples," Japan, with this help, would "win the hearts of the Chinese people."

The leaders of the Shōwa Research Association intended to unify foreign policy by rallying around the most obnoxious and counterproductive features of the army's program in China—the effort to detach the provinces of North China from the Nanking government by the so-called autonomy movement. Following its established strategy for promoting reforms, the board also labored to place the best light on the increasingly authoritarian demeanor of the government and armed forces after the mutiny of February 1936. The tone and thrust of the discussions indicated that these men chose to assign the most positive meaning possible to a rebellion in which the senior court adviser and the finance minister had been slaughtered and a cabinet commanding a parliamentary majority had been shattered. One member ascribed the motives of the rebels to their frustration with the "ignorance and ineptitude" of the Diet and the government in general; he added that the new bureaucrats shared the frustration of radical young officers. Indeed, he suggested that the rebellion exemplified the phenomenon of "juniors ruling seniors" (*gekokujō*) and that the rebels' behavior reflected a widespread demand for social change evident in the popular denunciation of Minobe Tatsukichi.[61] Gekokujō, a rebellious act of violence, was metamorphosed into something good and noble:

> I see the cause of "juniors ruling seniors" ultimately in the lack of response of the ruling class to the progress of science. Thus, if a leadership class at a certain time loses the ability to use scientific progress for the benefit of society and cannot properly respond to the demands of a new era, there arises the phenomenon of "juniors ruling seniors," where people calling for a new age do not recognize the authority of the past order, and, on the contrary, new people lead the era with some kind of ideology. "Juniors ruling seniors" in this sense is not a world-wide phenomenon. From the point of view of the destruction of the old order, it is truly a dark age; but from the view of the progress of science and discovery, one must say it is a brilliant age.[62]

This logic rationalized the actions of radical young officers who wanted to destroy parliamentary government and justified the policies that the Hirota cabinet insisted would "renovate" the state and society by placing controls on the Diet and the economy. This logic was also similar to that of Rōyama and Ryū, who viewed the army mutiny and increased pressure for a controlled economy as steps toward effective reforms.

The executive board cited the rise of the "new bureaucrats" within the government as another demand for social reforms. After debating whether these officials embodied a positive force for reform or a passive response to the incompetence of the political parties, "many of the members agreed with the assertion of one member . . . that although the new bureaucrats were not a great force today, they would gradually attain power in the near future; and, along with the army, they would become powerful elements in the construction of a new age." In apparent reference to European fascist models, the board concurred that a "corporativist" or "unionist" state would arise as the "future political form" for Japan and that dictatorial politics were necessary as a transitional stage.[63]

To guide Japan to its destined shape, the Shōwa Research Association sought to outline dramatic new policies. To this end, in June 1937 the executive board produced a comprehensive program that created research groups to investigate political, economic, budgetary, agricultural, educational, and foreign policies. Endeavoring to explain the general purpose of the association, the board stated: "In these times, it is urgent to establish a correct basic knowledge of the situation; and, on this basis, to plan the unity of national opinion regarding foreign and domestic policy to bind the union of each group —the business world, officials, and the army. This association now takes the clarification and establishment of such a comprehensive view of the situation as its most important responsibility."[64] The aim of the Shōwa Research Association was nothing less than the design of a totally new national polity, or form, for Japan.

This aim had motivated the Shōwa Research Association since its inception. The perception that Japan faced a crisis that demanded new and imaginative government policies drew members from various sectors of the society. Although their views diverged on specific issues, many members shared a belief that the times required a new political force and a reinforced ethic of individual service to the state or society as an entity that transcended the interests of private organizations. Optimistic about future trends, leaders of the association envisioned a corporatist state and Japan's leadership of China. When hostilities erupted in China during July, the need for mobilization would provide a compelling rationale for reforms to unify and strengthen the nation and inculcate a spirit of national service.

The mood in the Shōwa Research Association confirmed Rōyama Masamichi's perception of the political and foreign problems facing Japan and his attraction to European fascist policies. By 1938, Ryū Shintarō and Miki Kiyoshi had joined with Rōyama to design a new course for Japan. Ryū and Miki found the association to be a comfortable and stimulating environment because their ideas meshed with those of the leadership. Miki's quest for a new "thought" to dominate China fit the goal of "winning the hearts of the Chinese people," and his desire for a new ideology to replace "bourgeois" liberalism and to emphasize loyalty to a new "totality" suited the demand for a new national ethic. Ryū's attacks on the economic establishment and his advocacy of economic planning assumed the priority of public over private welfare. In addition, by providing access to important government officials, the association gave these intellectuals the chance to fulfill their long-held goal of influencing national policies.

Participation in the Shōwa Research Association guaranteed protection from censorship and distribution of their proposals to the highest levels of government. Discussions with sympathetic officials helped convince these writers that basic political and economic reforms were imminent. This interaction also led Rōyama, Ryū, and Miki to assume a primary concern of these public officials—designing policies for expanding Japanese influence on the Asian continent and for mobilizing the nation to support this effort. The closer that Rōyama, Ryū, and Miki thought they were getting to political power, the more they phrased their proposals toward achieving these goals.

7. Designing a New Order

After 1936 Japan's role in China and mobilization for a major war became central issues for the government and captured the attention of Miki Kiyoshi and Ryū Shintarō in the Shōwa Research Association. Ryū continued to study European fascism for models of future economic policies in Japan, and Miki began to affirm some of fascism's basic concepts as ideals for Japan to emulate. Both writers accepted the need for Japanese direction of Chinese affairs.

Some army officers and civilians questioned the need for military dominance. As its strategic priority, the Army General Staff prepared for war with the Soviet Union and vowed to avoid a war with China. Because the General Staff wanted time to achieve economic reforms at home and to integrate Manchuria into the defense economy in accordance with its five-year economic plan, military planners judged that Japan could not risk a confrontation with the Western powers. "To guarantee the neutrality of Britain and the United States, avoidance of war with China [was] crucial."[1]

From a different perspective, some prominent civilians criticized the army's extension of control by establishing "autonomous" governments within demilitarized zones in North China. In the popular press, Professor Yanaihara Tadao openly opposed Japan's aggression on the mainland by arguing in 1937 that the Nationalist government of Generalissimo Chiang Kai-shek would inevitably succeed in unifying China politically and in promoting economic development through a modern capitalist system.[2] Japanese policy should recognize and encourage this trend. The alternative was continual conflict between Japanese and Chinese nationalism. Japan had no right to interfere in Chinese affairs, and if Japan desired peace, it should not provoke China. Yanaihara did not see the need for a new world order to benefit the "poor" nations and did not advocate a "new thought" to unify East Asia, as had Miki Kiyoshi, but simply argued for the right of China to develop as an independent modern nation. These views represented a minority position, and Yanaihara was soon forced to leave his university post; but together with the adverse reaction of many Diet politicians and business leaders to the army's domestic reform program, his writings reflected an increased questioning of military policies.

In July 1937, as if to underscore Professor Yanaihara's prophecy, war broke out between China and Japan. Hostilities began with a small encounter between Japanese and Chinese troops near Peking. When Chiang Kai-shek refused a local settlement of the incident, Premier Konoe found himself in a difficult political situation. His army minister favored dispatching more troops to China, but the General Staff opposed escalation. Finally, announcing his desire for a "fundamental solution of Sino-Japanese relations" on July 27, Konoe sent reinforcements. The inner cabinet decided in August that Japan's terms should include de facto recognition of Manchukuo by the Nationalist government, as well as the creation of an enlarged demilitarized zone in North China.³ These terms were unacceptable to the Kuomintang.

As the war expanded and continued into 1938, it posed two dilemmas for Japanese policymakers: terminating the conflict without sacrificing Japan's prestige and developing Japan's economic strength to maintain a war effort. These two issues dominated discussions in the Shōwa Research Association and the writings of Miki Kiyoshi, Ryū Shintarō, and Rōyama Masamichi after 1937. Significantly, these writers did not lend support to the Army General Staff in its efforts to limit the fighting, and they did not urge the unilateral withdrawal of Japanese troops, as Yanaihara Tadao had done. Instead these men sought their own unique solution to the "China Incident" in an "East Asian cooperative body."

A New East Asian Order

The committees of the Shōwa Research Association that discussed the China Incident anticipated and generally concurred with government policies.⁴ On July 15, 1937, the administrative bureau published an outline entitled "Policies for the Incident in North China."⁵ While calling for the "independence of foreign policy from the military," the report demanded a "complete readjustment of Sino-Japanese relations." The cause of the incident was not the Japanese military but the "unstable situation in North China." The situation required direct negotiations with the Nanking government to establish an enlarged demilitarized zone in North China as one way to achieve stability.

In August, as the Japanese cabinet set forth its negotiating demands for a "fundamental solution of relations" with China, the mood within the Shōwa Research Association was optimistic about an early settlement. One member expressed his faith in Japan's military might: When the North was secure and "when Shanghai is suppressed, and Nanking bombed, Chiang or someone in place of him will arise and stop the resistance to Japan."⁶ Then Japan could withdraw its troops, end the privilege of extraterritoriality, and initiate a policy of cooperation with China. Another member was concerned about international criticism of the China War and argued that to justify its actions Japan "must have basic concepts and a thought that can serve as a basis for propaganda."[7]

The tone of discussions within the association became more exasperated in four months. Despite great victories and the seizure of China's capital, Nanking, Chiang had not capitulated. One participant in a committee asked in December, "How do we make the Nationalist government give up its will quickly?" Replying that the Nationalists "will not give up so easily," a colleague recommended more military pressure.[8] The members of one committee agreed finally that the "Nanking government is a false government" and that the creation of a new central government for China was desirable.[9] Another position paper was more conciliatory in supporting the recognition in principle of the unity of China under the Kuomintang, aid for China's "development as a modern nation," and direct negotiations between Japan and Chiang. Yet, even this draft affirmed the Japanese government's goal of hegemony over North China through the creation of demilitarized zones and a mandatory end to anti-Japanese activities there.[10] In contrast to Professor Yanaihara, the members of the Shōwa Research Association who were most sympathetic to the force of Chinese nationalism did not challenge basic government policies.

The association also advised that responsibility for the determination of China policy be removed from the Foreign Ministry to a new organ that would include military officers, diplomats, and other civilian officials. The reasons for this urgent proposal were not explained in detail; the draft stated vaguely that preparations for a diplomatic initiative were necessary because "[we] expect a Bismarckian turn in China policy and [we expect] to resolve the situation peacefully from the standpoint of pursuing Japan's world policies as well as securing the fruits of war."[11] During 1938 the army also demanded the establishment of such a body to seize control of China policy from the Foreign Ministry, and in October 1938, Premier Konoe created the China Affairs Bureau (Taishiin) over the vigorous protests of professional diplomats.

Similarities between policy recommendations of the association and announcements of governmental policy suggest the influence of Shōwa Research Association proposals on Konoe.[12] On July 15, for example, the association advocated a "complete readjustment of Sino-Japanese relations," and within twelve days Premier Konoe announced the need for a "fundamental solution to Sino-Japanese relations." Throughout 1937 the association anticipated or concurred with the thrust of Foreign Minister Hirota Kōki's demands on Chiang Kai-shek, especially the creation of an enlarged demilitarized zone in North China and an end to anti-Japanese activities. The members of the association, however, were still divided on the issue of creating a new Chinese government to replace the Kuomintang.

In 1938, Konoe was also unsure of his attitudes toward China. In January he proclaimed the nonrecognition of the Nanking government, but in May, judging that tactic a failure, he replaced Hirota with General Ugaki Kazushige, who wanted to initiate negotiations immediately with the Nationalist government. Accordingly, in June the Shōwa Research Association created an updated outline, "General Goals and Policies for Resolving the China Incident."[13] The association viewed China policy within the framework of four long-term goals of Japanese diplomacy: avoidance of war with the Soviet Union, the neutralization of the United States and France, the strengthening of the Anti-Comintern Pact with Germany, and the ultimate ouster of Britain from Asia. One immediate aim was to sever relations between Britain and the Kuomintang. To accomplish peace within this context the association offered two plans. One plan called for recognition of the Nationalist government and negotiations with it. Japanese terms were to be similar to those already decided: a demilitarized zone, an end to anti-Japanese acts, recognition of Manchukuo, Chinese participation in the Anti-Comintern Pact, and an indemnity. The other plan assumed the destruction of the Kuomintang and the creation of a new government.

The Five Ministers Conference, the policymaking group of the Konoe cabinet, soon determined a similar set of alternatives. The ministers' goals were identical to those outlined by the Shōwa Research Association, except that they explicitly emphasized the creation of a new Chinese government.[14] If Chiang surrendered, the Nationalists would be required to participate in a new government, consent to the reform of the old regime, and adopt a pro-Japanese and anticommunist policy; Chiang would be asked to retire from politics. If the generalissimo did not yield, Japan would smash his government and establish a new one. A week later, the five ministers envisioned the shape of a new Chinese government as a loose confederation (*bunji gassaku*) of local regimes. The main requirement for this body would be a friendly policy toward Japan.[15]

The main impetus for a new government in China came from the Imperial Army, which was overseeing the occupation of the mainland. Officers like General Ishiwara Kanji championed the union of Manchuria, China, and Japan into an East Asian league.[16] Believing the main problem in China was enlisting the "autonomous cooperation" of the Chinese people, the Army Ministry proposed that Japan follow the confederation strategy to create a new central government with just a few Japanese advisers.[17] Meanwhile, Lieutenant General Doihara Kenji began negotiations with the Chinese politician

Wu P'ei-fu to head a new Chinese regime, and Colonel Kagesa Sadaaki contacted Wang Ching-wei, vice-president of the Kuomintang, as a potential leader.[18]

Propaganda was to play an important role in these political machinations. The Army Ministry stressed the need for a new thought that could "revere the individual culture of the Chinese race, especially the common culture of China and Japan, revive the civilization and spirit of the Orient and encourage Sino-Japanese cooperation." Japan had to "establish an ideology that can be a basis of the realization of Sino-Japanese cooperation for the pursuit of the policies of the new regime."[19] Doihara explained that "the current incident is a war for the creation of a new culture" and urged Japanese intellectuals to become "cultural warriors" to ensure the survival of Oriental culture and the "progress" of Japan. In a world in which "democratic civilization" had "lost its progressive character completely" and the "objective trends of the world" indicated that Western ideologies were "bankrupt," Japan could give the world a "new order."[20]

To take advantage of this opportunity the leaders of the Shōwa Research Association invited Miki Kiyoshi to form the Cultural Problems Research Group (Bunka mondai kenkyūkai) in 1938. Having married the daughter of Professor Tōhata Seiichi, a charter member, Miki was known to association members through personal contacts and through participation in discussions of educational reform. His writings and his constant prodding of intellectuals to speak out on political issues indicated an intense interest in matters of national policy. Impressed by Miki's broad perspective on current events and by his energy, Sakai Saburō invited him to head the Cultural Problems Group, which would attempt to produce a theory to guide the various research projects of the association.[21] The group furnished a chance for Miki to complete his quest for designing a new ideology, a new "totality" in the form of a comprehensive plan for a new Japan, and to convey his ideas to important officials.

Miki agreed with the public pronouncements of the government that the "objectives of the military actions of Japan in China are to establish peace in the Orient and friendly relations between the two countries." Because "military activities cannot be carried on permanently, Japan had to resort to the measure of influencing China by means of ideas. . . . 'The spirit of Japan' [could] serve as the ideological basis for such a relationship between the two countries. . . . This [was] the challenge with which Japanese culture [was] confronted, now that it [had] started to extend its sphere of influence over the Asiatic continent. This challenge [was] sufficient to stimulate the Japanese intelligentsia to rise to the occasion."[22]

As Japanese troops advanced into central China in June 1938, Miki's appeals became more urgent. He pleaded with the Japanese intelligentsia to recognize the "gravity of the reality that present-day Japan faces," and wrote that all Japanese were wrapped up in one "fate." It was the appropriate time "for the intelligentsia to rise up to this fate aggressively and to participate dynamically in the solution of real problems."[23] "Thus, the autonomous contribution of the intellectual class [was] necessary for the progress of present politics. The politics of tomorrow [would] be possible because the intellectual class [would] influence politics from its own position and [would] give it flexibility." Not only Japan, but the whole "world [was] agonizing, while searching for a new order."[24] Japan could point the way to a "new order," and "Japan's military actions, because of their scale, [would] have world historical impact. . . . It [was] expected that there must be a grand thought to correspond to grand actions. . . . For example, Nazi thought had [assumed] the general name of national socialism. What Japan need[ed was] a world, not a regional thought."[25]

In a private report to the Shōwa Research Association, Miki first expounded on the historical significance of the China Incident by labeling the incident a "world war" that marked the "beginning of the twentieth century" for the Orient.[26] The incident represented not a human tragedy but a Japanese opportunity, the fulfillment of "Japan's historic mission, in spatial terms, . . . the unification of Asia," in general terms, "the resolution of the contradictions of capitalist societies."

The culture group began its work during the summer of 1938 by sponsoring a series of lectures on current economic and intellectual developments. Ryū Shintarō, for example, spoke on "economic reorganization"; Keio University Professor Kawada Tetsuji discussed "Japanism"; and Miki himself interpreted the "meaning and special character of Confucianism."[27] By the winter the members had drafted *The Principles of Thought for a New Japan*. The thrust of this report was that Japan could lead the way in creating a new East Asian culture of international significance. As a "self-criticism of Europeanism," World War I had ended the era in which world history had centered on Europe. Now another war, the China Incident, would "clarify a new idea of world history." Achievement of this goal required domestic reform within Japan and a "qualitative change" in the nature of Japanese culture.[28]

The report reflected Miki's perspective on Japanese culture. Japan's superiority depended on a capability to absorb and combine foreign influences, to be a "subjective culture without form." Through the "breadth of [its] heart" Japanese culture could unite seemingly incompatible ideas. The capacity to absorb foreign ideas had made Japanese culture "enterprising," as demonstrated by the rapid development of military power enhanced by the Japanese adoption of Western technology.[29] Miki's group believed that the Japanese should now set specific theoretical goals for cultural development. Japan should protect its "special characteristics," and "for Japanese culture to progress outward and to be recognized by all other peoples, Japanese culture must not settle for being without a form but it must develop as an objective culture with a form."[30] The main task before Japan was, therefore, the creation of a new cultural "form," a "cooperative body" (*kyōdōtai*) for East Asia.

The report assumed that as "action in world history always begins with one race," it was Japan's "moral mission" to lead the Orient. Japan would become a cultural center as ancient Greece had been: "Previously, so-called Hellenistic culture, which was represented by the Olympic games, blossomed because of the union of races in Greece. The mission of the East Asian cooperative body is to create a 'new East Asian culture' of world significance, as Hellenistic culture was, on the basis of the cooperation of all races in East Asia."[31] The philosophy of cooperativism (*kyōdōshugi*) would rescue Japan, East Asia, and perhaps the world.

The principles of cooperativism presumed that the creation of regional economic blocs was the fundamental economic and political trend in contemporary international relations. The Soviet Union, for example, represented one self-sufficient bloc, as did the American-dollar bloc of the Western Hemisphere. Japan's future lay in forming an East Asian bloc, united by the ideology of cooperativism. A major goal, then, was the "liberation" of China from Western imperialism so that the Orient could determine its own destiny. Another principle was a mutual respect between China and Japan that demanded that Japan transcend "racialism" in leading East Asia. "Japan must not prevent the national unity of China. . . . However, it is required that, at the same time, China rise above simple nationalism in order to enter into the new order."[32] The culture study group proposed to reconcile what many observers saw as two irreconcilable forces—Chinese and Japanese nationalism.

As an alternative to liberalism and socialism, the philosophy of cooperativism would eliminate the "evils of capitalism," the strategy of "class struggle," and the "bureaucratization" of Japanese life. The state would have a unified economic structure: "Classes will cease being classes and become [incorporated into] an occupational order within a higher whole; and this occupational order will be considered functional and not stratified."[33] Because individual rights would be sacrificed for the welfare of the "whole," Japan's "new thought" had to depend upon a type of "totalitarianism" (*zentaishugi*). Although there was a need to preserve the "autonomy and creative power of the individual" and the influence of the "popular will," there must be "planning based on the whole and control of individual freedom. . . . In contrast to individualism, which considered the individual first and society second, co-operativism considers society first and the individual second. In other words, the individual is born from society, exists because of society, and can create the self completely within society."[34]

Finally, the report argued that the Orient could overcome the individualistic atomism of the modern world. Using the concepts of the German sociologist Ferdinand Toennies, Miki wrote that Oriental society was a type of *Gemeinschaft* society, one dominated by close ties of kinship as in a traditional rural community. Modern Western society, in contrast, constituted a *Gesellschaft*, an organization marked by rational and contractual relationships. The culture study group hoped that the *Gemeinschaft* of the East could somehow absorb the "scientific spirit" of the West's *Gesellschaft*, reject capitalism, root out "feudalism," and create a new *Gemeinschaft*. This ideal society would incorporate Western technology, but avoid the insidious doctrine of individualism. The emphasis of Confucian "humanism" on proper social relationships would provide a sound basis for the new community, in which the individual would have to place the welfare of the whole above his own selfish interests. The "cooperative body" would be a uniquely Asian product.[35]

Miki's explanation of the *kyōdōtai* indicated for the first time his concept of an ideal Japanese state. It also reflected themes borrowed from European fascism. The emphasis on constructing a national "occupational order" suggested a corporate state. Just as European fascists advocated a new type of freedom "within the collectivity," Miki stressed that individual "creativity" could be preserved through service to the cooperative body. However contradictory this stance was, it allowed him to argue for the submission of the individual to the nation while praising creative freedom. Complete identification of the individual with the nation would dissolve the distinction between liberty and submission to authority. He wrote two years later that when "all the people are working while united in the structure of the whole, control . . . will become freedom; each person will be able to revive the creativity of his self in his work."[36]

Miki glorified the national community in arguing that the formation of a national cooperative body was an essential step toward an East Asian cooperative body. His statement that cooperativism valued society over the individual echoed Alfredo Rocco's explanation of the primacy of the state in fascism. In 1939 he asserted that the nation would become the arbiter of all values, a "moral whole," which alone could resolve social and economic conflicts.[37] Although Miki did not praise an ancient era of national virility, of conquest and struggle, as Italian fascists glorified the Roman Empire and Nazi writers did the ancient *Volk*,[38] he cited the Confucian heritage and traditional values that facilitated social harmony and submission to the state. Moreover, Miki believed nationalistic sentiment and the power of the state could aid the rational reform of Japanese society.

Drafted when the Japanese government was plotting to create an alternative to the Nationalist regime, *The Principles for a New Japan* also provided a rationale for a "new order" of relations between Japan and China.[39] Thus, Miki's ideas suited the policies advocated by the military in China. He had at least indirect contact with army officers by becoming a director of a private group, the Shinyūsha (New Friends Society), which Lieutenant General Doihara funded to assemble Chinese and Japanese in a "new culture movement."[40] Although this organization disbanded within a year, Miki's participation in it demonstrated his enthusiasm for pursuing the establishment of a new Oriental bloc even through cooperation with army officers.

Since the early 1930s, Miki had argued that a new culture or ideology, a "new liberalism," could solve Japan's domestic political problems, that a "new thought" could unite East Asia, and that ideology could influence politics. Noting the political strains caused by the China War, Miki reiterated in 1939 the need for a theory to explain the China Incident, to guide domestic reform, and to inspire the people of Japan. This was a political necessity, because "theories" and "ideals" enabled people to anticipate and control events. "Intellectuals must be the custodians of theory and the protectors of ideals. . . . The brotherhood of intellectuals must cooperate, develop a theory which the times sincerely demand, and strive to promote ideals."[41]

Miki's efforts in the Shōwa Research Association to set forth a new "form" of Oriental culture paralleled the development in his private writings of a new "philosophy of action," which stressed the ability of people to invent new social and political forms of history through "imagination."[42] Convinced that history moved from "form to form," Miki thought in 1938 that the time had arrived to conceive a new form of Japanese and Chinese culture as the first step toward the realization of a new social structure—a possibility that was very real to him.

As Miki laid down abstract guidelines for an East Asian bloc, other leading members of the Shōwa Research Association made more specific policy suggestions for accomplishing that goal. A special task force, the China Incident Policy Committee (Shina jihen taisaku iinkai), labored over ways to end the China War honorably but quickly.[43] The committee issued a report on September 30, 1938, that called for the establishment of a new order in China by Japan's issuing soon after the expected fall of Wuhan "a declaration appealing to the Chinese people (both friends and enemies), Japan, and the world." The statement would stress the goals of Japan: "peace in the Orient," the "advancement of an anticommunist union," the creation of the independent power of the Orient, cooperation between Japan and China toward the "revival of the Orient," and the "cooperation of the Western powers for the construction of the new order."[44] Emphasizing that Japan wished to avoid a "great war," the committee advised that the declaration soften the announced policy of nonrecognition of the Nationalist government. Although the committee did not expect that the declaration would lead to immediate cooperation with China, it did hope that it could help signal a fresh Japanese stance toward China.

The members envisioned a new "representative" government evolving in China with close ties to Japan and Manchuria through an East Asian policy liaison body to coordinate military, economic, and diplomatic policies among the three nations and anchor a regional bloc in the form of an East Asian league.[45] While maintaining a forceful military presence and sponsoring "autonomous" governments, Japan should consider the needs of its "partner" and aid its economic development. Western trade and investment would be welcomed, but Britain would be induced to "give up aid to Chiang's government" and to "cooperate positively with Japan."[46] In effect, Japan would dominate China through a political and economic union.

This vision soon became government policy. Almost immediately after the fall of Wuhan, Premier Konoe, in a radio address on November 3, defined Japan's new war aim as the creation of an East Asian "new order."[47] The prince stated that Japan sought China's "cooperation and not conquest." Japan wanted a "new order of peace in the Far East," was determined to "fight it out with communism," and would "not exclude the cooperation of foreign powers." If the Nationalist government would effect radical reforms, Konoe promised that Japan "would not reject the participation of the National Government" in the "reconstruction of China." The premier was morally certain that in "pace with the progress of history" Japan had "entered upon a new stage of creation in all fields of human life."

The Shōwa Research Association influenced this speech. The assumption that the war now entailed a universally important moral purpose and creation of a new stage in world history through the new order indicated that Konoe shared Miki Kiyoshi's perspective on the China Incident and on the proper solution to it. Nakayama Yū, one of Konoe's speechwriters, composed the actual text of the declaration,[48] but the timing and the main content of the statement followed the guidelines put forth by the China Incident Policy Committee of the association one month beforehand. Like the committee, Konoe reiterated the stated goals of Japanese continental policy—specifically, peace, an anti-Comintern alliance, and an end to Chinese hostility. His offer to absorb the Chinese into an East Asian new order reflected the strategy of the committee to defuse the explosive force of Chinese nationalism through a policy aimed at incorporating the Kuomintang into a regional body.

The popular press during the 1930s suspected that the Shōwa Research Association was the brain trust of Premier Konoe,[49] and, indeed, important civil servants and cabinet officers did participate in the association. Committees sometimes anticipated significant developments in government policy and generally concurred with them. Cabinet Secretary Kazami Akira was active in discussions of China policy, and Konoe followed the advice of the China Incident Policy Committee by declaring Japan's aspirations for a new Asian order shortly after the fall of Wuhan. The claim that the association had no influence on national policy assumes that the group's aim was to harness the military, end the war in China, and reduce oppression at home.[50] The main goal of participants like Miki and Ryū, however, was to use the China conflict and national mobilization to effect basic reforms of capitalism and parliamentary democracy within Japan and to create an Asian utopia under Japanese guidance.

Demands for a Defense Economy

As the China War escalated, Japan's most immediate economic problem was a balance of payments deficit following a dramatic increase in imports during 1937. The stockpiling of strategic raw materials caused Japanese imports in 1937 to exceed exports by a huge amount.[51] In order to correct this deficit the Diet passed the Temporary Funds Adjustment Act and the Temporary Foreign Trade Control Act, which required prior governmental approval for large purchases of imports and restricted the volume and type of imported goods. The government also limited imports of raw cotton for Japan's textile industries and favored imports of raw iron and scrap steel for heavy industry. By the end of 1938 Japan had restored a favorable balance of trade.

Despite the short-term success of the new trade policies, new problems arose in Japan's economic situation. No new export-oriented industries emerged to replace the restricted textile industry. Japan, therefore, could not expand its capacity to earn foreign exchange outside of the yen bloc in order to buy imports of raw materials. Because Japan was dependent on countries outside its empire for iron ore, scrap iron, oil, and other essential items, raising imports and finding reliable sources of raw materials became key economic issues during the China War. The difficulties that Japan faced in purchasing raw materials were evidenced by the stagnation of imports after 1938, despite the economic mobilization program.

The economic demands of the China Incident, in addition, placed a serious strain on capital resources, as Japan attempted to create new sources of raw materials. Although North China and Manchuria had important reserves of fuels and metals, such as coal and iron ore, the cost of their long-term development was expensive. Japan poured investment into both regions between 1932 and 1937, mostly in exported machinery, but could not significantly augment its purchase of supplies. By 1937 the government realized that Japan was reaching its fiscal limits. Plans for future development stressed the need for Manchukuo to finance its own economic development and the necessity for Western investment.[52]

The growing military portion of the national budget, along with increased budget deficits, also presented a major problem. As the national budget expanded, the percentage comprising military expenditures rose from 31 percent in 1931 to 47 percent in 1936.[53] Cuts in civilian administration and domestic economic relief measures had reduced the annual deficit of the budget between 1934 and 1936. After the assassination of Finance Minister Takahashi in February 1936, however, the government resumed a policy of increased military expenditures and deficit financing. That policy stimulated inflation, and the retail price index jumped sharply.[54]

Given these difficulties, the need for more economic control by the state was obvious to military and bureaucratic circles. The most forceful call for a state-controlled economy came from the army. In December 1935, Miyazaki Masayoshi, an economist working for the South Manchurian Railway, and Colonel Ishiwara Kanji, head of the Operations Section of the General Staff, had organized the Japan-Manchuria Financial and Economic Research Association in order to draw up plans for the industrial development of Japan's empire.[55] Miyazaki's estimates of production targets for munitions-related industries in Manchuria evolved into the government's Five-Year Plan for Manchurian Industrial Development. His research also served as a basis for the Army Ministry's Five-Year Plan for Important Industries.[56]

Miyazaki's proposals for a restructuring of the Japanese economy to suit the needs of the military received wide support within the army. Miyazaki explained in 1938 that Japan's escape from dependence on the West began with the Manchurian Incident and the army's attempts to impose a planned economy in Manchukuo.[57] To him, Japan's future lay in an integrated East Asian bloc centered on China. A cooperative relationship between Japan and China based on a planned regional economy would enable Japan to provide economic aid to its neighbor and spur industrial development. The primary responsibility for directing the regional economy would be assigned to the Japanese military. Specifically, Miyazaki proposed the establishment of a supreme defense agency (*saikō kokubō kikan*) to supervise a central economic planning agency (*keizai chūsa kikan*) that would coordinate economic planning.[58]

Miyazaki did not advocate nationalization of industry. His objective was governmental economic planning as a means toward national defense, "to encourage the functioning of the economic system to its highest limits for the prosecution of war." He lauded the Nazi system, with its tight organization of cartels and restriction on profits, as a fine model of firm state guidance over the economy that also permitted private ownership and initiative.[59] Recognizing that there would be an immediate decline in nonmilitary industries, including textiles, he even argued that, because their long-term health depended on the growth of an East Asian regional bloc, a controlled economy would ultimately be beneficial to those sectors too.[60] Miyazaki articulated a complete prescription for a future East Asian economy designed to satisfy the needs of the military.

As one step toward this type of controlled economy, the Army Ministry pressured the government to adopt the Five-Year Plan for Important Industries. Although military economists rejected the nationalization of industry, they wished to control every sector of the economy.[61] Advocating the need to regulate investment and trade to the benefit of armament industries, the army also recognized the necessity for exports of consumer and textile goods to maintain a healthy trade balance and to ameliorate the effects of war mobilization on the population. The army wanted to limit the profits of private companies and to "strengthen price controls" to reduce Japan's inflation rate below 10 percent a year. Various welfare measures, such as crop insurance for farmers and health insurance, were urged to improve the "national livelihood."

The five-year plan in operation did not fulfill these early expectations. The government gained only modified authority over private enterprise during 1938.[62] The plan itself was poorly conceived because it merely described the funds, raw materials, and production goals necessary to reach the military's estimates of its production requirements.[63] Because planners had not set practical production targets for the different sectors of the economy, it was not surprising that even during the first year of the plan actual output was well below the original goals. In spite of this poor performance, a revised four-year plan established even higher production targets in 1938. The value and the effectiveness of the Army Ministry's economic planning warranted skepticism and stimulated alternative proposals for economic planning.

A realization that Japan's economic strength was a crucial factor in determining its capacity to create and lead an East Asian new order had already led the Shōwa Research Association to focus on the problems of Japanese industry. The economics section, under the direction of Takahashi Kamekichi and then Ryū Shintarō, drew up proposals for reforms to improve the productivity of Japanese enterprises. Ryū's recommendations, in particular, were a response to the severe trade and financial strains of the China War, the army's plans for mobilization, the growing admiration for Nazi economic policies among many Japanese, and the utopian vision of a new order propounded by Miki Kiyoshi.

The association devised its own plans for a program of national economic mobilization. The major architect of this initial plan was Takahashi, a distinguished economist and former editor of the *Far Eastern Economic Review*, who joined the executive board in 1936. An enthusiastic student of Roosevelt's New Deal, Takahashi had entered the association to "rethink fundamentally ways of conceiving and solving economic problems" with a view toward serving as Konoe's major economic adviser.[64] Takahashi thought that the Japanese adoption of economic policies similar to those in Nazi Germany was "inevitable." He, like many Japanese, hoped that Japan could induce China to surrender by demonstrating the economic capacity to carry on the war indefinitely.[65]

Takahashi's industrial research section within the Shōwa Research Association produced the "Draft for a Civilian Economic Central Body" in December 1937.[66] The report indicated the association's interest in war mobilization and the Nazi economy and provided a model which Ryū Shintarō could develop. It sketched a structure that would prompt Japanese businessmen to subordinate their individual goals to the welfare of the national economy.

Committee members were favorably impressed by the manner in which the National Chamber of Commerce in the United States had gradually formed itself into an autonomous and responsible organ that represented the interests of the business community to the federal government. They were also impressed by the efficient establishment of War Services Industrial committees that had cooperated successfully with the War Industry Board to promote America's economic mobilization during World War I,[67] and anticipated that the recently established Federation of Economic Organizations (Keizai dantai renmei), which encompassed the Japan Chamber of Commerce, the Japan Economic League, and other major business associations, could facilitate cooperation between private businessmen and the government. The federation would become a "parent body and establish a central organization that would truly respond to the needs of the times."[68]

Like Miyazaki Masayoshi, Takahashi's group also noticed the rapid development of a powerful munitions industry in Nazi Germany.[69] Accordingly, the committee proposed the creation of councils (*kyōgikai*) organized both on the basis of economic function and by regions. Participation would be compulsory, and each council would elect representatives to a national executive board (*rijikai*). Members of the executive board would elect a president and then join appropriate sections (*bukai*) of a national executive council—for example, trade, finance, small business, and large industry—where they would meet with special consultants, receive reports from local councils, and discuss national economic policies. These sections would formulate policy recommendations "on the basis of the national economy." Takahashi's committee hoped that by assembling businessmen in a comprehensive yet compartmentalized organization, selfish sectional motives would be eliminated and economic policy could be considered on a broad national basis to suit national ends: The government would have to force Japanese businessmen to form an autonomous national organization that would cooperate with the government in economic planning.

Takahashi's plan outlined a uniquely Japanese economic system based upon a fusion of what he perceived to be an American-style private interest group with the Nazi style of compulsory and comprehensive industrial councils. This combination presumably distinguished his proposals from dictatorial Nazism and would not dismantle Japanese capitalism.[70] The plan, unlike Miyazaki's proposals, was avowedly procapitalist in its rejection of profit limitation and insistence on capitalists' influencing policy, even with improved economic planning.

The report illustrated the ambivalent attitudes of association members toward fascism. The committee clearly saw Nazi policies as effective for increasing industrial production, but the group also recognized the dictatorial character of the Nazi economic structure. The report sought a compromise by importing the structure but preserving the independence of private companies through the formation of their own national organization. Still, the limits on the state's authority in this proposed structure were unclear. Because Ryū Shintarō refused to affirm the principles of capitalism, his adaptation of the Nazi model would be even more authoritarian, despite his own professed dislike for dictatorial government.

Ryū's Plans for Economic Reform

Ryū Shintarō joined the economic research section of the Shōwa Research Association in 1938 to explore even more radical methods of solving Japan's economic dilemmas. Sassa Hiroo, his colleague at the *Asahi*, probably introduced him to the group, and his arrival coincided with a split of the economic section into two segments. The study groups under Takahashi's direction focused on financial issues, such as increasing the absorption of government bonds and raising tax revenues.[71] Meanwhile, the newer participants in the association planned for a more drastic restructuring of Japanese capitalism. In response, the association established the Study Group of the Economic Situation (Keizai jōsei kenkyūkai) in 1938. Participants included Takahashi, Ryū, and several officials from the Cabinet Planning Board, a newly created agency charged with drawing up plans for economic mobilization. These men deplored that "the Japanese economy [was] still experiencing profound changes in confronting the effects of the China Incident and new industrial plans for defense, the economic development of Manchuria and North China, and the new trade situation." More specifically, the task force proposed to conduct "research relating to a future economic structure, ([that is,] research relating to the economic policies of the United States, Germany, Italy, and the Soviet Union and the future direction of Japan[ese economic policy])."[72]

The Japanese government's attempts to effect a wartime economic mobilization in the wake of the China Incident had encountered new difficulties. As growth in trade and industrial production remained sluggish, the National Mobilization Law in 1938 enhanced the emergency laws of 1937 and invested the government with broad economic powers, which could be implemented by imperial decree. However, when the Konoe cabinet attempted to enact some provisions, a fierce confrontation arose over limiting corporate profits. Supported by Home Minister Suetsugu Nobumasa, the army argued strongly for profit limitations, while Finance Minister Ikeda Seihin championed business interests by doggedly resisting this measure. After the government had already assumed the authority to control wages and the distribution of raw materials and manufactured goods, the antagonists finally reached a compromise in December 1938. Dividends were restricted to 10 percent, and businessmen promised to investigate "appropriate" means of disposing of surplus funds.[73] Despite this agreement, the army remained dissatisfied.

The Ministry of Commerce and Industry also coveted more authority to cope with inflation. The general retail price index had risen 9 percent in 1937 and 15 percent in 1938; prices of some items had increased as much as 50 percent.[74] Unable to impose effective unilateral price guidelines on certain goods, including textiles, the ministry created the Central Price Board in 1938. The board comprised the vice-ministers of several government ministries, businessmen, and outside experts, including Takahashi Kamekichi. This body moved toward instituting price guidelines for all goods and distribution control to prevent black markets.

Ryū Shintarō thought these measures would neither prevent black markets nor guarantee the cooperation of businessmen with government policy. In his view, a totally new economic system was necessary. In a year-end report to the Shōwa Research Association, Ryū defined the main national goal as the "building of a Japanese, Manchurian, and Chinese bloc which included the burden of military operations."[75] He agreed with many Japanese economists that the major problem was to provide sufficient capital to finance expanded investment in East Asia and to underwrite the military expenses of the China Incident. Worrying about the decline in those export industries that earned the money to pay for imports of raw materials and about the decline in the ratio of fixed capital to total capital, the growing amount of uninvested money in Japan, Ryū suggested more investment in textile industries, a program of cost cutting (including the reduction of wages), and the merger of small businesses into more efficient large units in order to increase the international competitiveness of Japanese goods.[76] He thought that "future price control must reach into the productive process of goods"; that the government should limit corporate dividends and supervise the investment of surplus profits; and that newly emerging "captains of industry" who, as managers, valued the social usefulness of their work over profit would comply with these policies.

In some respects, Ryū's new Japanese economic system was more politically astute than economically sound. His insistence on more investment in textile industries, for example, failed to deal adequately with the obstacles posed to Japanese textiles in foreign markets. Cheaper Japanese textiles with a small profit margin would not necessarily bring a significant rise in the value of Japanese exports, as Ryū himself had argued in 1934. The more important aspects of Ryū's program were: strict ceilings on profits, the control of inflation through austerity, the merger of small businesses, and economic planning. Along with supporting the popular positions within the Army Ministry and the Cabinet Planning Board, Ryū accepted Miki Kiyoshi's notion of a new "form" for the Orient. "The [China] War imposed various sacrifices. On the other hand, the war has given the people the grand ideal that they must build the East on the basis of a new system. War has brought a new form of life to the people."[77]

As the prospect of an East Asian cooperative body became the dominant ideal of the Shōwa Research Association, ardent supporters of a new Asian order assumed new positions of leadership. In May 1939 the association split into four major sections; Ryū Shintarō, Sassa Hiroo, Miki Kiyoshi, and Yabe Teiji received appointments as section chiefs (*kanjiyaku*). Ryū directed economic research; Sassa led the political section; Miki supervised investigations on cultural topics; and Yabe guided research on foreign affairs.[78] This group of intellectuals had ambitious aspirations for a comprehensive reform of Japanese domestic and foreign policies based upon the principles of "cooperativism." Ryū, for example, premised his consideration of economic policies on the emergence of an East Asian economic bloc.

Throughout 1939, Ryū actively participated in two economic research groups of the Shōwa Research Association that devised policies for an East Asian regional economy and a new Japanese economic system. The East Asian Economic Bloc Study Group (Tōa keizai burokku kenkyūkai), under Professor Kawada Tetsuji, aimed at a long-term "cooperative" economic relationship between Japan and East Asia. The committee's reports revealed a desire to build a self-sufficient bloc centering on Japan and China and encompassing the western Pacific area.[79] Although the members professed to seek equal cooperation with Asian neighbors, they were convinced that Japan should lead the bloc and carefully plan its operation.[80] Criticizing the capitalistic framework of the British empire for its lack of an "organic structure," they argued that the Asian economic union should "depend upon the principles of totalitarianism and collectivism as do Germany, Italy, and Russia."[81] Japanese interests would be paramount, as in the case of coal. The Chinese could tap their own rich deposits of coal, but monopolistic "sales control companies" would be necessary to prevent Chinese competition from challenging mines owned by Japanese citizens.[82] In addition, the sales companies would supervise all exports of Chinese coal. Economic cooperation, in this sense, entailed neither sacrifice on the part of Japan nor an equal relationship with China.

Ryū advocated a bloc economy, although he knew that Japan's trade with the West was as crucial as that with East Asia. Like Miyazaki, he underlined the "closeness of political relations between Japan and the continent since the Manchurian Incident of 1931 and the trend of the inevitable relationship of the 'East Asian new order' which took the China Incident as a turning point."[83] Japan had to lead the crusade against Western influence. Although Japan was becoming the leading economic power in China, it faced competition from British investment. Japan's role was now to build in Asia a "new order that would, as a method of economic development, internally cast off the old clothes of Western capitalism."[84]

Ryū's main activity centered on his own research committees, which included the Study Group for the Reorganization of the Japanese Economy (Nihon keizai saihensei kenkyūkai), whose purpose was to plan a reform of the national economy to serve more effectively Japan's war in China:

> This economic reorganization of Japan must make possible a rational use and conservation of present resources which are necessary to respond to all demands and preparations of the national defense economy in order to: (1) pursue the present war (2) bring about long-term construction of the economy (3) support the livelihood of the Manchurian, Chinese, and Japanese peoples and (4) manage present international economic difficulties. . . . However, because the achievement of the new mission of the holy war and the construction of the new East Asian order is imposing an unusual burden and sacrifice on the nation, the order that must be built must be rational to the extent that it (a) lessens, as much as possible, the friction and contradictions which must rise during the process of the economic reconstruction of East Asia; (b) brings rational economic development not only to Japan but also to China and Manchuria; and (c) makes the Chinese people realize the crime of their anti-Japanese movement.[85]

Ryū assembled a talented group of young economic specialists from a variety of backgrounds. His committee included two well-known economists —Hoashi Kei and Kimura Kihachirō. A director of the research division of the Japan Economic League (Nihon keizai renmeikai), Hoashi served as the lone spokesman for this group of businessmen. Kimura, in contrast, was a respected Marxist who favored the reform of Japanese capitalism.[86] The nucleus of Ryū's group consisted of five civil servants—Masaki Chifuyu, Okuyama Teijirō, Katsumata Seiichi, Inaba Hidezō, and Wada Kōsaku.[87] As original members of the Cabinet Investigation Bureau in 1935, Masaki, Okuyama, and Katsumata had survived its subsequent metamorphoses into first the Cabinet Planning Bureau and then the Cabinet Planning Board by 1937. Inaba had joined after leaving the Harmonization Society, and Wada joined after resigning from the Research Section of the South Manchurian Railway.

Ryū's rapport with these men was natural, because they belonged to the same generation and shared an elitist education and youthful interest in Marxism. Katsumata, Inaba, and Wada were 1930 graduates of the University of Kyōto; Masaki had attended the University of Tokyo. Except for Wada, all had been arrested in their youth on suspicion of being communist sympathizers, and Wada had been a member of the underground radical student group, the Social Science Research Association. They were enamored of socialist thought and social reform and had great faith in the bureaucracy as an active agent in the restructuring of Japanese society. In 1935, Katsumata,

Masaki, and Okuyama, together with their senior, Wada Hiroo from the Agriculture Ministry, formed a cohesive clique which, on moving into the Cabinet Planning Bureau, lobbied intensely for the establishment of a strong national policymaking council. When Wada Kōsaku and Inaba Hidezō joined the group in early 1937, all hoped the recently formed Cabinet Planning Bureau would assume more authority. Following the outbreak of the China Incident, the Konoe cabinet merged the Resources Bureau and the planning bureau into a Cabinet Planning Board that would draw up plans for munitions production. Katsumata and his colleagues tried unsuccessfully to resist this narrowing of the bureau's purpose.[88] Disappointed by the cabinet's decision, they joined the Shōwa Research Association to champion their views on national policies.[89]

When Ryū's economic section hammered out guidelines for a national system of economic control, members had to confront the question of how the government could institute controls without becoming more oppressive.[90] Ryū's article of April 1939, "The Urgency of Basic Policies," manifested a commitment to using state pressure to dampen inflation and prevent black markets.[91] Doubting that businessmen would sacrifice profit for the general welfare, Ryū criticized the current policy of allowing committees of business leaders to decide general price guidelines. He proposed the creation of new committees in each industrial sector; these would include government officials as well as businessmen and would set strict prices for goods. Ryū's attitude was clear: "If national power to a certain extent is not operating from above, I think that real basic prices will not evolve." Nonetheless, civilian cooperation was desirable: "That national power must have influence is one [possible] system, but if it stresses only national power and has no autonomous cooperation from the people at its base, it will bring about purely repressive policies."[92] To facilitate national supervision of industry, Ryū suggested a "new system"—that is, "'true self-government'"—in which industrialists, aware of their social responsibilities, would voluntarily regulate themselves instead of seeking more profits. Ryū's hope that independent cooperation from private citizens would moderate the severity of necessary authoritarian controls soon evolved into the ideal of officials and the people uniting into one body.

In September the administrative board of the Shōwa Research Association compiled a report that summarized the progress of the economic research section. This report, "The Basic Direction of Economic Reorganization," outlined major premises that Ryū soon incorporated in his influential and controversial *The Reorganization of the Japanese Economy*.[93] His task force enumerated two major problems facing Japanese economic policy: inflation, because it threatened to undermine industrial expansion for munitions production and the livelihood of the people, and the economic depression and unemployment that would follow the end of the China War, when munitions industries would cut production and the army would demobilize. From this perspective current measures to control prices without curbing profits were futile because even if the supply of goods were strictly regulated, businessmen would still seek to realize the same or greater profit from the sale of their goods. In the face of retail price controls, companies would reduce the quality of goods and lower working conditions in order to obtain the same level of profit. Industries with low profits would simply go bankrupt, and in other industries inefficient working conditions and low productivity would cause price rises in spite of restrictions. The pursuit of private profit could not aid the nation in resolving the grave economic problems of inflation and the depression yet to come with the end of hostilities in China.

The control of wages and profits, according to Ryū's group, was essential. The regulation of wages was relatively easy to implement, but profit limitation would require a new economic system for Japan.[94] Although the government had limited dividends to 10 percent, it did not yet supervise the use of profits beyond that level. Therefore, only a "complete public opening" of industrial management could assure that surplus funds would be used for a reduction of prices and an increase in productivity. Citing German economic legislation, the committee suggested that a set dividend be paid to stockholders and that excess profits be turned over to a national capital reserve for investment in industrial expansion.

Following Nazi economic policies, the group proposed the "establishment of compulsory trusts and cartels and a change in the character of the trusts and cartels."[95] Instead of seeking to protect profits of member companies, the new trusts and cartels would effect "low prices" as well as an "increase in productivity and the socialization of production." Again the line between the imposition of authority and the inducement of popular cooperation was blurred. While the framework for this new structure would be "provided by the authority of the state, . . . within this system, the activity of businessmen [would] extend itself autonomously; and, in this sense, the form of control [would] be 'self-regulation' in the truest sense."[96]

The spirit and substance of the proposals of this report were similar to the publicized policies of the Nazi economy. Previously, the economic research section of the Shōwa Research Association, under Takahashi Kamekichi's direction, had meticulously studied the German economy, and Ryū's committee indicated that the "managed economies" in Russia, Italy, and Germany had provided basic "reference" material. Ryū and his committee regarded the Nazi economy as an imaginative, effective, and adaptable model for a managed economy in Japan.[97]

Ryū set forth his personal opinions in December 1939 with the publication of *The Reorganization of the Japanese Economy*. This book immediately became a best-seller, and by the fall of 1940 it had gone through forty-four printings. As the most controversial and influential work published on the Japanese economy during the late 1930s, it defined the topics that dominated the public discussion of economic mobilization for the next year. Ryū was credited with inventing the phrase *reorganization of the economy* (*keizai saihensei*).[98] His suggestion that stockholders should have no active role in industrial management ignited a heated debate over the "separation of capital and management" (*shihon keiei no bunri*). His book also popularized the goal of creating an "economic cooperative body" (*keizai kyōdōtai*) infused with a new "economic ethic" (*keizai rinri*).

Influenced by Miki Kiyoshi's philosophy of cooperativism outlined in *The Principles of Thought for a New Japan*,[99] Ryū now insisted that his proposals for structural reform would be useless without the creation of a new cooperative economic ethic that would transcend "English liberalism." The new ethic stressed the importance of the individual's economic "function" in society and the "communal feeling" (the *Gemeinschaft*) of the Japanese people.

The basic tenets of Ryū's economic analysis in this book—the danger of inflation caused by deficit spending, the overemphasis on munitions industries, the dominance of finance capital over the economy, the exploitation of labor, and the disruption of the economic reproductive cycle—had marked his writings throughout the past decade. The new elements were a comprehensive program of policy reforms and an emphasis on the values of the "cooperative body." Ironically, Ryū was now looking to the great *zaibatsu* as the key to economic reform in Japan. The growth of these large family industrial concerns had caused a split between ownership of capital, usually by one family, and the actual daily management of the enterprises. Within these firms had arisen a new managerial class that did not own stock and had no incentive for increasing profits. "A manager has to pay a certain amount of dividends to capital [stockholders] through the company; but, beyond this, he has no responsibility towards capital. On the contrary, he bears a great responsibility regarding the national and social significance of the management of enterprises. It is his reward and responsibility in his social and national function to manage enterprises with the greatest efficiency."[100] The managerial class would play a crucial role in achieving economic reform and creating a new form of economic ethics.

Ryū argued that liberal capitalism in Japan was rooted in the profit motive and that it had reached the limits of its ability to respond effectively to the economic problems caused by the China War. It was, therefore, time to replace the ethic of the free pursuit of profit with a commitment to serve national interests by seeking the most efficient methods of increasing production and making goods at the lowest possible prices. This transformation mandated instilling a willingness for individuals to sacrifice personal gain for national goals. Similarly, enterprises would be administered by managers who thought of the whole economy and who would share technology and trade secrets. "Thus for functional activity to replace the first consideration of profit motive as a principle, the structure of social ethics must divorce itself from individualism and make its base the totality and the social character of the life of the nation." The new ethics would "abandon individual gain and give birth to the true self."[101] They would, as well, blend well with Japan's traditional national polity, which accented loyalty and obedience.

Despite the stress on Japan's unique culture, Ryū's specific proposals for the reorganization of the Japanese economy closely resembled those put forward in Nazi Germany. Ryū criticized the dictatorial bureaucratic control that distinguished the Nazi system in practice, but he wanted the Japanese government to legislate a totally new economic system: a series of cartels and trusts divided both by industry and region. Each cartel or trust would communicate closely with others in all sectors of its industrial group and with all those in its region. For example, each sector of the cotton industry—weaving, dyeing, importing, exporting, manufacturing—would form an industry guild (*dōgyō kumiai*). These guilds in turn would elect representatives to a cotton industry association (*rengōkai*). The cotton industry association, along with other sectors of the textile industry, such as rayon, wool, silk, and so forth, would send representatives to a major industry association (*jūyō sangyō rengōkai*) to represent the whole textile industry. This process would be duplicated in other major industrial sectors, such as steel, utilities, chemicals, and machine manufacturing. Each major industry association would send representatives to economic policy councils located at the municipal, prefectural, and national levels. At every level, special industrial councils would assemble representatives of the cartels and government officials to foster economic planning.[102]

Admitting that this outline for a new economic structure was borrowed from economist Miura Tetsutarō, Ryū, unlike Takahashi Kamekichi, argued explicitly that a new economic system should not serve the interests of Japanese capitalism and criticized Miura for accepting the ideal of the profit motive.[103] The new "economic ethic" of managers had to permeate the new economic structure.[104] The "technocrats" who administered each enterprise would also represent their organizations in the new cartels. In this arrangement, stockholders would be allowed to retain their shares, but the organization of industry would be so tight and so closely bound to government consultation and planning that management would, in effect, become open and responsible to the public.

Besides a system of national cartels, Ryū favored special sales organizations for some goods. Discussing the coal industry, he depicted the operations of his ideal distribution network and argued that under the present market economy in Japan, if an efficient mine produced a set amount of coal for ten yen and an inefficient mine for twenty yen, the market price would be twenty-one yen.[105] In the proposed managerial system with its cooperative ethic, this price would be too high and the profit for the efficient mine excessive. If a national coal cartel bought a set amount of coal from the efficient mine for twelve yen and from the inefficient mine for twenty-one yen, it could sell the coal for fifteen yen to the public. Thus, in spite of Ryū's constant stress on the need to improve the efficiency of Japanese industry, his utopian system would lower the prices of goods by reducing the profit of efficient enterprises.

Reactions to Ryū's Proposals

Ryū advanced a double-edged policy toward capital investments that included the limitation of dividends and the reinvestment of profits into production. Business leaders argued that profit limitations would discourage investment in industry. However, Ryū reasoned that if the government effected a flat 30-percent reduction in all individual dividends, there would still be a "gap" between high and low profit returns, and the capital available to individual investors would still flow to the sectors with relatively high profit return. "Besides if they hesitate to invest, what would the owners of capital gain?"[106]

Classical economists perceived Ryū's proposals as a poorly disguised attempt to destroy the free-market system in Japan. Yamamoto Katsuichi considered Ryū an unpatriotic communist and warned that his proposals would lead to economic disaster because continual reinvestment of profits within an industry by a cartel would block the flow of capital as needed from one sector of the economy to the other. Yamamoto noted that the new system would transfer responsibility for investment from the natural operation of the free market to the "arbitrary will" of economic planners, whom he doubted could "decide how to distribute and redistribute the entire resources of the nation."[107] Strengthening export industries—the "peace industries"—presented other difficulties for Ryū. He did not confront the problem of deciding which industries had the best potential for export or what policies Japan could pursue to persuade the Western powers to end restrictions against Japanese imports in many foreign markets.

Ryū's book *The Reorganization of the Japanese Economy* appeared as an imaginative attempt to achieve a compromise between advocates of state socialism and the principle of private property. His proposals constituted a radical restructuring of the economy by an eclectic and opportunistic ideology that appealed to a wide spectrum of politically active Japanese, embracing anticapitalist nationalists, military planners, and especially economic officials in his study group who all resented private profits being earned during the holy war in China. Ryū once again linked the cause of reform with the need for economic mobilization to build national strength for the construction of the new Asian order.

Obscuring the extent of bureaucratic control necessary for his economic new order, Ryū admitted that his proposed economic controls "resembled the system that Germany had adopted," even though it would not be as dictatorial. Ryū did not, however, mention any institutional safeguards against bureaucratic dictatorship; nor did he indicate how his system would deal with businessmen who refused to recognize their national duty. If the state would limit profits, the "object of businessmen's efforts could not help turning in the direction of the social and national meaning of management."[108] Thus, Ryū expected that businessmen could not challenge the state.

The Reorganization of the Japanese Economy rejected a Marxist analysis of historical development based on class conflict. Ryū asserted that the "competing interests" of labor and capital did not obscure their "common interests" and agreed with Alfredo Rocco's assertion that English liberalism and Marxism were the products of an individualistic view that stressed competition between individuals and, by extension, economic classes within society. Such doctrines had wrongly de-emphasized the independent power of the state as an economic force because the state did not have to represent class interests. "The political authority [of the state] can emerge as an independent force in relation to the economy and as a force mediating changes in the economic system."[109] Like Miki Kiyoshi, Ryū developed a mystical reverence for the national community as an ethical standard: "In order to build the new structure of our life, we must try to accept honestly and impartially the consciousness of national life that we possess, in other words, our group consciousness that has existed throughout history."

Some Japanese economic reviewers applauded Ryū's book as a brief for a totalitarian and fascist economic system. To some, Ryū's proposals "implie[d] the rebuilding of the nation on a totalitarian basis. So, to say the least, the volume provide[d] a good suggestion as to the possible future trend of Japan's economic policy."[110] Toda Takeo, a well-known economist, observed "that fascistic vocational principles were being taught anew from the standpoint of this progressive social thought."[111] The Shōwa Research Association, also regarding fascist principles as progressive social thought, accepted the totalitarian character of Ryū's proposals and the influence of fascist ideology on his ideas.

The association's *Draft for the Reorganization of the Japanese Economy*[112] reflected many of Ryū's ideas. This document proposed the separation of capital ownership and industrial management, a transformation of economic ethics, state-administered distribution organizations, a tightly organized economic structure, and comprehensive economic planning, which would be achieved through the establishment of a supreme economic council (*saikō keizai kaigi*). In contrast to Ryū's plan, that of the Shōwa Research Association underscored the role of the council, which would include civil servants, economists, and business leaders. They would gather information from the various cartels, formulate national goals, and then supervise the efforts of cartels, "complete organizations" (*zentai kumiai*), to reach their production targets. This plan indicated how well Ryū's ideas were suited to a comprehensive bureaucratic economic structure.

The proposal of the Shōwa Research Association was also similar to Miyazaki Masayoshi's plans for the economic structure of an East Asian league. Both affirmed the need to respond to the economic burdens of the China War; both aimed at the modification of capitalism through profit limitation and the creation of new economic organizations; and both advocated an economic planning council. Miyazaki, however, argued for the primacy of munitions production, whereas the Shōwa Research Association emphasized the cooperative welfare of Japanese and Asians.

The recommendations of the association accepted government policies for mobilizing a national defense economy and constructing a "new order" in China, and Ryū and the association avoided direct criticism of the policies of the Japanese military in China. In line with the strategy set in 1937 by the executive board, Ryū sought to influence military policy by "taking its hand." His aim was not to end the China War soon but to direct its goals beyond military conquest to the construction of a new economic and social system in Japan and East Asia, what he called a new "form of life."

Participation in the Shōwa Research Association prompted Ryū to view the China Incident as affording Japanese intellectuals an unprecedented opportunity for influence. "The most urgent task now is for the intellectual class to abandon small differences, unite in agreement, and participate positively in the establishment of political and economic guidelines for Japan that will open up the constructive directions that the China Incident suggests."[113] The association's goals fit the interests of both Miki and Ryū and encouraged important developments in their ideas of reform. Miki had argued the need for a new ideology in Japan since 1933; Ryū had considered policies of economic mobilization since 1935. Devising guidelines for national policies finally forced both men to specify their alternatives to capitalism and socialism. With the expressed desire of Konoe and the association's executive board for basic political and economic reforms and for an assertion of Japanese leadership as a "poor" nation, Miki and Ryū found a fertile atmosphere for elaborating their fascination with fascist policies and ideology and adapting them for Japan.

The philosophy of cooperativism rejected liberalism and rationalized state control of politics and economics. Both Miki and Ryū deplored bureaucratic dictatorship, but both advocated increased authority for the state. A cooperative ethic would ameliorate authoritarianism, but the question of how this ethic was going to arise was left unanswered. As Rōyama had suggested in 1931, only a massive program of education by the state could inculcate such a new communal awareness. The ideas of Miki and Ryū laid the basis for an authoritarian state without clear checks on the power of the state.

Far from accommodating Chinese nationalism, the ideal of the cooperative body justified Japan's expansionism.[114] If Miki's philosophy of cooperativism aimed at appealing to Chinese nationalism, it also presumed the dismantlement of the Nationalist government in China. Ryū and the East Asian Economic Bloc Committee wanted to enhance Japan's position of economic leadership at the expense of China.

A published discussion of "nationalism" between Miki and a Chinese politician, Chou Fo-hai, in 1940 revealed the former's disdain for Chinese aspirations.[115] When Chou explained that the Chinese wanted "independence, freedom, and equality" with other nations, Miki responded unsympathetically that "today . . . thinking only of the independence or freedom of peoples does not suffice." Asserting that Asia needed "something transcending nationalism" to prevent friction between nations, he then asked Chou whether he had considered the possibilities for a new political organization, such as an East Asian league or cooperative body. Chou indicated he had not. The obvious gap between the aims of Chinese nationalism and those of the Shōwa Research Association explains why few non-Japanese ever participated in the association's planning for the new Asian order.

The theory of the cooperative body has been called in retrospect the only Japanese "attempt at intellectual creation" during the China War.[116] The product of the sincere attempts of some of Japan's most able writers to resolve dilemmas facing the nation, this philosophy was designed to achieve international appeal by combining antimodern and promodern ideals. Miki wanted his philosophy to absorb the rational structure of industrial society into a revival of a unique Oriental *Gemeinschaft*, a concept that implied a preindustrial form of social relations. The cooperative ethic was to be similar to that advocated by ideologues like Tachibana Kōzaburō and Gondō Seikyō, who desired a return to agricultural, self-sufficient villages.[117] Miki and Ryū, however, placed the focus of the individual's loyalty on the nation and argued that their reforms would augment Japan's industrial strength.

8. Political Mobilization

The failure to end the China Incident and the threat of hostilities in Europe underscored the need for national mobilization in Japan. National unity was needed to maintain the war effort and to respond effectively to new international tensions that threatened to involve Japan in a new conflict. When Wang Ching-wei defected from the Chinese Nationalist government in December 1938, the Japanese encouraged him to form a new government in Nanking. Because Premier Konoe refused to give a deadline for the withdrawal of Japanese troops from the mainland, Wang hesitated and negotiations bogged down for more than a year. In Europe, six months after the Munich Agreement of September 1938, Hitler marched into Bohemia. The British government extended military guarantees to Poland and Rumania and made overtures to the Soviet Union. Since the signing of the Anti-Comintern Pact of 1936, the Japanese government had considered the possibility of a political alliance with Germany and Italy; Hitler insisted on a military pact. The Hiranuma cabinet (January–August 1939) met seventy-five times to discuss a military alliance with the Axis powers. The army's argument that an alliance would force China to surrender could not overcome the navy's fears of provoking the United States and Britain. In August, Germany and the Soviet Union concluded a nonaggression agreement; in September, Germany invaded Poland, and England declared war on Germany.

The need to respond to rapidly shifting European developments and to bear the continuing manpower and economic costs of the China War focused the attention of Japanese leaders on maintaining popular support for the government. Some politicians planned for a powerful new party that would unite the nation and revive the prestige of the Diet. Others promoted the creation of a monolithic "national organization" premised on the elimination of the Diet as a responsible political body. The army desired a national defense state that entailed drastic changes in government decision making, with the role of the Diet reduced and the authority of a national planning organ increased and favored the reorganization of the cabinet into two parts—a small national affairs board (*kokumuin*) and administrative directors for the various ministries.[1] Despite the abundance of reform proposals, the first Konoe cabinet had rejected radical political or administrative measures and instead created the National Spiritual Mobilization Movement under the supervision of the Cabinet Information Bureau and the Home and Education ministries. As the China War continued and developments in Europe remained unsettled, the debate on strategies for political mobilization intensified and dominated the activity of the political section of the Shōwa Research Association.

Responding to the ongoing events in China and Europe, the political section, led by Rōyama Masamichi and Sassa Hiroo, created guidelines for a new Japanese political system to aid mobilization for building a new order in East Asia. Thus, they hoped to continue their campaign to create a more rational political structure. In 1937, Kazami Akira had presented an association plan for the reform of the cabinet system to Premier Konoe. Following one of Rōyama's long-held ideals, the proposal stressed the need for a stronger cabinet to unify government policies and to carry out reforms, with some members able to concentrate on general policies of the nation rather than routine administration. This report is credited with inspiring Konoe to appoint ten cabinet "councillors" to advise him.[2] Now, the association promoted its proposals as a rationale for national mobilization.

During 1938 the political section agreed that the formation of a regional economic bloc required a "reorganization" of the established political system. The old political system, a report announced, could not be reconciled with the "self-consciousness of Japan's mission in East Asia and the racial consciousness that has arisen recently [in Japan]."[3] The association thus began to incorporate considerations of China policy in studies of domestic political reform. The East Asian Politics Study Group in 1939 started to research the political relations of Japan, Manchuria, and China and the political structure of an East Asian bloc and to reexamine the theory of the East Asian cooperative body.[4] Meanwhile, the Political Trends Study Group investigated the influence of the extension of the China Incident and of the formation of the East Asian cooperative body on Japanese domestic politics. This committee also discussed reforms of the cabinet system and the administrative structure in general, and "methods of popular cooperation with the government."

Sassa Hiroo's "Problems of a National Organization" exemplified the mood of the political section.[5] He cited the need for a new political system to strengthen Japan for leading the East Asian new order, judged that the new party movement in Japan was "close to hopeless," and asserted that the government's National Spiritual Mobilization Movement was futile because it was not a movement "from the people." For a solution, Sassa could put forth only a vague proposal for a partnership between a nonexistent cabinet office and the Social Mass party. In order to effect a viable national mobilization to support the war in China, a new propaganda bureau under the direct supervision of the cabinet had to control the campaign. This office, in turn, would cooperate with rural agricultural associations and the Agricultural National Service Movement of the Social Mass party to establish "research associations" throughout the nation. These "semiofficial and semiprivate" groups would usurp the rural political bases of the established parties and displace the latter as "mediating groups" between the government and the people. The research groups would represent a movement "from the people" and would become the new "pillars of the state." They would "settle into the parallel use of both regional and occupational divisions" and "send representatives to the Diet." Sassa desired an entirely new national organization based primarily on occupational representation, and his view reflected a consensus within the Shōwa Research Association.

The association launched its Research Association for a National Movement (Kokumin undō kenkyūkai) in February 1939 in order to gather support for a new political system. The movement was one of a series of attempts to spread the ideas of the Shōwa Research Association. The Shōwa Brotherhood (Shōwa dōjinkai), for example, had been founded in July 1938 to facilitate contact between outstanding young men in various sectors of Japanese society, especially within the bureaucracy, and to foster discussion of current issues in a context provided by the published policies of the association.[6] By the fall many association members, including Gotō Ryūnosuke, Ryū, and Sassa, were participating in the Shōwa Academy (Shōwa juku), which featured evening discussions with university students.[7] The Research Association for a National Movement purported to create popular support for a new national political organization based on the principles of cooperativism.[8] The group sponsored conferences, often in local facilities of the Youth Association, and distributed pamphlets. Although the movement attracted several thousand participants in its programs and subscribers to its newsletter, it did not develop any concrete political strength. This failure, however, did not dampen the enthusiasm of the Shōwa Research Association for basic political reforms.

Rōyama's View of the Cooperative Body

As the Shōwa Research Association sought to spread understanding of the philosophy of cooperativism, Rōyama Masamichi elaborated the justification for the East Asian cooperative body and explored its implications for national policy. Instead of criticizing Japan's aggression, he argued that Japanese dominance of Asia was beneficial and affirmed the historical destiny demanded by the "economic, political, and military ability of the Japanese race."[9] Because China's naive adoption of the Western ideology of nationalism had brought war with Japan, its mission was to correct China's mistake by producing a "new regional cultural unit." While Miki Kiyoshi outlined the philosophical principles of the cooperative body, Rōyama set forth its political configuration, albeit at a general level. When the fighting ended, China should adopt the political structure of a confederacy, and Japan should establish a "confederacy" together with China and Manchuria.[10] Local governments would be as autonomous as possible, but central organs of the confederation, in which Japan would be the "guiding power," would have to control tariff policies, and Japan would have to protect the entire region from Western pressure. Although the ideal of the East Asian cooperative body called for equality among nations, reality dictated otherwise.

In May 1939, Rōyama's "Formation of a National Cooperative Body" linked the fashioning of the East Asian cooperative body with the creation of a new political system in Japan. "The theory and the policies for building the East Asian cooperative body . . . call forth a new order for the Japanese nation and the Japanese people."[11] The new order would entail the establishment of a national cooperative body and a reorganization of the economy. Drawing heavily on Ryū Shintarō's economic views and Miki's philosophical writings, Rōyama articulated his own conception of the desired economic cooperative body. He honestly acknowledged the immediate influence of Nazism in citing the writings of Rudolf Brinkman, vice-minister of the German Economics Ministry, as a splendid exposition of how the "freedom of the [individual] personality is to recognize by oneself the higher necessity of the cooperative body, to enter into it, and to be placed under it."[12] Rōyama believed, though, that Japan could not fully incorporate the Nazi "racial cooperative body."[13]

Rōyama openly espoused totalitarian political ideals, if with a Japanese twist. Because Japan's national polity would not sanction an exact imitation of German policies, the new national political organization could "not be a dictatorial party like the Nazis, but [we] must await the emergence of a party that must achieve internal unity similar to the Nazis through a democratic means unique to Japan."[14] If the ideal of national unity was clear, the "democratic means" were less so. Rōyama advised the creation of an entirely new organ of government to decide national policies; this body would encompass Diet politicians and representatives of private enterprises who would "participate in policy decisions and in administration just like officials."[15] The exact function of a new body—whether it would be an advisory board to the cabinet or a second legislature—was not clear. Aware of substantial political and legal obstacles to realizing this body, Rōyama proposed that a special administrative order would suffice. Thus, the state would provide the "democratic means" by decree.

Rōyama hoped that Japan's unique heritage of the "duty as subjects toward the national polity" could ease the construction of a new political order based on a cooperative ethic. The "ethical feelings of the people" had to form the base of a new national organization. Still, Rōyama thought the reforms would emulate the Nazi system: "Compared to the past division of authority based on the theory of liberalism, the new national organization will certainly be totalitarian."[16]

Rōyama recognized that basic political reform in Japan would raise serious constitutional issues. He realized, as did others, that although the 1889 Meiji Constitution granted the military the independence of supreme command, the powers of the elected Diet blocked the emergence of an overt dictatorship.[17] This realization, however, did not prevent him from arguing that provisions of the constitution would have to be changed. Significantly, Rōyama concluded his 1939 essay on the national cooperative body with a brief commentary on the constitution.

Citing the seventh-century constitution of Shōtoku Taishi and the creation of the Meiji state, he stated that the "principle of Japan's political formation is the formation of a new order"—that Japan always adjusted to changed circumstances by creating a new political system and maintaining a basic unity.[18] Thus, the Meiji Constitution was a unique nineteenth-century compromise between the monarchy and new demands for popular participation in politics. A new national organization should not violate the constitution, but the constitution should not be subjected to superficial "legalistic interpretations." Instead, "in our country constitutionalism must stand on the internal principle of the political formation of the nation that centers on Japan's national polity."[19] The constitution should be revered not for its specific regulations but for its embodiment of national unity and its flexibility. The Meiji Constitution had to change to allow the creation of a totally new political system in Japan.

Just as Rōyama used Nazi ideology in his version of the national cooperative body, he used German foreign policy as a model for the foreign policy of Japan. Because of their late arrival on the imperialistic scene, both Japan and Germany were economically "have not" nations and had common interests in revamping the existing structure of international relations. Germany's seizure of Czechoslovakia was part of the regional cooperative body being created by the Nazis in Europe, and Japan was engaged in a similar venture with its "new order" in Asia.[20]

Regarding Japan's specific relationship with Germany, Rōyama never criticized the consensus view of the Shōwa Research Association that the general cooperation provided by the Anti-Comintern Pact would suffice to effect a new world order. Members did not want a tight military alliance that might draw Japan into a European war, and they criticized the overt racism of Nazi ideology and its assertion of Aryan supremacy.[21]

Because of his enthusiasm for a new world order, Rōyama welcomed the German-Soviet Non-Aggression Pact, which stunned the Japanese government. Unconcerned that the treaty enhanced the Soviet Union's position in Asia, he depicted the pact as a step toward the creation of regional blocs. Nazi Germany and the Soviet Union were compatible partners because they shared new political and economic principles. Both of their political systems were based on "totalitarian dictatorship"; their economies exemplified "national socialism" and "national capitalism," respectively; and they both despised the European order established by the Versailles Treaty. Therefore, Nazi Germany and the Soviet Union should cooperate to build a "new political and economic order" in Eastern Europe.[22] The "old" imperialists—Britain and France—had imposed the principle of nationalism on Europe through the Versailles settlement, which established many small nations, including Czechoslovakia and Poland. The assault of the "new imperialism" of Germany, Italy, and the Soviet Union on this old principle of nationalism raised a central question: "In the process of the war between the new and the old imperialism, how will the principles of the 'nation' and 'nationalism' be managed?" Would the "old imperialist" view of self-determination be neglected, respected, or somehow reformed and recognized in a new form?[23] Rōyama anticipated a new form in East Asia and in Europe.

Launching the New Order Movement

As Rōyama rationalized the need for an East Asian cooperative body and a national cooperative body, the various study groups of the Shōwa Research Association deliberated concrete proposals for political reform. These centered on the problems of supreme command, reform of the Diet, improvement of local government, and institution of more efficient administration. From 1939 to 1940 many distinguished civil servants, politicans, and academics participated in these studies. A special task force, composed of Sassa Hiroo, Yabe Teiji, and Miwa Jusō, formulated specific political proposals in the spring of 1940. In June, Yabe's "Outline for the Reform of the Political Structure" summarized and integrated all of the recommendations of the Shōwa Research Association for a new political order.[24]

Yabe denounced liberal democracy as an outmoded "form of the nineteenth century" and declared the Japanese constitutional system a failure in its primary task to "assist imperial rule based on the unique national polity." The people were alienated from the government, which itself had become divided. Only the creation of a "cooperative body [type of] planned or managed economy and a centralized administrative form based on the masses" could correct these faults and remain faithful to Japan's unique polity.[25]

The new political prospectus of the Shōwa Research Association enunciated radical changes for the Meiji constitutional state, some of which the army had championed.[26] It proposed to reduce the number of ministers of state and to divide their duties. A special selection committee (*sōsen kikan*) of elder statesmen, including the lord keeper of the privy seal, would choose "national ministers" to consider broad affairs of state. The ministers would delegate routine administration to vice-ministers. The cabinet planning agency would expand and advise the cabinet on foreign and domestic affairs. The Diet would lose authority: "The cabinet must attend to the guiding plans and recommendations for national policy; the Diet must not." The Diet would cooperate with the cabinet "through constructive criticism" and "promote appropriate political, social, economic, and cultural propaganda to the masses of the nation." Standing committees in the Diet would consider national issues on a full-time basis, and "newspaper reporters" would participate in these committees as a means of involving intellectuals in government. Rather than the "main assembly," these committees would become the center of the Diet's activity. In wartime, though, the government would have to limit the length of Diet debates regarding important legislation and the right of representatives to question cabinet ministers.

The Shōwa Research Association shaped the new political order to implement the ideal of a cooperative body and to complement the new economic order outlined by Ryū Shintarō. It envisioned new political organs that in many respects would functionally displace the existing Diet and political parties through the "establishment of an organization of vocational groups covering the areas of culture and economics." These vocational groups would be "closely merged with a cabinet planning bureau and participate internally in the planning of economic policy." They would be "closely united with the political structure at each level," and they would elect one-third (one hundred) of the members of the new House of Peers.

The new political order would thus create one mass organization in which persons would participate on the basis of their occupations. The organization would follow the principle of democratic centralism; that is, the individual would participate in the administration and discussions of his local vocational unit, and leaders of each unit would represent it in the national unit of that occupation. Local units could influence local government policies, while the national unit would be responsible for transmitting the will of the people to the cabinet's planning agency, the proposed new policymaking body. The entire national mass organization would provide the state with a powerful means of enforcing its policies.

The vocational organizations would "guarantee organic unity" among the various sectors of government and form a system in which there was no "class, occupational, or economic conflict." The details of how the new political order would evolve were not clear, but the change would be peaceful and take the form of a "patriotic movement." The plan for the "driving force" of the national organization to comprise "superior elements of the army, the bureaucracy and the people" indicated that a new party would play a crucial role. Later the Shōwa Research Association cited the need for a party as a nucleus of the movement and eventually for the "political section of the national organization" to establish a "Japanese form of one nation, one party."[27]

Fascist regimes were attractive models for these reforms. Referring presumably to the general aim of creating a mass party, Arima Yoriyasu, a confidant of Konoe, recognized that the theory for reorganizing the nation was similar to the political ideas of the Nazis.[28] In detail, the system of occupational organizations proposed by the Shōwa Research Association was actually more akin to the provincial councils of corporative economy established in Italy in 1934. Although the Italian corporative state never functioned according to legislated plans, its structure provided for cooperation between economic classes and for mass participation in politics. The local councils were composed of appointed government officials and selected representatives of syndical (occupational) organizations in each province. They were, in theory, to assist in economic planning and general administration through their mandate to "represent in a unitary and integral manner the interests of the economic activities of their respective provinces, and assure and promote their coordination and development in harmony with the general interests of the nation." The corporate councils were also supposed to act as sources of information and channels of liaison for government administration and to nominate candidates for the National Council of Corporations, a body that had initially advised the government on economic matters. In 1938, when the elected Chamber of Deputies dissolved, the council became the legislative assembly for the Italian government.[29]

The June report represented a hurried effort to bring together the various proposals for political reform that study groups had investigated since the China Incident. Despite the rudimentary and abstract nature of Yabe's proposals, several important themes stand out. The creation of the East Asian cooperative body mandated drastic domestic political reforms. The role of the Diet, which was dominated by the political parties, would diminish, and in its place occupational organizations would not only displace the political parties but, as part of a comprehensive economic planning structure, would also reform Japanese capitalism. For the sake of administrative efficiency the report recommended enlarged powers for a cabinet planning agency, a reduction in the number of state ministers, and a delegation of administrative authority over ministries to "directors." Although Yabe Teiji composed this outline, the reform proposals were drawn from previous Shōwa Research Association reports and reflected basic ideas that had been developed by Rōyama Masamichi —the need for occupational representation, administrative efficiency, centralized planning, and the ideal of the cooperative body.

This comprehensive political statement of the Shōwa Research Association embodied Konoe's strategy of seizing the initiative from the army. During the early months of 1940 members consulted with army officers.[30] Major Tada Tokuji from the Army General Staff even confided to one association official that the army wished to manipulate Konoe and suggested that "those assembled in the association and the Army General Staff become the brains of a [Konoe] cabinet." The association did not collaborate formally with the General Staff, but Yabe touted the goal of a new Asian order and proposed two reforms that the army had pushed since 1936: a more powerful planning agency and fewer state ministers. Yabe's report further accommodated the military by encouraging members of the armed forces to join the "driving force" of the new order, along with civil servants and ordinary citizens. There was little, though, that the military would gain by joining the proposed fascist political order, and without an affirmation of the principle of the independence of supreme command the military might well lose its autonomy. Thus, the June report, as a culmination of the political thought of the Shōwa Research Association, represented a severe case of political psychosis in that it envisioned radical alterations of the influence of Japan's three most powerful interest groups—the political parties, big business, and the military. Amazingly, these ideas were taken seriously at the highest levels of government.

In the spring of 1940 the German army launched its blitzkrieg across France and appeared on the verge of conquering England as well. The imminent victory of the fascist powers in Europe stimulated demands for a new order in Japan to enable the nation to keep abreast of world trends. Diet politicians, including Nakajima Chikuhei and Kuhara Fusanosuke, wanted a new order in the form of a new political party that would revive the power of party politicians.[31] The military preferred a political reorganization to guarantee support for its policies. The intellectuals and bureaucrats in the Shōwa Research Association wanted a new order to eliminate the evils of capitalism and parliamentary democracy in Japan.

All of these proponents of political reform hoped Prince Konoe, who had resigned as premier in 1939, would take the initiative in organizing a new order movement in Japan. Gotō Ryūnosuke began to recruit personnel in the spring of 1940 by asking Hanyū Shinshichi, a leader of the Research Association for a National Movement, to recommend someone "appropriate" for a new Konoe cabinet.[32] Hanyū nominated Tomita Kenji, then the governor of Nagano Prefecture and former head of the Peace Preservation (police) Section of the Home Ministry. After Gotō and Ryū Shintarō conferred with Tomita, he was invited to Konoe's summer resort in Karuizawa, where he agreed to serve as executive secretary in the projected new order.[33] On June 1, at Gotō's request, Yabe Teiji discussed with Konoe the plans of the Shōwa Research Association for a new political system, and Konoe revealed to Yabe his intention to create a new party movement.[34] Proclaiming his wish for a "new order,"[35] Konoe resigned as head of the Privy Council on June 24 and, on the same day, asked Yabe to draft plans for a new political system. Gotō Ryūnosuke, meanwhile, formed a small group that included Ryū Shintarō and Gotō Fumio to consider implementing a new order.[36]

Konoe's resignation signaled his availability for the premiership; in a press conference on July 7 he affirmed his desire to realize a new order within the limits of the Meiji Constitution. Immediately thereafter, Konoe conferred with his advisers about detailed plans. According to Yabe Teiji, he and Gotō Ryūnosuke presented Konoe with two draft proposals on July 9, one written by Yabe and the other a "plan with stages number one, two, and three drawn up by Ryū [Shintarō], Sassa [Hiroo], Gotō Fumio, and others."[37] Yabe's plan enunciated the need for "harmony of national administration and supreme command," "cooperation between the Diet and cabinet," "strengthening of rule within the cabinet," and a "national organization" based on "occupational organizations." Avoiding reliance on the political parties, the new order would begin with a "planning organ" in the cabinet to formulate strategy and then expand into a national movement.[38]

Developments would proceed swiftly. Within one or two months the existing political parties would disband voluntarily; a new [Konoe] cabinet would emerge; and the nucleus of a national organization would form. During the next one or two months, a new party would arise, committed to building a national organization. Election laws would be revised by imperial edict; the Diet would be "reformed"; and new elections would be held. In this manner, the national organization would spread "across the nation and to the masses," and Konoe would have his new order within two to four months.

Konoe's New Order Movement gained momentum quickly during the summer of 1940. Support among Diet politicians remained strong, and the army desired a replacement for the cabinet of Admiral Yonai Mitsumasa, who balked at concluding a military alliance with the Axis powers. Expecting that the New Order Movement could lead to a "high degree defense state," the army backed Konoe's candidacy and schemed to topple the existing cabinet. Within less than a month of Konoe's resignation from the Privy Council on July 16, Army Minister Hata Shunroku resigned, announcing that the army believed there was an urgent need to reform the "hearts of the people" and to construct a national defense state.[39] The army toppled Yonai's cabinet by refusing to name a successor. Receiving an imperial request to become premier, Prince Konoe interpreted his appointment as a mandate to effect a new domestic order according to the plans of the Shōwa Research Association.[40]

Konoe picked his cabinet to carry out a basic change of Japan's political system.[41] Yasui Eiichi and Arima Yoriyasu, two of Konoe's closest colleagues in the House of Peers and ardent enthusiasts for a new order, became home minister and agricultural minister, respectively. Kazami Akira, a leading figure in the Shōwa Research Association and an active instigator of the Diet's new party movement, was minister of justice. Kishi Nobusuke, a firm proponent of centralized economic controls, was offered the Ministry of Commerce and Industry, but he preferred to serve as a vice-minister and to have a prominent businessman openly responsible for new policies. Konoe, therefore, selected Kobayashi Ichizō, the president of the Tokyo Electric Company, as minister of commerce and industry. Murase Naoki, a vice-minister of commerce and industry and, like Kishi, a member of the Shōwa Brotherhood, accepted the post of cabinet legal secretary. Because of his reputedly close personal connections with the army and right-wing organizations and the approval of the Shōwa Research Association, Tomita Kenji became chief cabinet secretary and the official cabinet spokesman for the New Order Movement.

Konoe's zeal for pursuing the Asian new order was evident in the appointment of Matsuoka Yōsuke, who had led the Japanese delegation out of the League of Nations in 1933, as foreign minister. A defector from the Seiyūkai, Matsuoka had become a well-known opponent of the parties and a resolute advocate of an aggressive foreign policy.[42] The cabinet promptly delineated the essential principles of national policy as the strategy of "southern advancement" and an alliance with Italy and Germany. Soon afterward, Matsuoka publicly committed Japan to the construction of the Greater East Asian Coprosperity Sphere (Daitōa kyōeiken), and the cabinet decided that a new political structure was essential in order to accomplish that task.

The initial response to the New Order Movement was enthusiastic. By August 16 the political parties had dissolved voluntarily and various groups and ministries had submitted over fifty different new order plans to the government. Konoe relied upon the advice of two competing groups of advisers. One camp—Kazami Akira, Maeda Yonezō, Nagai Ryūtarō, Nakajima Chikuhei, and Arima Yoriyasu—favored a merger of the former political parties into one single party and a substantial role for established Diet politicians. The other camp—Yabe Teiji, Sassa Hiroo, Tomita Kenji, Yasui Eiichi, and Gotō Ryūnosuke—advocated diminishing the power of political party members and building a new system based on occupational organizations.[43]

Miki Kiyoshi and Rōyama Masamichi supported a radical new order movement. Miki argued for a new political organization separated completely from currently active party politicians: a national organization was essential to effect a basic change in national character, to make awareness of the nation spontaneous, and to produce Japanese citizens truly committed to a new order.[44] Recognizing the impossibility of a "spontaneous" mass movement, Rōyama hoped a new national organization would include occupational representation.[45] Although the New Order Movement was a domestic campaign, Rōyama stressed its vital relationship with foreign policy. "Party politics [had] become possible while linked to a definite international foreign policy," the "cooperative diplomacy" with the Anglo-American powers. The European war was now a "heaven-sent opportunity" because it allowed Japan to pursue a new policy of building the Greater East Asian Coprosperity Sphere by expanding its influence toward the southern Pacific area. Moreover, the historical mandate to create a regional bloc constituted a "world trend" that demanded political reform leading toward a more unified Japan.[46]

This interpretation of contemporary events also informed the official proposal of the Shōwa Research Association for a new order in all areas of national life. This outline, which summarized the political, economic, cultural, and educational proposals of the association, was unique among the many plans submitted to the government because the outline justified all reforms by the creation of an Asian bloc. Whereas many plans touted the need for a "high degree national defense state," the Shōwa Research Association argued that domestic reforms were essential for the specific goal of constructing an East Asian cooperative body: that is, "of liberating Asia from her current humiliating position and expecting the establishment of an Asian self-supporting system based on the principles of harmony and autonomy of all races."[47] The leaders of the association believed that Japan's Asian and domestic policies were inseparable, and their views dominated the early New Order Movement.

In August, Premier Konoe appointed twenty-six leading representatives from all sectors of Japanese society to the Preparation Committee for the New Order. The initial membership of the committee's secretariat (*kanjikai*) signaled a victory for the antiparty clique of Konoe's advisers, as Gotō Ryūnosuke, Tomita Kenji, and Murase Naoki joined. Tomita had also asked Yabe to join the secretariat,[48] but he demurred, perhaps because he realized by this time the utter impossibility of realizing the specific plans projected by the Shōwa Research Association. The five other members of the secretariat were Obata Tadayoshi, an officer of the Sumitomo combine and a vice-director of the Cabinet Planning Board; Major-General Mutō Akira, head of the Military Affairs Bureau of the army; Admiral Abe Katsuo, head of the Military Affairs Bureau of the navy; Hasama Shigeki of the Home Ministry; and Matsumoto Shigeharu of the Dōmei news agency. There were no representatives of the political parties or independent businessmen in the group.

By August 27 the secretariat had prepared a draft for the new order with features that resembled proposals devised earlier by the political and economic sections of the Shōwa Research Association.[49] The draft called for the establishment of a "nuclear body" as a step toward the creation of a national organization that would constitute a political "system of united assistance to imperial rule" and "effect an occupational principle." The head of this new body would be the premier, and the "central leadership section" would consist of two parts. An administrative bureau directly responsible to the premier would manage the organization, and national cooperative councils would "guarantee direct contact with the people" through local branches. The national-level cooperative council would, in effect, supersede the Diet, while prefectural, county (*gun*), and municipal councils would assume the tasks of local assemblies.

As part of its economic program the secretariat ventured that a "functional standard" would replace the "profit standard." "For this [change] it is necessary to separate management from capital, to determine new authority for managerial leaders and to establish their position. (In other words, to change the locus of the responsibility of managerial leaders from stockholders to national service.)" The creation of "systematic cartel organizations divided by industry" would accompany the "dissolution" of the *zaibatsu*. A supreme economic council, including representatives from the various industrial organizations, would institute economic planning on a national scale.

Premier Konoe endorsed these proposals before the full preparation committee on August 28. Whatever his hidden political motives might have been,[50] he justified the New Order Movement by a special historical framework similar to that expounded by the association. This perspective, which pervaded the reports of the association and the writings of Rōyama, Ryū, and

Miki after 1937, argued that the division of the world into economic blocs mandated the immediate creation of an East Asian cooperative body led by Japan. This achievement would parallel an overhaul of the fractious and inefficient parliamentary and capitalist systems that had outlived their historical roles. Significantly, Konoe selected Yabe Teiji to compose his initial address to the preparation committee.

The premier's speech began with an affirmation of Japan's commitment to the "unparalleled task" of creating an East Asian new order and a "new world order."[51] This necessitated an "internal structure" to "unite the energies of the State and the people." The deficiencies of the old political structure had failed to unite the people and the government. The new government structure would aspire to "superseding the old party politics postulated upon liberalism." Without any popular political base under his personal control, Konoe's only hope for success in accomplishing reforms was the expectation that members of the preparation committee would also recognize the passing of democratic liberalism and the dawning of a new age in Asia and in Japan.

The Economic New Order

As the deliberations of the preparation committee began, the Cabinet Planning Board compiled its specific recommendations for the institution of a planned economy on the basis of many of the ideas articulated by Ryū Shintarō. Ryū had great expectations that the Cabinet Planning Board would become an effective national economic planning agency. He explained in June 1940 that his proposed reorganization of the Japanese economy would facilitate planning because a tight system of industrial cartels would guarantee both the cooperation of private enterprises with the board and the efficient collection of accurate data.[52] The new control structure had to "take the form that individual managements actually participate[d] in the [creation of] comprehensive economic plans." In view of his close cooperation with younger members of the Cabinet Planning Board, Ryū's insistence that the board become the pinnacle of a national organization of cartels was not surprising. He "seemed to place hope for [reform] in radical elements then present in the bureaucracy and the army."[53]

If the Konoe cabinet initially supported economic reform, it made no new concrete proposals during the summer of 1940. The cabinet's "Outline of Basic Policies" of August 1 simply indicated that it favored "enforcement of a planned economy between government and business." Minister of Commerce and Industry Kobayashi blandly promised to increase production and to lower prices and hinted that "private business will be invited to cooperate in the enforcement of national policy."⁵⁴ The middle-level bureaucrats of the Cabinet Planning Board, however, schemed to force business into a tightly regimented control system.

The board's plans for a new economic order evolved in its council (shingishitsu) of high-level bureaucrats known as enthusiasts for national planning. The most prominent members were Minobe Yōji of the Ministry of Commerce and Industry; Colonel Akinaga Gessan of the army; Okumura Kiwao, the original drafter of the 1937 Electric Power Control Law; Sakumizu Hisatsune of the Finance Ministry; and Mori Hideoto of the China Affairs Bureau. Each of these men had graduated from the University of Tokyo during 1925–26. The leader of the group was Minobe, a member of the Shōwa Brotherhood and an official of the Ministry of Commerce and Industry. He had served for three years in Manchuria, where the army had imposed severe controls on economic development. During the fall of 1940 he served as the leading government proponent and defender of the new economic order, thereby earning the nickname "Minobe of the new economic order."⁵⁵

The clique of junior bureaucrats from Ryū's economic committee in the Shōwa Research Association channeled their ideas to Minobe, who integrated them into the planning board's drafts for a new economic order. Acknowledging that his consideration of economic policies had been influenced by "Katsumata and his group" (Katsumata *atari*), Minobe referred specifically to their concern for the lack of growth in nonmunitions sectors of the economy and the ominous disruption of the economic reproductive process—two ideas central to Ryū Shintarō's analysis of the Japanese economy.⁵⁶

The outline for creating the economic new order, which the planning board issued on September 28, reflected many of Ryū's ideas.⁵⁷ It also shocked the leaders of big business. This document called for a "national defense economy," "reform of the free enterprise system," "rejection of the pursuit of private gain," "high productivity," and a "comprehensively planned cooperative body for production." "Enterprises [would] be freed from the domination of capital," and management would be liberated to fulfill national goals for industrial production. Echoing Ryū's *Reorganization of the Japanese Economy*, the board advised, "[We] must control dividends and entrust managers with the national responsibility of preserving and strengthening production and increasing economic reproduction without being bound by capital in the management of enterprises, and [we] must encourage their ability and creativity."

The Cabinet Planning Board reiterated other suggestions that Ryū had put forth. It proposed the merger of small companies and the formation of a national system of tightly organized cartel associations, one for each industry. The leaders of the cartels would be subject to governmental approval, and the cartels would be regulated by a supreme economic council that would be "under the supervision of the cabinet (the planning board)."

Ryū's *Reorganization of the Japanese Economy* served as the wellspring for many of the recommendations of the Cabinet Planning Board—for example, the creation of a new economic ethic of public service, comprehensive economic planning, elimination of stockholders from company management, recognition of a new managerial class, a national organization of industrial cartels, and increased authority for the board. The authoritarian features of these proposals also dovetailed with Ryū's views. Since 1939, Ryū had publicly advocated a totalitarian economic system and promoted the planning board as the focus of a new economic structure. Although Ryū had stated that the planning board should not exercise dictatorial power over the economy, there were no specific safeguards in his proposed reorganization of the Japanese economy to prevent the growth of bureaucratic power. Ryū, himself, expected to receive an appointment to direct economic planning in the new order.[58]

Many of the ideas put forward by the Cabinet Planning Board were similar to those advanced by the Ministry of Commerce and Industry and the Army Ministry. The Commerce Ministry, under the influence of Vice-Minister Kishi, also drafted a new economic order that emphasized bureaucratic control and a new system of cartel organizations.[59] This plan urged neither the elimination of stockholders from industrial management nor the location of ultimate authority over the economy in the Cabinet Planning Board. Instead, this power would reside in the Commerce Ministry.

The Army Ministry supported limits on profits and increased state control over the economy. In the spring of 1940 the army had caused a sharp slump in the Japanese stock market by implementing strict profit controls over enterprises that manufactured munitions. Later, a spokesman proclaimed:

> This new economic structure of the high degree national defense state aims at the completion of military preparations, expansion of productivity, and . . . a mobilization of the entire personnel and material resources of the country. This means an epoch-making development not only in the munitions industries. Such a rapid and large-scale reorganization of the industrial structure is practically impossible under the old liberal economic structure without causing disturbances to the entire national economic structure. Therefore, it is essential first of all to intensify thoroughly planned economic control.[60]

Influential segments of the government bureaucracy and the army agreed with Ryū's quest for a new economic order. The major point of debate was only what agency would control economic planning. A major political obstacle to creating the new order, though, was the constitutional authority invested in the Diet.

The Failure of Radical Reforms

Whereas some civilian and military officials voiced strong support for radical economic reforms, criticism of the new order campaign as a communist or totalitarian movement aroused serious opposition in the preparation committee. Led by a group of former party politicians that included Kanemitsu Tsuneo and Okada Tadahiko of the Seiyūkai, the committee rejected the secretariat's views on economic reorganization and a political body based on occupational groups. Despite Premier Konoe's constant avowals of respect for the constitution and the principle of imperial rule, committee members openly reproached him for attempting to create a new government separate from the emperor's authority. Referring to the dual structure of the Tokugawa government from 1600 to 1868, when the shogun ruled Japan through his personal government (*bakufu*) separate from the emperor's interference, some members even accused the premier of forming a new *bakufu* in the guise of the "national organization" proposed by the secretariat.[61] Others feared a lessening of the Diet's powers in the new political order.

By its sixth and final meeting the preparation committee had eliminated the radical proposals submitted by the secretariat and had endorsed the creation of the Imperial Rule Assistance Association (IRAA) in place of the fascist political organization envisioned by the Shōwa Research Association. Before disbanding, the committee established an eleven-man board of permanent directors for the IRAA and decided that it should include an administrative bureau and a hierarchical series of cooperative councils. The composition of the councils remained undetermined, but by early October the permanent directors had entrusted control of the prefectural branches to the Home Ministry. Konoe's euphoric new order rhetoric of July and August was no longer evident in October, when he launched the IRAA: "The program of the present movement will be fulfilled in the realization of the way of the subject in assisting Imperial rule. Outside of this, there are no programs or proclamations."[62]

Disregarding Konoe's new reluctance to support substantial reforms, members of the Shōwa Research Association participated actively in the formal organization of the IRAA. Gotō Ryūnosuke accepted an appointment as director of the important Organization Section and persuaded several other association members to work under him. Two members of Ryū's economic committee, Wada Kōsaku and Katsumata Seiichi, became head of the General Affairs Bureau and director of the Kyūshū area, respectively. Sakai Saburō joined the Culture Section, while Miki Kiyoshi served as a consultant.[63] Association members thus attempted to carry out the New Order Movement that they had helped to design and that they had convinced Konoe to lead.

As Gotō tried to staff the branches of the IRAA with persons sympathetic to substantive reforms, the army, the Home Ministry, and former party politicians battled for control of the organization.[64] The parties had dissolved, because politicians had anticipated gaining influence over national policy through the Diet Bureau of the IRAA, but, realizing the bias of leaders like Gotō against former party members, Diet representatives soon began to view the IRAA as a threat. They lobbied for disassociation from the new body and, in a protest, even refused to fund it. Opposition from the Diet was a major factor in the failure of the New Order Movement.[65] Finally, Konoe acted to settle the controversy by asking Justice Minister Kazami and Home Minister Yasui to resign in December. Baron Hiranuma Kiichirō, an opponent of radical political reforms, then joined the cabinet. Within two months the Diet declared its independence from the IRAA, and the organization passed into the control of the Home Ministry as a movement for "spiritual mobilization."[66] Contrary to its ambitious goals, the New Order Movement of Prince Konoe ended up leaving the political structure of Japan basically unaltered. The disappearance of the political parties had not reduced their members' prerogatives in the Diet, because a new mass political organization had not emerged.[67]

The struggle over the new economic order was just as vicious.[68] The reaction of the business world to the bureaucratic plans for a new economic order was vehemently negative. One major defender of private enterprise was Hoashi Kei, a research director for the Japan Economic League and a secretary for the Council of Important Industry Cartels (Jūyō sangyō karuteru kondankai). Because Hoashi had participated in Ryū's economic research group, he was well acquainted with the rationale behind the plans for economic reorganization. Hoashi agreed that the times demanded increased productivity and an orientation of business toward national goals. Still, he maintained, the principle of private property was crucial to economic prosperity: "Especially in new industry and small businesses, 'property' has a close and indivisible relationship with management as an important dynamic of business management. Therefore 'killing the bull by trimming its horns,' by mechanically dividing property and management or by having bureaucrats directly interfere in management, must be avoided by all means."[69] In addition, Hoashi argued that Japan could not emulate the German managed economy, because Japan's industrial structure was comparatively underdeveloped. He suggested, as Takahashi Kamekichi had in 1937, that Japanese businessmen should form an autonomous organization, an "industrial league," which as part of the New Order Movement would foster public spirit and provide a leadership section for the new order to promote cooperation between officials and private entrepreneurs in economic planning.

In early December the Japan Economic League confronted Konoe with a bitter denunciation of the idea of the new economic order. After stating that it regretted the "misunderstanding" that private profit contradicted national goals, the league warned that removing the profit motive would bring a "contraction of business, a decrease in production, and a drastic drop in tax revenues."[70] In the view of Japan's prominent businessmen, the Cabinet Planning Board was infested with communists because those who touted the "concept of the superiority of public welfare" were trying "to destroy our economic world and make our country into Russia."

Gradually, the Cabinet Planning Board modified its plans for a new economic order. Each successive draft became more moderate, to the point that direct references to the "separation of capital and mangement" disappeared. Following a series of November cabinet conferences on economic policy, the service ministries even complained that the government's plans were becoming too procapitalist.[71] The cabinet finally agreed on an outline for the construction of a new economic order on December 7, 1940. This version was sufficiently vague to satisfy both the advocates of increased state economic planning and the leaders of private business.[72] The outline omitted any references to the nationalization of industry or the "separation of management and capital," sanctioned "proper profits," and even permitted "productive" firms to increase their profits. In return, big business agreed in principle to the priority of "public welfare," in that the government would have the right to regulate excess profits and to encourage the reorganization of businesses. Corporate leaders affirmed the need to establish a new economic structure based on cartels and promised to cooperate with the government.[73]

The major victor in this struggle was big business. Government bureaucrats gained very little substantive authority, as the provisions for profit limitation were similar to the compromise that Finance Minister Ikeda Seihin had worked out with the army in 1938, and the locus of economic planning remained unclear. Business leaders had prevented the enactment of any form of covert or overt nationalization. The cabinet outline also indicated the probable need for a "supreme economic organ to embrace all industries"; Minobe Yōji, in particular, was concerned about this item, which business groups supported because it would create a powerful lobby for big business within the government.[74] Furthermore, the official implementation of the diluted new economic order was delayed for almost another year. The battle over the new economic order was interpreted as a basic struggle between the "state authority" of the bureaucracy and the "real power" of big business,[75] and eighteen months after the formation of the Konoe cabinet and the summons to a new order, this battle still raged.

The animosity of businessmen toward the "reds" in the Cabinet Planning Board forced the government to turn against the most controversial advocates of the new economic order. Quickly sensing the shift in political momentum, Ogata Taketora, editor in chief of the *Asahi*, encouraged Ryū to leave in October 1940 as a special correspondent to Germany. The key members of Ryū's research group in the Shōwa Research Association could not escape. The police arrested Katsumata Seiichi, Wada Kōsaku, Inaba Hidezō, and Masaki Chifuyu in April 1941 on charges of trying to effect socialism under the guise of national defense policies prepared in the Cabinet Planning Board. Rumors were rife that Minobe Yōji would also be imprisoned, but his senior civil service rank apparently spared him this humiliation.[76] The "Cabinet Planning Board Incident" symbolized the demise of radical economic reforms within the New Order Movement.

The Shōwa Research Association dissolved in November 1940. The attendance of over two hundred dignitaries from academia, business, politics, government, and journalism at the final ceremonies testified to the prestige of the organization. The immediate reasons for the sudden decision to dissolve the association are unclear, especially in light of the enthusiasm of some important members, like Miki Kiyoshi, to continue. Former members claim there was no capable replacement for Gotō Ryūnosuke, who had resigned as chief organizer when he assumed a post in the IRAA,[77] but this does not explain why finding a successor proved so difficult. The leaders of the association perhaps thought the IRAA deserved their full attention, and because of the widespread charges of communist infiltration of the group, they might well have disbanded to quell criticism of the premier and the IRAA.

By providing close contact with important public officials, the Shōwa Research Association had given Rōyama, Ryū, and Miki the chance to fulfill their dreams of creating a new society. The government's preoccupation with national mobilization and the need to rationalize the China War had encouraged those writers to envision fundamental changes in both political and economic policies and to interpret the conflict as an opportunity to create a regional bloc based on the moral ideology of cooperativism. The New Order Movement represented the most vigorous attempt of Japanese intellectuals to influence directly national policies in the prewar period. For a brief moment when Konoe formed his second cabinet, Rōyama, Ryū, and Miki felt that their ideas would at last be transformed into action, as their ideas found significant support in some sections of the bureaucracy.

However, the rapid evanescence of the association revealed a vulnerability that had long been present. It had not succeeded in building a popular political movement; nor had it cultivated independent financial resources. Its prestige and influence had resulted not from its own power but from its access to government officials and the patronage of Prince Konoe. Determined opposition from sectors of the political and economic establishment had crushed its program of radical reforms.

9. Intellectuals, Fascism, and the Quest for Power

The Shōwa Research Association afforded a select group of Japanese intellectuals the passing illusion of power and influence. They had impact, when their proposals fit the needs of established leaders or political forces without threatening too many major interest groups. Konoe accepted the idea of appointing cabinet councillors in 1937 because of his interest in bolstering his own authority. In 1938 the proposal to establish a special agency to determine policy for China concurred with the desires of the army, which overcame resistance from the Foreign Ministry. The association succeeded in encouraging Konoe to conceive of the China War as an event of worldwide significance and as an opportunity for progress toward a new order because these ideas rationalized the conflict.

As a body without a power base of its own, the Shōwa Research Association had to gain cooperation from powerful political forces to obtain influence. Contrary to Rōyama's assertion that the impartiality of intellectuals would lead to benevolent government, a lack of specific political support led members of the association to adapt to the interests of Prince Konoe, the army, and the "new bureaucrats," who all favored national mobilization and increased government intervention in politics and the economy. The association hailed its program for the domestic new order as leading to efficiency, productivity, and greater national strength. Its success would intimidate China into surrender and show the way to a moral East Asian order. Thus, the leaders of the association adopted the role of ideologues for those officials whom the association wanted to influence.[1] The experiences of Rōyama, Ryū, and Miki indicate how seductive that role can be for independent intellectuals who try to influence national policies directly.[2]

Fascism was an attractive model of reform for Rōyama, Ryū, and Miki. The similarities between the initial proposals for a New Order Movement and the structure of Mussolini's corporate state were clear in 1940.[3] A single, national political organization based on occupational units would replace the political parties and lead to a "Japanese form of one nation, one party." The new economic order emulated the policies of Nazi Germany: limits on profits, government supervision of excess profits, economic planning, a national organization of regional and industrial cartels, and the recognition of the primacy of national goals.

Rōyama, Ryū, and Miki's view of the state by 1940 accorded with what they understood as the fascist perception of the nation. They believed the state should incorporate all economic groups into its structure, and they upheld the right of the government to intervene in all aspects of society. Moreover, they defined the state as a "cooperative body," a community that constituted a moral force and an ethical basis for action. In their ideal political and economic order the individual would rise above his own selfish desires and base his actions on the collective welfare of the nation. The theory of the national cooperative body rested on the elaboration of a "national mystique" similar to that common in the ideology of European fascism, because Rōyama, Ryū, and Miki construed Japan's traditional national polity as centered on reverence for the emperor and as leading naturally to the ethics of the cooperative body.[4] These writers glorified the nation and those elements in Japan's past that were conducive to an ethic of national service.

Like fascist ideologues in Europe, Rōyama, Ryū, and Miki envisioned a new type of freedom. European fascists prescribed freedom in a "true community," in which men "voluntarily join together on a basis of a common origin, attitude, and purpose." A Nazi pamphlet proclaimed: "He who can do what he wants is not free, but he is free who does what he should."[5] Similarly, Rōyama, Ryū, and Miki argued that in the "cooperative body," "control" would metamorphose into "freedom" and that freedom would consist of the citizen's autonomously realizing the needs of the whole nation. Ryū advocated abandoning "individual interests" and discovering the "true self."[6] This aspect of fascism was crucial to these writers because it allowed them to argue that, far from seeking to suppress liberty like reactionary Japanists, they favored a superior type of freedom.

However, these intellectuals did not imitate some aspects of fascism. Although they longed for a strong leader to carry out their program and ultimately relied upon Konoe, they did not explicitly call for a charismatic dictator.[7] Of course, such an idea would have prompted immediate charges of lese majesty. Nor did these writers glorify struggle and violence for their own sake, as was often the case in European fascism.[8] European fascists often referred to the glory of the Roman Empire or the savagery of the ancient *Volk* to stress the values of struggle and martial valor. Rōyama, Ryū, and Miki did not emphasize those qualities, despite the presence of the *samurai* tradition as a convenient reference. Their proposals, though, did imply the use of force exerted by the state for implementing reforms and inducing the compliance of citizens.

Fascism appealed to Rōyama, Ryū, and Miki because it presented solutions to serious economic and political problems of industrial society, addressing such concerns as Japan's national role in Asia, social peace, and economic justice. Moreover, fascism promised to break the deadlock of parliamentary democracy, raise productivity, and end economic strife. Rōyama, Ryū, and Miki believed that even the emotional aspect of fascism, the ethic of national service, could facilitate rational reforms of society.

In Europe too the rational aspects of fascism, retrospectively termed *left fascism* or *managerial fascism*, attracted intellectuals.[9] Some maintained their idealistic view of fascism for the rest of their careers, and others quickly grew disillusioned.[10] The reformist elements in European fascism eased its acceptance by the intellectual community, and this appeal of fascism is important to recognize in order to understand its complex attraction to different constituencies in a society.[11]

In some respects the ideals of the East Asian and the national cooperative bodies were reactions against the conflicts of modern society.[12] Miki discussed the preservation of rationality and individual creativity and, together with Ryū and Rōyama, aspired to create a new universal ideology; but these men repudiated the principles of individualism and universalism based on the doctrines of liberalism and Marxism. The pride of these men in Japan's economic development and new power was obvious; yet they fretted about conflicts between individuals, classes, economic groups, and political parties within Japan, which they termed harmful to national solidarity. They advocated the revival of a unique Oriental *Gemeinschaft* in which political and economic relationships among Japanese would be cooperative, as in a small traditional and tightly knit community.

The New Order Movement of the Shōwa Research Association also emphasized national industrial development. The proposed cooperative body did not call for a return to self-sufficient agricultural villages, a position typical of "agrarianists" in the 1930s, but beckoned the individual to merge with the nation as a whole in the new *Gemeinschaft*. Moreover, the state would direct the economy. One important aim of the new *Gemeinschaft* was to absorb the *Gesellschaft* of modern industry and to raise industrial productivity. The Shōwa Research Association wanted to augment national military strength by increasing Japan's industrial production in a national defense state.

Neither the theme of antimodernism nor that of state-directed accelerated industrial development by itself is helpful in delineating fascism in prewar Japan. The New Order Movement of the Shōwa Research Association embraced both themes in seeking a return to a premodern form of social relations and an increase in Japan's economic power. In addition, calls for a return to traditional social values were common to many groups in prewar Japan, and many government officials, civilian and military, underscored the need for rapid industrial development directed by the state. This study suggests that useful criteria for defining the association's New Order Movement as fascist are the advocacy of a single mass party or "national organization" based on the leadership principle, strict state controls over the economy through corporatist organizations, and inculcation of a national service ethic for the purpose of augmenting national strength. These policies were common to fascist Italy, Nazi Germany, and the initial New Order Movement.

The prewar Japanese government was not fascist. Interpreting the IRAA as a special type of "emperor-system fascism" institutionally different from European fascism creates paradoxes in explaining the thought and behavior of Rōyama, Ryū, Miki, and other intellectuals involved in the Shōwa Research Association.[13] They knew Japan was not a fascist state in the 1930s, that the armed forces and the bureaucracy held political power, and that the major political parties and the business community were waging a long battle against the extension of state controls that accompanied the continuation of the war in China. These intellectuals looked to Nazi Germany and fascist Italy for better and more reasonable ways to free an industrialized Japan from the political and economic system of the Meiji constitutional state. One paradox of interpreting the prewar Japanese state as fascist is that the initial New Order Movement used fascist ideas in an attempt to restructure the political and economic institutions of that state.

The issue of why intellectuals like Rōyama Masamichi, Miki Kiyoshi, and Ryū Shintarō ended up leading the New Order Movement is important for understanding central political trends in prewar Japan. In contrast to the widespread assertion that prominent intellectuals resisted fascism, Rōyama, Ryū, and Miki led the creation of a fascist movement in 1940. The basic patterns of the activity of these men indicate why there were so few protests from intellectuals against Japan's policies of domestic oppression and foreign aggression. These patterns help explain why the ideals of party democracy and of cooperative diplomacy disappeared so quickly into what historians have called the "dark valley" of the early Shōwa period.

The concept of apostasy, that intellectuals suddenly changed their beliefs due to external pressures, is not useful for analyzing the writings of Rōyama, Ryū, and Miki, because it neglects important continuities in their thought. Rōyama, for example, responded to new problems and trends in domestic and foreign affairs, but his constant concern in domestic politics was to eliminate the conflicts caused by party rivalry and class struggle within Japanese capitalism. He never lost his conviction that the major problem facing industrial Japanese society was competition between occupational interest groups and that some form of occupational representation coupled with adminstrative guidance from the state was necessary to moderate this friction. Although Rōyama developed the idea of an East Asian cooperative body led by Japan after 1937, he had long been a supporter of Japanese dominance over China.

Ryū retrospectively endorsed the concept of apostasy in saying that because Japanese Marxists did not adjust their imported theory to the persisting reality of traditional social values in Japan, Marxists were too easily disappointed when their revolutionary credo failed. This disappointment led to apostasy.[14] Ryū's own analysis of the Japanese economy in the 1930s showed considerable flexibility; he adjusted Marxism to the reality of the need for a defense economy by drawing upon Nazi economic policies and by echoing the Home Ministry's propaganda on behalf of social harmony and popular unity. Developments in the thought of Rōyama and Ryū and their reliance on the state to implement their ideals of economic and political reform constituted neither apostasy nor false apostasy.

In the early 1930s, Miki Kiyoshi refuted charges that he had committed apostasy by arguing that all thought should change in a dialectical fashion. He expected that some of his ideas would change gradually to meet new demands; and they did. The philosophy of cooperativism, a product of Miki's work in the Shōwa Research Association, was his first attempt to create a political and economic ideology. It addressed specific dilemmas confronting Japan in 1938 by providing guidelines for national mobilization, a rationale for a new Chinese government supported by Japan, and goals for Japanese leadership of Asia. Still, the theory of cooperativism rested on assumptions that had been consistent themes in Miki's writings during the previous decade—that is, that Japan was experiencing a profound crisis, that its established political and economic systems were outmoded, and that a "new culture" was necessary for both Japan and China. Indeed, the belief that they should help design a new Japan was a constant element in the writings of Rōyama, Ryū, and Miki and helped lead to their creation of a fascist movement.

A combination of factors resulted in the participation of these writers in the New Order Movement: a determination to influence national policy, a sense of crisis based on a conviction that Japan needed radical political and economic reforms, a rejection of individualistic values, flexibility in adjusting to major trends in Japan and in Europe, and nationalistic sentiment. In particular, the persistence of a strong sense of mission among these intellectuals was impressive during the entire interwar period. Rōyama, Ryū, and Miki could have easily avoided politics in pursuing academic careers, but they insisted on overcoming the isolation of Japanese intellectuals from political influence. Although they identified themselves as members of an intellectual elite, they agonized over how they could contribute to resolving contemporary problems in a concrete way. Rōyama, Ryū, and Miki first looked to the moderate proletarian parties as agents of potential influence, but when that movement failed, they searched for another avenue of influence and thought they had found it in the power of the state bureaucracy.

The Shōwa Research Association provided these men with direct access to powerful officials.[15] They viewed the resolution of Japan's crises as their obligation as intellectuals. When the second Konoe cabinet in 1940 began to ape the rhetoric of the cooperative body by calling for a Greater East Asian Coprosperity Sphere and a new national organization, they must have felt that their political influence was increasing. In retrospect, the military used this rhetoric to rationalize its own domestic and foreign policies. At the time, however, the intellectuals in the Shōwa Research Association may well have believed that they were directing the government's policies toward goals beyond domestic oppression and foreign military conquest. The association gave these three intellectuals the hope that they could fulfill their self-appointed mission to remold Japan.

Rōyama, Ryū and Miki presumed that contemporary Japanese society needed drastic reforms. In the 1930s this conviction developed into a sense of crisis, into the feeling that the economic and political systems might even collapse. They severely criticized the forms of liberalism in Japan as favoring special interest groups.[16] They castigated the corruption and ineffectiveness of the main political parties—the Minseitō and the Seiyūkai—rejected traditional liberalism, and advocated an overhaul of the free-market economy in Japan. The appeal of fascism to Rōyama, Ryū, and Miki was its promise of radical reforms through the power of the state.

These men were not liberals in the sense of defending the rights of the individual against the authority of the state. In the 1920s they decided that the values of individualism were obsolete and emphasized the importance of occupational groups and economic classes as the basic units of society. This stance facilitated their later advocacy of the nation as the focus of loyalty for the individual.

The premise of Miki's philosophy of cooperativism in 1938 was the priority of the welfare of the "whole" society or nation over that of the individual. Rōyama's vision of the new political order centered on a comprehensive national organization that would bind the individual to the state. Ryū's proposed economic structure would encompass business enterprises so that they all could become extensions of the central planning organ by participating in the planning process. Although these men nominally criticized bureaucratic government in Japan, they placed the welfare of the whole over the protection of the individual. They sought to correct this fault in their policy proposals not by limiting bureaucratic authority but by encouraging cooperative relationships between civilians and officials. In their scheme every Japanese citizen would spontaneously become aware of his responsibility as a public servant of the nation, but they did not describe exactly how this attitude would emerge.

The flexibility in the ideas of these men was another reason for their adoption of fascist ideology. Throughout the interwar period they remained sensitive to intellectual and political trends in the West. Because their earliest writings drew inspiration from Western socialism, they followed closely the fate of left-wing movements in Europe and the rise of fascism. One of the attractions of fascist policies to the Shōwa Research Association was that these seemed to be the latest and most effective Western models for economic and political reform.

Finally, the force of nationalism affected these Japanese writers. As the military waged war, first in Manchuria and then in China, none of these men doubted that Japan should be the leader of Asia. They recognized the rise of popular nationalism at home and the later mobilization for war as powerful domestic trends and adapted their ideas to these developments. The strategy of not confronting these trends but directing them toward visionary goals seemed to Miki, Rōyama, and Ryū the most promising for gaining political influence. Thus, Miki could view the humiliation of Minobe Tatsukichi, a respected academic, as a progressive sign of popular dissatisfaction with the political establishment; Rōyama could interpret the violent mutiny of 1936 in a similar manner; and Ryū could see the military's desire to extend state control over the economy as a chance to dismantle capitalism. Unlike some other writers, these three intellectuals did not challenge the army's presence in China. Instead, they tried to redefine the quest to conquer the mainland as one step toward an Asian utopia.

The eclecticism of Rōyama, Ryū, and Miki allowed them to adapt their ideas to new situations and influences, but it also made their proposals infeasible. Combining ideas from the ideologies of Marxism, guild socialism, and fascism and from the sociological theories of Toennies into their ideal of a cooperative body, Rōyama, Ryū, and Miki failed to consider whether discrete ideas or policies drawn from different ideologies could fit together in practice. It is not surprising that antagonists criticized the plans of the association as unrealistic schemes concocted by intellectuals with no experience in politics or economics.

Leaders of the Shōwa Research Association, like Rōyama, Ryū, and Miki, were not simply victims of the force of events during the prewar era; nor were they opponents of those trends. During the mid-1930s the desire of these intellectuals for influence dictated a turn to the state as an expedient choice for implementing their strategy of reform. Their basic assumptions about the need for reform and the type of change necessary impelled them to desert the parliamentary system in Japan and the values of individualism. These writers reinforced the development of state control over the economy and the Japanese sense of mission to dominate Asia. Although the Shōwa period, in retrospect, was a dark era, to these men it offered the prospect of a bright new society.

Notes

Chapter 1

1. For an example of the use of the term "dark valley," see Ōuchi, *Fuashizumu e no michi*, p. 422.
2. For descriptions and interpretations of the Shōwa Research Association by former members, see Shōwa dōjinkai, *Shōwa kenkyūkai*, and Sakai, *Shōwa kenkyūkai*. A chronology of Ryū's life is contained in Ryū, *Zenshū*, 6:605–48. Remembrances of Ryū composed by many of his former colleagues are collected in Ebata, *Kaisō Ryū Shintarō*. Some biographical data on Rōyama Masamichi are available in Matsuzawa, "Minshū shakaishugi no hitobito," pp. 249–307. A revised version of this essay appears in Matsuzawa, *Nihon shakaishugi*, pp. 289–382. Miyakawa, *Miki Kiyoshi*, pp. 157–82, and Miki, *Zenshū*, 19:853–932, present detailed chronologies of the life of Miki Kiyoshi.

Rōyama and Ryū remained active in the postwar period. Purged from public office after his service in the wartime Diet, Rōyama became a vice-president of the prestigious journal *Chūō kōron* and president of Ochanomizu University; he was also a prominent participant in the democratic socialist movement. Ryū returned to Japan in 1948, after eight years in Europe, to assume the post of editor in chief of the *Asahi* newspaper, Japan's largest.

Miki was arrested by the police in 1945 and died of illness in prison. He is considered the most eminent philosopher of his generation.

3. There is much controversy about the character of fascism as a European and international phenomenon. Weber, *Varieties of Fascism*, argues that fascism was a reform movement which appealed to laborers in Europe. Weiss, *The Fascist Tradition*, contends that fascism was a conservative movement.

More recently, debate has centered on whether fascism was a promodern or antimodern movement. Among those who view fascism as promoting modernity are Gregor, *The Fascist Persuasion*, especially pp. 181–82, and "The Ideology of Fascism," p. 288; Joes, *Fascism in the Contemporary World*, pp. 201–206. Advocates of the antimodern character of fascism include Nolte, *Three Faces of Fascism*, and Turner, "Fascism and Modernization," pp. 547–64 (this essay is reprinted in Turner, *Reappraisals of Fascism*, pp. 117–39). Cassels, "Janus," pp. 69–92, argues that fascism could be either promodern or antimodern.

4. The contention that the initial New Order Movement of 1940 was a fascist movement that failed challenges two different but common interpretations of Japanese fascism—that Japan by 1940 was fascist and that there was no such thing as fascism in Japan. Many Japanese scholars believe that fascism evolved "from above" through the state bureaucracy and triumphed with the creation of the IRAA. See Tōyama, Imai, and Fujiwara, *Shōwa shi*; Maruyama, *Gendai seiji no shisō to kōdō*, pp. 32, 39, 58, 80–82 (in English, Maruyama, *Thought and Behavior in Modern Japanese Politics*, pp. 33–34, 51–52, and 82); Ōuchi, *Fuashizumu e no michi*, pp. 314–15, 479–82; Hashikawa, "Nihon fuashizumu no shisōteki tokushitsu," pp. 332–34; Chō, *Shōwa kyōkō*, pp. 181–82, 195–98; Furuya, "Nihon fuashizumuron," pp. 83–86, 120–21.

This study shares the opposing view that because there were few institutional similarities between prewar Japan and fascist Italy or Nazi Germany, the Japanese state was not fascist. See Hayashi "Japan and Germany in the Interwar Period," especially pp. 477–78, 483–86, and Wilson, "A New Look at the Problem of Japanese Fascism," pp. 401–12 (this article is reprinted in Turner, *Reappraisals of Fascism*, pp. 117–39).

Some historians contend that the lack of an accepted definition of fascism has undermined its utility as an analytical tool. See Itō, "Shōwa seiji shi kenkyū," pp. 215–28; Duus and Okimoto, "Fascism and the History of Prewar Japan," pp. 65–76; Allardyce, "What Fascism Is Not," pp. 376–88.

In contrast, this study seeks to find common themes between European fascist movements and the New Order Movement in Japan. For a recent attempt to define common "assumptions" in European fascism, see Mosse, "Towards a General Theory of Fascism."

In reply to critics of the concept of fascism, some scholars have noted that most categories of political thought—liberalism, conservatism, socialism, nationalism, democracy, militarism—are complex and elastic and that complexity does not necessarily vitiate an analytical concept. For example, see Nolte's reply to Allardyce, "What Fascism Is Not," in the *American Historical Review* 85 (April 1979): 391–94.

5. For example, the most influential Japanese analysis of the prewar period, Maruyama's *Thought and Behavior in Modern Japanese Politics*, virtually ignores the role of prominent intellectuals, saying they attempted "passive resistance" to fascism (p. 58). The defensive attitude of many Japanese intellectuals has also hindered investigations of their role. Ryū Shintarō, for example, claims that when he returned to Japan from Europe, where he spent the war as a reporter, he tossed his diary of the prewar years into the ocean. See Ryū, "Kaigai de no hachigatsu jūgo nichi," p. 215.

6. Japanese scholars have emphasized the phenomenon of "apostasy," of an intellectual's sudden abandonment of liberal or socialist beliefs due to "pressure exerted by the state." See Shisō no kagaku kenkyūkai, *Tenkō*, 3 vols., especially the introduction by Tsurumi Shunsuke to the first volume, "Tenkō no kyōdō kenkyū ni tsuite," pp. 1–27. (A partial English translation of this piece appears in the *Journal of Social and Political Ideas in Japan* 2 (1964): 54–58.) Western historians have tended to stress continuities rather than changes in the ideas of various individuals during this period. See, for example, Najita, "Nakano Seigō," pp. 375–421; Duus, "Ōyama Ikuo," pp. 423–58; Bernstein, *Japanese Marxist*. For an exception, see Johnson, *Instance of Treason*, pp. 114–18.

Morley, "Introduction: Choice and Consequences," p. 27, argues that the thought of Japanese writers became increasingly irrational during this period, and Reischauer, "What Went Wrong?" pp. 502–3, posits that "centrist" intellectuals supported the parliamentary system.

7. Less than 2 percent of students entering the school system each year continued at the university level. See Smith, *Japan's First Student Radicals*, p. 3.

8. Passin, "Modernization and the Japanese Intellectual," pp. 466–73; Passin, "Intellectuals in the Decision-Making Process," pp. 252–53; Harootunian, "Introduction: The Sense of Ending and the Problem of Taishō," pp. 12–28; Arima, *The Failure of Freedom*, pp. 1–14.

9. Smith, *Japan's First Student Radicals*, describes the campus mood well; this topic receives more attention in the next chapter.

10. For discussions of this problem, see Bourne, *War and the Intellectuals*, pp. 3–14, and Hofstadter, *Anti-Intellectualism in American Life*, pp. 428–29.

11. Bowen, *German Theories of the Corporative State*, pp. 164–72.

12. Ibid., pp. 173–209.

13. Nazi economic policies will be discussed in more detail in chapter 5. The ideal of the Italian corporate state is explained in chapter 4.

14. There is increasing recognition of the rational, intellectual appeal of fascism. Robert Soucy argues French writer and fascist Drieu La Rochelle viewed fascism as a "highly rationalistic creed" and an answer to "industrialism, liberalism, and socialism" (*Fascist Intellectual*, pp. 17–19). David D. Roberts argues that the syndicalist Sergio Panunzio converted to fascism because of its "revolutionary potential" for replacing the liberal state and making Italian life "more practical and productive." Roberts calls Panunzio's ideology "left fascism" (*The Syndicalist Tradition and Italian Fascism*, chaps. 9 and 10).

Chapter 2

1. Endō, "Shokugyōteki chishikijin," pp. 285–89. See also Pierson, *Tokutomi Sohō*, pp. 99 and 197, for the views of one famous Japanese journalist on his role in society.

2. Yamada, "Miki Kiyoshi," pp. 302–4.

3. See Miki Kiyoshi's review of Ryū's *Shupengurā no rekishishugiteki tachiba* in Ryū, *Zenshū*, 8:214–17. The review originally appeared in the *Teikoku daigaku shimbun* on December 10, 1928.

4. Pyle, *The New Generation in Meiji Japan*.

5. Pyle, "Advantages of Followership," pp. 127–64.

6. For an excellent summary of the economic developments in Japan during the twenties, see Patrick, "Economic Muddle," pp. 211–66. See also Nakamura, *Nihon keizai seichō*, pp. 127–37.

7. Smith, *Japan's First Student Radicals*, pp. 29–30. For an analysis of the Yūaikai, see Large, *The Rise of Labor in Japan*.

8. Smith, *Japan's First Student Radicals*, pp. 58–59. See also Watanabe, "Nihon no marukusushugi undō," pp. 169–72.

9. For a summary of the labor movement in Japan at this time, see Imai, *Taishō demokurashii*, pp. 282–309.

10. Mitchell, "Japan's Peace Preservation Law," pp. 317–45; Mitchell, *Thought Control*, chaps. 2–3; Fridell, "Government Ethics Textbooks," pp. 823–33.

11. Smethurst, *Social Basis*.

12. Kano, *Taishō demokurashii no teiryū*, pp. 14–18, and Itō, *Jūgo nen sensō*, pp. 16–18.

13. Rōyama, *Gendai no shakai shisō*, pp. 5–6.

14. Quoted in Silberman, "Yoshino Sakuzō," p. 316. See also, Tsurumi and Kuno, *Gendai nihon no shisō*, p. 154.

15. See Smith, *Japan's First Student Radicals*.
16. Quoted in ibid., p. 57.
17. Ibid., pp. 52, 288.
18. Taira Teizō, a classmate of Rōyama at the University of Tokyo and a prominent member of the Social Thought Association, described the split in Taira, "Shakai shisōsha kessei no koro," pp. 195–99. Taira relates the split to the struggle between syndicalists and moderate socialists within the entire Japanese socialist movement.
19. Ibid.; this work is the fullest available account of the Social Thought Association.
20. Quoted in ibid., p. 197.
21. Rōyama, "Gyōsei seiri no shakaiteki igi," p. 2. At Tōdai, Rōyama studied administrative theory under Professor Onotsuka Kiheiji and eventually took over his courses. See Matsuzawa, *Nihon shakaishugi no shisō*, pp. 308–10.
22. Rōyama, "Sengo shinkenpō," p. 175.
23. Ibid., p. 174.
24. An interesting discussion of the Esher Report as an example of the thought of "national efficiency" in Britain appears in Searle, *The Quest for National Efficiency*, p. 216. For a concise summary of the Esher Report, see Benians et al., *The Empire-Commonwealth, 1870–1919*, pp. 567–69.
25. Rōyama, "Rikken seido," p. 17.
26. Rōyama, "Rikken seido," pp. 18, 13.
27. Cole, *Self Government in Industry*, pp. 252–69.
28. Wright, "Guild Socialism Revisited," p. 175.
29. Rōyama, "Sengo shinkenpō," p. 172. The Christian leader Kagawa Toyohiko was also attracted to the doctrine of guild socialism (Bickle, *Kagawa Toyohiko*).
30. Rōyama, "Sengo shinkenpō," p. 171.
31. Ibid., p. 172.
32. Carpenter, *G. D. H. Cole*, pp. 69–70.
33. Maruyama, *Intellectual History of Tokugawa Japan*, p. xxiii.
34. Ibid., p. xxiv. For Maruyama's view of the meaning of Marxism in the history of Japanese thought, see Maruyama, *Nihon no shisō*, pp. 55–57. For an analysis of initial Japanese interpretations of Marxism, see Ikimatsu, *Taishō ki no shisō to bunka*, pp. 139–66.
35. These essays are presented in Miki, *Chosakushū*, 3:1–115. In Japan, they were published first in separate journals and then in a single volume, *Yuibutsu shikan to gendai no ishiki*, in 1928. Funayama, *Shōwa yuibutsuron shi*, pp. 111–51, contains a summary of Miki's interpretation of Marxism.
36. Quoted in Miyakawa, *Nishida, Miki, Tosaka no tetsugaku*, pp. 51–52.
37. Miyakawa, *Miki*, p. 44; Piovesana, "Miki Kiyoshi," p. 135.
38. Quoted in Miyakawa, *Miki*, pp. 46–47.
39. Miki, "Ningengaku no marukusuteki keitai," p. 2.
40. Ibid., p. 7.
41. Ibid., p. 25.
42. Ibid., p. 35.
43. Quoted in Funayama, *Shōwa yuibutsuron shi*, p. 150.
44. Miki, "Marukusushugi to yuibutsuron," p. 70.
45. Ibid., pp. 58–60.
46. Miki, "Puragumachizumu no tetsugaku," pp. 111–14.

47. Miki, "Murukusushugi to yuibutsuron," p. 70.
48. Quoted in Miyakawa, *Miki*, p. 20.
49. Miki, "Ningengaku no marukusuteki keitai," pp. 3–4, and Miki, "Haidegga no sonzairon," p. 75.
50. Charles E. Scott, "Heidegger and Consciousness," p. 97. For an explanation of Marx's materialist view of society, see Bottomore and Rubel, *Karl Marx*, introduction, pp. 35–38, 66–81.
51. Matsuzawa, "Minshū shakaishugi no hitobito," p. 252.
52. A. James Gregor makes a similar point in analyzing the attraction of socialists to fascism in Italy ("The Ideology of Fascism," pp. 264–66).
53. Taira, "Shakai shisōsha kessei no koro," p. 200, and Taira, "Shakai shisōsha no koro," p. 150. In an interview with the author on May 31, 1974, Ryū's classmate at Hitotsubashi Nakayama Ichirō suggested that Ryū had a loose association with the Social Thought Association. Matsumoto Shigeharu, a member of the association, indicated to the author during an interview on January 18, 1973, that Ryū was not a formal member.
54. Ryū's graduation thesis was published as an article: Ryū, "Supengura no keizai kan."
55. For a chronology of the life of Miura Shinshichi, see Masubuchi, "Miura Shinshichi sensei nenpu," pp. 483–92. Ryū describes his relationship with his mentor in Ryū, "Miura Shinshichi hakase," pp. 410–13; Ryū's professor in graduate school suggests that there was a strained relationship between Ryū and Miura in Takagaki, "Ryū kun," p. 77.

For Spengler's views, see Spengler, *The Decline of the West*, vol. 1, and Spengler, "Prussianism and Socialism." For estimates of Spengler's importance, see Hale, *Challenge to Defeat*, and Hughes, *Oswald Spengler*.
56. Ryū, "Supengura no keizai kan," p. 186.
57. Spengler, *Decline of the West*, 2:504.
58. Ryū, "Supengura no keizai kan," pp. 166–67.
59. Ibid., p. 185.
60. Ibid., p. 187.
61. Spengler, "Prussianism and Socialism," pp. 92–94.
62. Ryū even asserted that Spengler's thought and socialist theory each had a debt to Hegelian philosophy (*Shupengurā no rekishishugiteki tachiba*, pp. 3–4).
63. Ibid., p. 170.
64. Ibid., p. 171.
65. Ibid., p. 172.
66. Ibid.
67. Ibid., pp. 171–72. For an explication of these Marxist principles, see Mandel, *Marxist Economic Theory*, pp. 13–20, 41–45.
68. Kushida, "Yuibutsu shikan no chii," pp. 6–18. For an assessment of Kushida's importance, see Ōuchi, "Kushida Tamizō," pp. 150–67. Ryū claimed his relationship to Kushida was close in Ryū and Aochi, "Taiwa ni yoru kaisetsu," p. 406.
69. Ryū, "Shiteki yuibutsuron," p. 123.
70. Ibid., pp. 125–26.
71. McClellan, *Marx before Marxism*, p. 271. For an example of George Lukacs's interpretation of Marxism with a stress on its affinity with the dialectic of Hegel, see

Lukacs, *Marxism and Human Revolution*, pp. 20–48.

72. See Ryū, *Zenshū*, 8:214–17.

73. For one evaluation of the British Labour party by an active member of the Social Thought Association, see Sassa, "Eikoku kindai shakaishugi undō," pp. 143–47.

74. Rōyama, "Kaku kuni rōdō kaikyū to futsu senkyo," p. 16.

75. Ibid., p. 18.

76. Ibid.

77. Ibid., p. 9.

78. Ibid., p. 16.

79. Ibid., p. 17.

80. Rōyama, "Toshi keikaku to rōdōsha kaikyū," pp. 27–28.

81. For a brief summary of the movement to establish a Japanese proletarian party, see Yanaga, *Japan since Perry*, pp. 474–82, and Ōuchi, *Fuashizumu e no michi*, pp. 120–27.

82. Totten, *The Social Democratic Movement*, p. 147. See also Ōshima, *Takano Iwasaburō*. A concise history of the Ohara Institute is presented by Ohara shakai mondai kenkyūjo, *Ohara shakai mondai kenkyūjo sanjū nen shi*.

83. Ryū and Aochi, "Taiwa ni yoru kaisetsu," p. 403.

84. This was Ryū, *Beikoku kanzei chōsa*.

85. For a description of the links between the Social Thought Association and the Ōsaka Labor School, see Ōsaka rōdō gakkō jū nen shi hensan iinkai, *Ōsaka rōdō gakkō*, pp. 32–33; Ōshima, *Takano Iwasaburō*, pp. 281–84; Taira, "Shakai shisōsha kessei no koro," p. 202. Nakamura, *Saikin no shakai undō*, pp. 958–60, gives a summary of the development of the workers' education movement in Japan.

86. Ōsaka rōdō gakkō jū nen shi hensan iinkai, *Ōsaka rōdō gakkō*, pp. 19–76, describes the curriculum of the school.

87. Miyakawa, *Miki*, pp. 72–73, summarizes these arguments, made by Kuno Osamu and others.

88. Yamada, "Miki Kiyoshi," p. 308.

Chapter 3

1. For example, see Kano, *Taishō demokurashii no teiryū*, pp. 257–60.

2. Rōyama, *Seijigaku no ninmu to taishō*, pp. 507–9, 524–27.

3. Rōyama, *Japan's Position in Manchuria*, pp. 100–103.

4. For the response of the press to the Manchurian Incident, see Eguchi, "Manshū jihen to taishimbun," pp. 98–113. See also Eguchi, "Shinryaku sensō," pp. 231–52.

5. *Manshū mondai kaiketsu an*. The other members were Matsukata Gisaburō, Yamanaka Tokutarō, and Uramatsu Sabitarō.

6. Ibid., pp. 51–55.

7. Matsumoto, *Shanhai jidai*, vol. 1, p. 36, and Mitani, *Taishō demokurashii*, p. 242.

8. *Manshū mondai kaiketsu an*, p. 53.

9. Ibid., pp. 53–54.

10. Ibid., p. 79.

11. Ibid., pp. 85–89.

12. Ibid., pp. 67–68, 82.
13. Ibid., p. 97.
14. Mitani, *Taishō demokurashii*, pp. 234–35.
15. *Manshū mondai kaiketsu an*, pp. 79–81.
16. Ibid., appendix, pp. 4, 10–11.
17. Rōyama, *Nihon seiji dōkō*, p. 59.
18. Mitani, *Taishō demokurashii*, p. 242.
19. Rōyama and Masui, "Sekai kyōkō to burokku keizai," pp. 91–92.
20. Wilson, *Revolutionary Nationalist*, pp. 70–72.
21. Havens, *Farm and Nation*, pp. 163–274.
22. Rekishigaku kenkyūkai, *Nitchū sensō 1, 1932–1937*, pp. 83–84. For a description of the anticapitalist ideology of the young officers who participated in the Manchurian Incident, see Ogata, *Defiance in Manchuria*, pp. 23–33, 120–28.
23. Crowley, *Japan's Quest for Autonomy*, chap. 1.
24. Berger, *Parties out of Power*, pp. 12–18, and Allinson, *Japanese Urbanism*, pp. 78–80.
25. Rōyama, *Kōmin seiji*, p. 18.
26. Ibid., p. 19.
27. Ibid., p. 28. For the results of the general elections of 1928 and 1930, see George Totten, *The Social Democratic Movement*, p. 293.
28. Rōyama, *Kōmin seiji*, p. 28.
29. Ibid., p. 163.
30. Ibid., pp. 163–65. Following the 1932 Theses of the Comintern, the Japan Communist party called for a revolution against the entire political order, which was defined as the "emperor system" (Beckmann and Okubo, *The Japan Communist Party*, pp. 332–51).
31. Rōyama, *Kōmin seiji*, pp. 174–77.
32. The following analysis of Ryū's attitudes relies on the unsigned forewards [*Shogen*] to the *Nihon rōdō nenkan*, which Ryū edited from 1928 to 1935. His former colleagues at the Ohara Institute have confirmed that Ryū composed the foreword to each volume during this period. See Ōuchi, "Ohara shaken nyūjo no koro," p. 308, and Kimura, "Wasurenokori no ki," p. 4. See "Shogen—shōwa sannendo taikan" [Foreword—An overview of 1928], *Nihon rōdō nenkan, 1929*, p. 3.
33. "Shogen—shōwa gonendo taikan" [Foreword—An overview of 1930], *Nihon rōdō nenkan, 1931*, p. 4.
34. Rōyama, *Kōmin seiji*, pp. 184–94.
35. Ibid., pp. 175–78.
36. Ibid., p. 178.
37. Ibid., p. 165.
38. Ibid., p. 182.
39. Ibid., p. 183.
40. Ibid., pp. 9–11, 13.
41. Ibid., p. 9.
42. Ibid., pp. 30–33.
43. Rōyama, "Nōchi no shoyū to kōsaku jōtai," 74–80.
44. Roberts, *The Syndicalist Tradition and Italian Fascism*, p. 253.
45. For a discussion of the rise of "opinion magazines" during the interwar period,

see Kurihara, Katō, and Yamada, "Jānarizumu no shisōteki yakuwari," pp. 168-73.

46. Patrick, "Economic Muddle," pp. 247-49, gives a succinct description of the 1927 banking crisis.

47. Ryū, "Ginkō kyōkō no haigo," pp. 23-34.

48. Ibid., p. 32.

49. Ibid., p. 34.

50. Patrick, "Economic Muddle," p. 248.

51. In 1928 the exchange rate of the yen had fluctuated ninety times. See Chō, *Shōwa kyōkō*, p. 39.

52. Quoted in ibid., p. 40.

53. Yamamuro Sōbun, "Call for a Peaceful Japan," pp. 757-58.

54. For a good summary of the effects of the economic depression in Japan during 1930, see Chō, *Shōwa kyōkō*, pp. 111-42. In English, see Chō, "From the Shōwa Economic Crisis," pp. 568-96.

55. Chō, *Shōwa kyōkō*, pp. 113-16.

56. Ibid., pp. 134-39.

57. Patrick, "Economic Muddle," pp. 216-20.

58. Chō, *Shōwa kyōkō*, pp. 114-26. The semiofficial Kyōchōkai reported government estimates of unemployment at 5.25 percent of the labor force; labor unions suspected the real figure was much higher, perhaps as much as quadruple the government's figure. See *Shakai seisaku jihō*, monthly journal of Kyōchōkai, no. 118, English supplement, July 1930, pp. 1-2.

59. Chō, *Shōwa kyōkō*, p. 130.

60. Ryū, "Kin yushutsu saikinshi," pp. 83-94.

61. Eugen Varga's concept of the "third stage" is explained in Chō, *Shōwa kyōkō*, pp. 83-86.

62. Ryū, "Kin yushutsu saikinshi," p. 83.

63. Ibid., pp. 84-87.

64. Ibid., pp. 88-90.

65. Ibid., p. 90.

66. For Ryū's views on the importance of the gold standard in the capitalist currency system, see Ryū, "Kahei ni okeru burujoa ideorogii," pp. 441-63.

67. Ibid., p. 458.

68. Ibid., p. 459.

69. Ibid., p. 462.

70. Tiedemann, "Big Business and Politics," pp. 287-93.

71. Chō, "From the Shōwa Economic Crisis," p. 570, and Schumpeter, "Industrial Development," p. 798.

72. See Rekishigaku kenkyūkai, *Nitchū sensō 1, 1932-1937*, pp. 69-72. Nakamura, *Nihon keizai seichō*, pp. 214-16, stresses the effects of government subsidies on shipbuilding and of the development of an independent Japanese automobile industry on the growth of metal-manufacturing industries.

73. Ryū, "Infureshonka no shihon to rōdō," p. 415.

74. Ibid., p. 416.

75. Ibid., p. 421.

76. Miki, "Kiki ni okeru rironteki imi," pp. 4, 11-12, 16.

77. Piovesana, "Miki Kiyoshi," p. 152, and Miyakawa, *Miki*, p. 75.

78. Miki, "Fuan no shisō to sono chōkoku," p. 134.
79. Ibid., p. 143.
80. Ibid., pp. 147, 136–37.
81. Ibid., pp. 151–52.
82. Ibid., pp. 153–57.
83. Rōyama, "Kiki no shihai," pp. 139–45.
84. Rōyama, "Jo," *Nihon seiji dōkō*, pp. 4–5.
85. Rōyama, "Kiki no shihai," p. 141.
86. Mosse, "Towards a General Theory of Fascism," pp. 29–30. For the statements by Mussolini, see Mussolini, "Fascism: Doctrine and Institutions," pp. 92–94. In 1934, Rōyama said he had read works on fascism by Benito Mussolini and Alfredo Rocco. See Rōyama, *Gendai no shakai shisō*, pp. 63, 68–69.
87. Miyakawa, *Miki*, p. 84.
88. For a summary of Miki's book *Rekishi tetsugaku*, see ibid., pp. 79–86.
89. For example, see ibid., p. 76; Uotsu, "Aru jiyūshugi saha no chishikijin Miki Kiyoshi," pp. 366–82.
90. Miki, "Setcho hihyō ni kotau," p. 205.
91. Ibid., pp. 223–24.

Chapter 4

1. This statement challenges the argument that intellectuals like Rōyama, Ryū, and Miki committed *tenkō*, a sudden rejection of liberal or socialist beliefs due to pressure from the state. See Ryū, "Japanese Thought in Post-Meiji Times," pp. 151–71.
2. For the comments on Ryū, see Rōyama, "Shinjoteki nashionarisuto," pp. 141–42. For an analysis of the right wing, see Itō, "The Role of Right-Wing Organizations," pp. 491–93; for an explanation of the "Minobe Incident," see Miller, *Minobe Tatsukichi*, chap. 7.
3. For a description of the Imperial Reservist Association, see Smethurst, *A Social Basis*; for a study of the government's thought-control policies, see Mitchell, *Thought Control*, esp. chaps. 4–5.
4. Sassa, *Nihon fuashizumu*, p. 17. Sassa's interpretation of fascism represented a popular view. See Kanda, "Shōwa kyōkōki," pp. 308–16.
5. Sassa, *Nihon fuashizumu*, p. 11.
6. Ibid., p. 3.
7. Ibid., "Jo," p. 1.
8. Ibid., pp. 99–113.
9. Sassa, *Seiji no hinkon*, pp. 54–55.
10. Ibid., p. 68, and Sassa, *Nihon fuashizumu*, pp. 194–95.
11. See Rōyama, Sassa, and Akamatsu, "Fuashizumu hihan," pp. 37–66.
12. Ibid., p. 47.
13. Ibid., p. 50.
14. Ibid., pp. 50, 53–54.
15. Ibid., pp. 56–57.
16. Ibid., p. 56.
17. Ibid., p. 48.

18. Rōyama, *Gendai no shakai shisō*, pp. 46–47.
19. Rōyama, *Nihon seiji dōkō*, "Jo," p. 2.
20. Rōyama, *Gendai no shakai shisō*, pp. 5–6.
21. Ibid., pp. 20–21.
22. Ibid., p. 62.
23. Rocco, "The Political Doctrine of Fascism," pp. 389–445. This includes an explanation of recent fascist legislation establishing the Ministry of Corporations. The following description of fascist ideology is taken from Rocco's article.
24. Rōyama, *Gendai no shakai shisō*, p. 71.
25. Ibid., p. 74.
26. Ibid., pp. 149–54.
27. Ibid., pp. 165–68.
28. Ibid., p. 183.
29. Rōyama, *Nihon seiji dōkō*, p. 47.
30. Ibid., pp. 55–56.
31. Rōyama, *Gendai no shakai shisō*, p. 34.
32. Ibid., p. 71.
33. Rōyama, "Keizai kaigi no hikaku seido kenkyū," p. 95.
34. Ibid., pp. 83–89.
35. Rōyama, *Nihon seiji dōkō*, p. 358.
36. Ibid., p. 342.
37. Ibid.
38. Ibid., pp. 349–51, 359.
39. Ibid., pp. 353–54, 341–42.
40. Ibid., pp. 61–62.
41. Ibid., pp. 310–12.
42. Rocco, "The Political Doctrine of Fascism."
43. Miki, "Jiyūshugi igo," p. 68.
44. Ibid., p. 73. Miki also joined the League for Academic Freedom (Gakugei jiyū dōmei) in 1932 to protest the burning of books and the destruction of culture in Nazi Germany. See Kanda, "Shōwa kyōkōki," p. 315.
45. Miki, "Jiyūshugi igo," p. 74.
46. Ibid., pp. 73–75.
47. Miki's views on the China issue are expressed in Miki, "Nisshi shisō mondai," pp. 16–23.
48. Miki, "Seiji to bunka," pp. 20–31.
49. Eguchi, "Nitchū sensō no zenmenka," pp. 128–30.
50. Ryū, *Tsūka shinyō tōsei hihan*, pp. 60–61. Ryū listed all of the recently formed cartels on pp. 64–67.
51. Ibid., pp. 62–63.
52. For an explanation of the reproductive economic cycle, see Sweezy, *The Theory of Capitalist Development*, pp. 75–79, or Mandel, *Marxist Economic Theory*, pp. 41–44.
53. Ryū, *Tsūka shinyō tōsei hihan*, p. 54.
54. Ibid., pp. 238–39.
55. Ibid., p. 254.
56. For indices of inflation during this period, see ibid., pp. 27–28, and Schum-

peter, "Industrial Development," pp. 852-53.

57. Ryū, *Tsūka shinyō tōsei hihan*, p. 256.

58. Ibid., pp. 16-21. The aim of the Foreign Exchange Control Law was to monitor exports of capital and to prevent speculation against the yen. There were no restrictions on foreign trade transactions.

59. Ibid., p. 261.

60. Ibid., pp. 22-24.

61. Ibid., pp. 254-55.

62. Ibid., pp. 264-72.

63. For example, see "Shogen—shōwa rokunendo taikan" [Foreword—An overview of 1931], *Nihon rōdō nenkan, 1932*, pp. 7-8; "Shogen—shōwa shichinendo taikan" [Foreword—An overview of 1932], *Nihon rōdō nenkan, 1933*, pp. 6-11; "Shogen—shōwa hachinendo taikan" [Foreword—An overview of 1933], *Nihon rōdō nenkan, 1934*, pp. 6, 9-10. Ryū's interpretation of fascism was common among some factions of the social democratic movement in Japan. See Kanda, "Shōwa kyōkōki," pp. 296-300.

64. "Shogen—shōwa hachinendo taikan," pp. 11-12. "Kokka" can also be translated as "state."

65. Ryū, " 'Kokusai' no taijo," pp. 11-12.

66. "Kokubō no hongi to sono kyōka teishō" [The basic principles of national defense and proposals to strengthen it], quoted in Rekishigaku kenkyūkai, *Nitchū sensō 1, 1932-1937*, pp. 154-55.

67. Ryu, " 'Kokusai' no taijo," p. 12.

68. Ibid., p. 13.

69. Maier, *Recasting Bourgeois Europe*, defines "corporatism" in interwar Europe as a structure in which major organized economic interest groups—primarily industry, labor, and agriculture—began to bargain directly through nonparliamentary channels over the distribution of wealth. Often, as in both Weimar Germany and fascist Italy, state ministries intervened in the economies to mediate disputes.

Chapter 5

1. Details of Ryū's move to the *Asahi* are given in Anagaki, "Ningen Ryū san," p. 207; Kawano, "Rōdō nenkan o buntan shite," p. 69; and a letter from Ryū Shintarō to Matsuyama Akira, July 1935, *Zenshū*, 6:552. Ebata Kiyoshi also discussed Ryū's decision in an interview with the author on July 7, 1973 in Tokyo, Japan. Ryū discussed his reasons for leaving the Ohara Institute in Ryū and Aochi, "Taiwa ni yoru kaisetsu," pp. 414-15. Ōuchi Hyōe claims Ryū could have been a great Marxist scholar in "Ohara shaken nyūjo no koro," pp. 308-9.

2. The estimate of the *Asahi*'s readership is in Eguchi, "Manshū jihen to taishimbun," p. 104, fn. 2. According to Eguchi, the newspaper has not released its circulation figures for the 1930s. For an example of Marxist criticism of newspaper companies, see Tosaka, "Shimbun genshō no bunseki," pp. 268-72.

3. Rōyama and Masui, "Sekai kyōkō to burokku keizai," p. i.

4. Ryū, "Konoe kō no jidai," pp. 607-9.

5. Between June 1933 and June 1936, Germany's industrial production rose 56

percent; employment increased 36 percent; and wholesale prices climbed 12 percent (Knauerhase, *An Introduction to National Socialism*, p. 112).

6. Crowley, *Quest for Autonomy*, pp. 291–300. Hirota Kōki denki kankōkai, *Hirota Kōki*, pp. 205–6.
7. Aritake, *Shōwa keizai sokumen shi*, p. 348.
8. Ryū, "Hashigaki," *Junsenji tōsei keizai*, p. 276.
9. Ibid., p. 513.
10. Ibid., p. 275.
11. Ibid., pp. 286–87.
12. Ibid., pp. 452–53. Ryū's general analysis of Yūki's policies is contained in pp. 442–75.
13. Ibid., p. 450.
14. For background on the law, see Hashikawa, "Shinkanryō no seiji shisō," pp. 286–87, and Rekishigaku kenkyūkai, *Nitchū sensō 2, 1937–1945*, p. 90.
15. Ryū, *Junsenji tōsei keizai*, pp. 349–58.
16. Ibid., p. 357.
17. Ibid., pp. 290, 449.
18. Ibid., pp. 366–67.
19. Ibid., p. 361.
20. Ibid., pp. 366, 345.
21. Ibid., p. 369.
22. Ibid., p. 370.
23. Ibid., p. 371. Also, Ryū, "Denryoku mondai," p. 81.
24. Ryū, *Junsenji tōsei keizai*, p. 358.
25. Baba, "Hostilities and Parliament," pp. 596–97.
26. Ryū, *Junsenji tōsei keizai*, p. 345.
27. Ryū, "Konoe kō no jidai," pp. 607–9.
28. Ryū, *Junsenji tōsei keizai*, pp. 385–94.
29. Ibid., p. 280.
30. Ibid., p. 281.
31. Ibid., p. 450.
32. Ibid., pp. 283, 336–37.
33. Ibid., pp. 323–25.
34. This description of the Nazi economy depends on material from Nathan, *The Nazi Economic System*, pp. 71–73, 120–23, 129–30, 222–27; Ermath, *The New Germany*, pp. 124–26; and Schacht, *My First Seventy-six Years*, pp. 327–29. The consensus of postwar scholarly opinion is that the Nazi reforms did not basically affect the economic structure or induce much efficiency. See Carroll, *Design for Total War*, and Milward, *The German Economy at War*.
35. Ryū, *Junsenji tōsei keizai*, pp. 498–99.
36. Ibid., pp. 340–45.
37. Ibid., p. 277.
38. Ibid., pp. 504–5.
39. Ibid., p. 508.
40. Arthur Tiedemann, "Big Business and Politics," pp. 294–96.
41. Gordon M. Berger, *Parties out of Power*, pp. 93–95.
42. Ibid., p. 107.

43. Hashikawa, "Teikōsha no seiji shisō," pp. 400–401.
44. Rōyama, *Gikai, seitō, senkyo*, pp. 79–81, 240–45, and Rōyama, "Gikai no sasshin," pp. 37, 40–41.
45. Rōyama, "Gikai no sasshin," pp. 34 and 40–41.
46. Ibid., pp. 42–44.
47. Rōyama, *Gendai shakai shisō kōwa*, p. 293.
48. Ibid., p. 299.
49. Ibid., pp. 264–68.
50. Ibid., p. 252.
51. Ibid., pp. 60–61.
52. Ibid., pp. 281–86.
53. Ibid., pp. 159–62.
54. Ibid., pp. 172–75. See also Rōyama, "Gyōsei kikō kaikaku," pp. 56–62. For the reform proposals of the army, see Spaulding, "The Bureaucracy as a Political Force," p. 73.
55. Rōyama, *Gendai shakai shisō kōwa*, p. 198.
56. Ibid., p. 203.
57. Ibid., pp. 317–18.
58. Ibid., pp. 308–22, esp. p. 320.
59. Ibid., p. 186.
60. Monbushō, *Kokutai no hongi*, pp. 50–51, 63.
61. Ibid., pp. 137–39.
62. Ibid., pp. 155–56.
63. Miki, "Chishiki kaikyū to dentō," pp. 195–215.
64. Miyakawa, *Miki*, pp. 97–98.
65. Miki, "Nihonteki seikaku to fuashizumu," pp. 122–23.
66. Miki, "Chishiki kaikyū to dentō," pp. 203–6.
67. Miki, "Nihonteki seikaku to fuashizumu," p. 134.
68. Ibid., pp. 132–33. See also Miki, "Nihon bunka," pp. 475–77.
69. Miki, "Chishiki kaikyū to dentō," p. 208.
70. Miki, "Nihonteki seikaku to fuashizumu," p. 139.
71. Ibid., p. 138, and Miki, "Chishiki kaikyū to dentō," pp. 213–15.
72. Quoted in Arakawa, "1930 nendai," p. 10.
73. Miki, "Shakai jihyō," pp. 82–83.
74. Ibid., pp. 73–77, 84–87.
75. Miki, "Higorishugi keikō," p. 386.
76. Miki, "Shakai jihyō," pp. 76–77; Miki, "Ningen saisei," p. 86; Miki, "Nihonteki seikaku to fuashizumu," p. 142.
77. Miki, "Zentaishugi hihan," pp. 665–72, and Miki, "Jiyūshugi kannen," pp. 682–85. Miki and his mentor, Nishida Kitarō, discussed the new "totalitarianism" in Miki, "Hyūmanizumu no gendaiteki igi," pp. 492–98.
78. In contrast to this argument, several Japanese scholars have categorized these intellectuals as liberals. See Matsuzawa, "Minshū shakaishugi no hitobito," pp. 251–53, 302, and Tsurumi, "Yokusan undō no gakumon ron," pp. 182–83.

For a discussion of Japanese attitudes toward liberalism in the 1930s, see Ishida, *Nihon kindai shisō*, pp. 223–47.

For the importance of a belief in the guarantees of the basic rights of individuals to the doctrine of liberalism, see Smith, "Liberalism," p. 276; Berlin, *Four Essays on Liberty*, pp. 163–66; de Ruggiero, *European Liberalism*, pp. 363–68, 377–78.

79. Mosse, "Towards a General Theory of Fascism," pp. 6–7.

80. Miki, "Jikyoku to shisō no dōkō," pp. 64–66.

Chapter 6

1. The Shōwa Research Association has been the subject of an array of conflicting interpretations; it has been labeled a group of, variously, reactionaries, communists, apostatizers from liberalism, "social liberals," and "technocrats." Murata, "Shōwa kenkyūkai ni taisuru hyōka," pp. 59–72, summarizes many of these arguments. See also Arakawa, "1930 nendai," p. 11.

Former members have claimed that their main aim was to control the military and that they failed. See Shōwa dōjinkai, *Shōwa kenkyūkai*, pp. 21, 275, and Sakai, *Shōwa kenkyūkai*, pp. 289–300.

2. After its formation, the Shōwa Research Association maintained the Education Study Group.

3. Tsurumi, "Yokusan undō no sekkeisha," p. 72.

4. *Shōwa shi no tennō*, pp. 136–37; Shōwa dōjinkai, *Shōwa kenkyūkai*, p. 31; XYZ, "Shōwa kenkyūkai no tanbō," p. 281.

5. Shōwa dōjinkai, *Shōwa kenkyūkai*, pp. 6–7.

6. Ibid., p. 7.

7. Yatsugi, *Shōwa dōran shishi*, 1:93–103, and foreword, 1:2–3.

8. Shōwa dōjinkai, *Shōwa kenkyūkai*, p. 7.

9. See Baba, "1930 nendai ni okeru Nihon chishikijin," pp. 117–18. Also a good source for background on members of the Shōwa Research Association is Itō, " 'Kyokoku itchi' naikaku," pp. 94–106.

10. Shōwa dōjinkai, *Shōwa kenkyūkai*, pp. 33–36.

11. Tazawa Yoshiharu, *Seiji kyōiku kōza* [Lectures on political education] (1926), quoted in Itō, *Shōwa shoki seiji shi*, pp. 55–56; Tazawa, *Seinendan no shimei*, pp. 108–115.

12. Ibid., pp. 114–15.

13. Interview with Gotō Ryūnosuke by the author in Tokyo on December 12, 1973; Sakai, *Shōwa kenkyūkai*, pp. 170–71. This movement is described briefly in chapter 8.

14. Itō, *Shōwa shoki seiji shi*, pp. 48–60; Maruyama, *Nanajū nen tokoro dokoro*, pp. 200–204.

15. Itō, *Shōwa shoki seiji shi*, pp. 58–59.

16. Shōwa dōjinkai, *Shōwa kenkyūkai*, p. 200. Also interview with Gotō Ryūnosuke by the author on December 12, 1973, in Tokyo.

17. Shōwa dōjinkai, *Shōwa kenkyūkai*, p. 179. Also Taira et al., "Shōwa kenkyūkai no rekishiteki yakuwari," pp. 21–23.

18. This report, "Kyōiku seido kaikaku an" [A draft for reforming the educational system], is reprinted in Ishikawa, *Sōgō kokusaku to kyōiku kaikaku an*, pp. 702–7. The following paragraph is based on this report, which also contains a membership list of the Education Study Group.

19. For a description of the origins, structure, and militarization of the youth

schools established by the Education Ministry, see Nakajima, *Kindai nihon kyōiku seido shi*, pp. 783–815.

20. Sakai, Iwasaki, and Gotō, "Shōwa shi no katsukazan—Shōwa kenkyūkai," p. 197.
21. Sassa, *Zoku: Jinbutsu shunjū*, pp. 17–20.
22. Oka, *Konoe Fumimaro*, pp. 32–33, 35.
23. Rōyama, "Nichibei kankei sho mondai ni kansuru beikoku sho homen no iken gaiyō" [An outline of various opinions in America regarding problems in U.S.-Japanese relations], quoted in Yabe, *Konoe Fumimaro*, 1:286–87. See also, Konoe, *Konoe kō seidanroku*, pp. 63–87, for Konoe's own impressions of his trip to America.
24. Oka, *Konoe Fumimaro*, pp. 41–43.
25. Baba, "1930 nendai ni okeru Nihon chishikijin," p. 102. Sakai, *Shōwa kenkyūkai*, p. 17.
26. Sakai, Iwasaki, and Gotō, "Shōwa shi no katsukazan—Shōwa kenkyūkai," p. 198.
27. Shōwa dōjinkai, *Shōwa kenkyūkai*, pp. 9–10.
28. "Sakai memo," in ibid., pp. 85–86.
29. Ishikawa, *Sōgō kokusaku to kyōiku kaikaku an*, p. 30.
30. "Kokusaku kenkyūkai kaigō yōroku" [Digest of a meeting of the National Policy Study Group], March 15, 1935, reprinted in Kido Kōichi nikki kenkyūkai, *Kido Kōichi kankei monjo*, pp. 193–95 (hereafter cited as *KKKM*).
31. Ibid., p. 195.
32. Ibid., p. 193.
33. Ibid., p. 195.
34. Yoshida Shigeru denki kankō henshū iinkai, *Yoshida Shigeru*, p. 202.
35. Itō, " 'Kyokoku itchi' naikaku," pp. 63–66, presents a list of members of the Investigation Bureau.
36. Spaulding, "The Bureaucracy as a Political Force," p. 69. Yoshida Shigeru (1885–1955) was a civil servant in the Home Ministry and had served as the chief cabinet secretary for Okada Keisuke. He should not be confused with the Yoshida Shigeru who became premier in post-World War II Japan.
37. "Kokusaku kenkyūkai kaigō yōroku" [Digest of a meeting of the National Policy Research Group], June 18, 1935, *KKKM*, p. 198.
38. "Seiji kikō kaikaku kenkyūkai kaigō yōroku" [Digest of a meeting of the study group to reform the political structure], June 13, 1935, *KKKM*, p. 206.
39. Sassa, *Zoku: Jimbutsu shunjū*, p. 244. For an analysis of Minobe's political views, see Miller, *Minobe Tatsukichi*, pp. 187–90.
40. "Kokusaku kenkyūkai kaigō yōroku," March 15, 1935, *KKKM*, p. 194.
41. Soma, *Nihon senkyo keihatsu shi*, p. 128.
42. Senkyo shukusei undō dōrenmei, *Senkyo shukusei*, pp. 313–16.
43. "Kokusaku kenkyūkai kaigō yōroku," March 15, 1935, *KKKM*, p. 193.
44. Sassa, "Shintō keikaku," p. 310.
45. "Seiji kikō kaikaku mondai kenkyūkai kaigō yōroku" [Digest of a meeting of the study group to reform the political structure], May 9, 1935, *KKKM*, p. 201; Sassa, "Shinseitō no mondai," pp. 322–28.
46. Shōwa dōjinkai, *Shōwa kenkyūkai*, pp. 13–15.
47. Baba, "1930 nendai ni okeru Nihon chishikijin," pp. 111–17.

48. The most extensive available list of members of study groups is for 1939. The list is reprinted in Shōwa dōjinkai, *Shōwa kenkyūkai*, appendix, pp. 37–40. For the role of the executive board, see Sakai, *Shōwa kenkyūkai*, pp. 58–59.

49. Baba Shūichi analyzes the personnel of the Shōwa Research Association in "1930 nendai ni okeru nihon chishikijin," pp. 117–25. The earliest remaining list of personnel of the executive board is presented in *Shōwa kenkyūkai kankei shiryō*, item 229. These are unpublished materials collected by the Shōwa dōjinkai and kept at the University of Tokyo (hereafter cited as *SKKS*). On microfilm, these materials are divided into 248 categories, which are numbered sequentially; the item number will thus indicate the location on microfilm of the documents cited. For an evaluation of the "new bureaucrats" in prewar Japan, see Spaulding, "The Bureaucracy as a Political Force," pp. 61–80.

50. Nor did Kawai Eijirō, one of the few democratic socialists in prewar Japan recognized for not having changed his original beliefs. In the postwar era, Rōyama expressed great respect for the integrity of Kawai, a friend and colleague at the University of Tokyo. See Matsuzawa, *Nihon shakaishugi*, p. 310.

51. Yoshino Shinji would serve as commerce minister in the first Konoe cabinet of 1937–38, and Arita Hachirō would assume the post of foreign minister in the same cabinet in October 1938. Ōkochi was a member of the House of Peers, a professor at the University of Tokyo, and an expert on industrial technology; Taniguchi and Miura were well-known economists.

52. The records for this series of meetings are in two sources. The records for the sessions of November 12 and 26, December 3, 10, 17, and 23, 1936, and February 22, 1937, are in *SKKS*, items 2 and 227. Records for the meetings of November 19 and 26, December 3, 10, 17 and 23, 1936, are in *KKKM*, pp. 218–41.

53. "Shōwa kenkyūkai jōnin iinkai" [The executive committee of the Shōwa Research Association], November 12, 1936, *SKKS*, item 227, p. 2.

54. Baba, "Kanryō seiji ron," pp. 155–62.

55. "Shōwa kenkyūkai jōnin iinkai," November 12, 1936, *SKKS*, item 227, pp. 2–3.

56. "Shōwa kenkyūkai jōnin iinkai," November 26, 1936, *SKKS*, item 2, pp. 3–4, and *KKKM*, p. 221.

57. "Shōwa kenkyūkai jōnin iinkai," November 19, 1936, *KKKM*, p. 220.

58. "Shōwa kenkyūkai jōnin iinkai," December 10, 1936, *SKKS*, item 2, pp. 14–15, and *KKKM*, p. 231.

59. "Shōwa kenkyūkai jōnin iinkai," November 12, 1936, *SKKS*, item 227, p. 10.

60. "Shōwa kenkyūkai jōnin iinkai," December 10, 1936, *SKKS*, item 2, pp. 5–8, and *KKKM*, p. 229.

61. "Shōwa kenkyūkai jōnin iinkai," December 17, 1936, *SKKS*, item 2, pp. 4–5, and *KKKM*, p. 233.

62. "Shōwa kenkyūkai jōnin iinkai," December 17, 1936, *SKKS*, item 2, pp. 1–2, and *KKKM*, p. 232.

63. "Shōwa kenkyūkai jōnin iinkai," December 17, 1936, *SKKS*, item 2, pp. 10–12, and *KKKM*, p. 235.

64. "Shōwa kenkyūkai no kenkyū taikō" [The research outline for the Shōwa Research Association], June 1937, *SKKS*, item 1, p. 1.

Chapter 7

1. Sanbō honbu dainika, August 1936, "Taiso sensō shidō keikaku taikō" [An outline of plans for directing a war against the Soviet Union], reprinted in Shimada and Inaba, *Nitchū sensō, 1*, p. 686.
2. Yanaihara, "Shina mondai no shozai," pp. 4–17.
3. Crowley, *Quest for Autonomy*, pp. 338, 341.
4. Analyses of some of the activity of the Shōwa Research Association in regard to Japan's China policy are contained in Baba, "1930 nendai ni okeru nihon chishikijin," pp. 140–57, and Crowley, "Intellectuals as Visionaries," pp. 319–73.
5. Shōwa kenkyūkai jimukyoku, "Hokushi jihen no taisaku" [Policies for the incident in North China], July 15, 1937, in *SKKS* (unpublished documents collected by the Shōwa dōjinkai and kept at the University of Tokyo), item 41.
6. "Hokushi genka no zaisei, keizai, tsūka, kinyū no shomondai ni kansuru kaigō yōroku" [A digest of a meeting relating to current problems of finance, economics, currency, and credit in North China], August 28, 1937, *SKKS*, item 41, pp. 15–16.
7. Ibid., p. 14.
8. "Ippan gaikō iinkai daigokai kaigō yōroku" [A digest of the fifth meeting of the General Foreign Affairs Committee], December 1937, *SKKS*, item 37, pp. 6–7.
9. Ibid., p. 9; "Shina mondai iinkai daigokai kaigō yōroku" [A digest of the fifth meeting of the China Problems Study Committee], December 15, 1937, in *SKKS*, item 38; and "Hokushi kōsaku kenkyūkai kaigō yōroku" [A digest of a meeting of the North China Policy Study Committee], December 1937, in *SKKS*, item 41, p. 8.
10. "Shina jihen kaiketsu oyobi sengo hokushi keiei no ippanteki hōshin naranni kore ni tomanau shotaisaku (shikian)" [Policies to accompany the resolution of the China Incident and the general direction of managing North China after the war—A draft], December 1937, *SKKS*, item 41, pp. 1–5.
11. Ibid., p. 10.
12. Shōwa dōjinkai, *Shōwa kenkyūkai*, p. 15. Gotō claims that Cabinet Secretary Kazami Akira and others funneled association proposals to Konoe.
13. Shōwa kenkyūkai jimukyoku, "Shina jihen shūshū ni ippanteki hōshin naranni mokuhyō" [General goals and policies for resolving the China Incident], June 1938, *SKKS*, item 52. Crowley also summarizes this document in Crowley, "Intellectuals as Visionaries," pp. 359–60.
14. Goshō kaigi kettei, "Shina genchūō seifu kuppuku no bawai no taisaku" [Policies in the event of the surrender of the current Chinese central government], July 8, 1938, Japanese Foreign Ministry Archives, Library of Congress, S series, reel 491.
15. Goshō kaigi kettei, "Shina shinchūō seifu juritsu shidō hōsaku" [Guiding policies for creating a new Chinese central government], July 15, 1938, Japanese Foreign Ministry Archives, Library of Congress, S series, reel 491. For a description of the idea of *bunji gassaku*, see Boyle, *China and Japan at War*, pp. 119–20.
16. Peattie, *Ishiwara Kanji*, pp. 281–84.
17. Rikugunshō an, "Shina seiken naimen shidō taikō" [An outline for directing the inner workings of Chinese political power], June 2, 1938, Selected Archives of the Japanese Army, Navy, and other Government Agencies, 1868–1945, Library of Congress, reel WT 46, item 357.

18. Boyle, *China and Japan at War*, p. 160.
19. Rikugunshō an, "Shina seiken naimen shidō taikō."
20. Doihara, "Taishi kokumin kōryō no kondan," pp. 116–24.
21. Shōwa kenkyūkai, "Shōwa kenkyūkai no kenkyū taikō," June 1937, pp. 25–27, lists Miki as a participant in the committee on educational reform. Also, see Sakai, *Shōwa kenkyūkai*, pp. 150–54.
22. Miki, "The China Affair and Japanese Thought," pp. 606–9.
23. Quoted in Arakawa, *1930 nendai—shōwa shisō shi*, pp. 226–27.
24. Miki, "Chishiki kaikyū ni atae," p. 711.
25. Miki, "Sekaiteki shisō no yōbō," pp. 708–9.
26. Crowley, "Intellectuals as Visionaries," pp. 363–66. The original talk is presented in Miki, "Shina jihen no sekaishiteki igi," August 1938, *SKKS*, item 52.
27. "Shōwa 14 nendo Shōwa kenkyūkai kenkyū taikō (fu shōwa 13 nendo jigyō hōkoku)" [Research outline of the Shōwa Research Association for 1939—With a report on activities during 1938], *SKKS*, item 229, pp. 65–66. See also Shimizu, "Miki Kiyoshi to Shōwa kenkyūkai," pp. 57–65.
28. Shōwa kenkyūkai, *Shinnihon*. This item also appears in vol. 17 of Miki, *Zenshū*. It did not appear in the earlier *Chosakushū*.
29. Shōwa kenkyūkai, *Shinnihon*, pp. 26–27.
30. Ibid., pp. 27–28.
31. Ibid., pp. 11, 28, 6.
32. Ibid., pp. 12–13.
33. Ibid., p. 17.
34. Ibid., pp. 13, 19.
35. Ibid., pp. 7–10. Arakawa Ikuo notes that the term *cooperative body* (*kyōdōtai*) first appeared in articles by Sugiwara Masaoto in the magazine *Kaibō jidai* during 1937 (*1930 nendai—Shōwa shisō shi*, p. 232).
36. Shōwa kenkyūkai, *Kyōdōshugi no keizai rinri* (1940), reprinted in Sakai, *Shōwa kenkyūkai*, p. 355. Miki Kiyoshi and Ryū Shintarō composed this work. Mosse, "Towards a General Theory of Fascism," pp. 29–30, discusses the theme of individual fulfillment through the collectivity in fascism.
37. Shōwa kenkyūkai, *Shinnihon no shisō genri, zokuhen—kyōdōshugi no tetsugakuteki kiso* (1939), reprinted in Miki, *Zenshū* 17:577.
38. Mosse, "Towards a General Theory of Fascism," pp. 4–7, and Sternhell, "Fascist Ideology," pp. 339–41.
39. Some scholars argue that Miki's intent was to question army policies in China. See Ishizeki, "Chishikijin no kokka ishiki," pp. 11–15. Others believe Miki supported the army's goals because he wanted to influence national policy. See Takeyama, *Shōwa seishin shi*, pp. 81, 124–26. One of Miki's colleagues in the Culture Study Group has claimed that Miki became convinced of his nation's moral mission to create a new Asian order. See Shimizu, "Miki Kiyoshi to Shōwa kenkyūkai."
40. Yabe Teiji nikki kankōkai, *Yabe Teiji nikki*, pp. 163–64 (hereafter cited as *Yabe Teiji nikki*).
41. Miki, "Seiji no hinkon," p. 180.
42. Miki, *Kōsōryoku no ronri*, especially the preface, pp. 6–7.
43. "Shōwa 14 nendo shōwa kenkyūkai kenkyū taikō (fu shōwa 13 nendo jigyō hōkoku)," p. 62.

A membership roster for this special research group does not exist, as far as I know. Its members came from the China Problems Research Committee and the Political Trends Committee.

The China Problems Research Group included Kazami Akira, Ozaki Hotsumi, Shōbara Susumu, Ozawa Shōgen, Yamakami Masayoshi, Tanaka Kanae, Horie Eiichi, Gotō Teiji, Higuchi Hiroshi, Nakamura Tsunezō, Tanigawa Kōhei, Okazaki Saburō, Murakami Atsushi, Wada Kōsaku, Iguchi Tōsuke, Kuramochi Hiroshi, Suzuki Tokuichi, Sakai Saburō, Ōyama Iwao, Taira Teizō, Gotō Ryūnosuke, Sassa Hiroo, Ōnishi Sai, Takagaki Enjirō, Kobayashi Ikujirō, and Tsuchiya Keisayū.

The politics section (*seiji bukai*) for 1938 consisted of Rōyama Masamichi, Sassa Hiroo, Gotō Ryūnosuke, Hirai Yōzō, Matsui Haruo, Horie Eiichi, Ōyama Iwao, Karazawa Toshiki, Taira Teizō, Sakai Saburō, Suzuki Tokuichi, and Takagi Hajime.

Members of the politics section are listed in "Shōwa kenkyūkai setsuritsu shui naranni honnendo kenkyū taikō" [Research outline for this year and the reasons for founding the Shōwa Research Association], *SKKS*, item 7, pp. 10–11, and participants in the China Problems Group on pp. 37–39. "Shina mondai iinkai naran kenkyūkai" [The study groups and committees on China problems], *SKKS*, item 5, and "Shina mondai kenkyūkai kankei mono" [People related to the China Problems Research Group], *SKKS*, item 39, also list participants in this latter group.

44. Shina jihen taisaku iinkai, "Shina jihen taisaku sōan, kankō senshūryo zengo ni okeru" [A draft for policies toward the China Incident, at the seizure of Hankow], *SKKS*, item 56, pp. 2–3.

45. Ibid., pp. 6–7.

46. Ibid., p. 10.

47. A translation of Konoe's radio speech of November 3, 1938, is presented in United States Department of State, *Foreign Relations of the United States—Japan, 1931–1941*, pp. 478–81. For the Japanese text, see Yabe, *Konoe Fumimaro*, 1:165–68.

48. Bunker, *The Peace Conspiracy*, p. 94.

49. XYZ, "Shōwa kenkyūkai no tanbō," pp. 280–81.

50. Shōwa dōjinkai, *Shōwa kenkyūkai*, p. 75.

51. Bank of Japan, *Economic Statistics of Japan, 1937*, p. 76.

52. Kinney, "Japanese Investment," pp. 148–49. See also Chō, "Importing American Capital into Manchuria," pp. 377–410.

53. Chō, "From the Shōwa Economic Crisis," p. 587.

54. Schumpeter, "Industrial Development," p. 853, and Hayashi, *Taiheiyō sensō*, p. 93.

55. Nakamura, *Nihon keizai seichō*, p. 235; Peattie, *Ishiwara Kanji*, pp. 207–16; Berger, *Parties out of Power*, pp. 111–12.

56. Nakamura, *Nihon keizai seichō*, pp. 237–39. See also Yatsugi, *Shōwa dōran shishi*, 1:228–29.

57. Miyazaki, *Tōa renmei ron*, p. 92.

58. Ibid., pp. 96–97, 170.

59. Ibid., pp. 103–6.

60. Ibid., p. 200.

61. "Jūyō sangyō gokanen keikaku yōkō jisshi ni kansuru seisaku taikō (an)" [An outline of plans for implementing the principles of the five-year plan for important

industries—A draft] (Rikugun shikian, June 10, 1937), reprinted in Shimada and Inaba, *Nitchū sensō, 1*, pp. 733–44.

62. Berger, *Parties out of Power*, p. 157.
63. Nakamura, *Nihon keizai seichō*, pp. 245–53, 262.
64. Shōwa dōjinkai, *Shōwa kenkyūkai*, p. 68.
65. Takahashi, "Nihon keizai 1930 nendai," pp. 178, 182.
66. Shōwa kenkyūkai jimukyoku, "Minkan keizai chūsū kikan shikian," December 1937, *SKKS*, item 132. This report was also reprinted by the administrative bureau of the Shōwa Research Association for public distribution in 1939. The creation of this draft as a project of the economic section of the Shōwa Research Association under the supervision of Takahashi Kamekichi is projected in "Shōwa kenkyūkai no kenkyū taikō," June 1937, *SKKS*, item 1, pp. 19–20.
67. Shōwa kenkyūkai jimukyoku, "Minkan keizai chūsū kikan shikian," reprint, p. 4, and appendix, pp. 1–10.
68. Ibid., p. 2.
69. Ibid., appendix, pp. 16–28. The proposals are outlined on pp. 7–21 in the text.
70. Ibid., p. 22.
71. For a comprehensive overview of the economic research conducted by the Shōwa Research Association, see Fujimura, "Shōwa kenkyūkai no keizai seisaku," (1) pp. 14–19; (2) pp. 15–31; (3) pp. 12–18; (4) pp. 22–31.
72. Shōwa kenkyūkai, "Shōwa kenkyūkai setsuritsu shui naranni honnendo kenkyū taikō," March 1938, *SKKS*, item 7, pp. 15–17.
73. Rekishigaku kenkyūkai, *Nitchū sensō 2, 1937–1945*, pp. 131–32, 167–69.
74. For statistics, see ibid., p. 127; Schumpeter, "Industrial Development," p. 853; Fujimura, "Shōwa kenkyūkai no keizai seisaku," (2) p. 23; (3) p. 15.
75. Shōwa kenkyūkai jimukyoku, "Nihon keizai no saihensei ni tsuite—R shi kenkyū hōkoku ni yoru" [About the reorganization of the Japanese economy—Based on a research report by Mr. R], *Nōgyō mondai kenkyūkai shiryō*, December 22, 1938, p. 10. In December, Ryū published "Nihon keizai no saihensei," pp. 4–18. The report and the article present the same basic arguments for economic reform.
76. Shōwa kenkyūkai jimukyoku, "Nihon keizai no saihensei ni tsuite—R shi kenkyū hōkoku ni yoru," pp. 8–9, 11–17, 21.
77. Ryū, "Nihon keizai no saihensei," p. 18.
78. *Yabe Teiji nikki*, p. 218. See also Shōwa dōjinkai, *Shōwa kenkyūkai*, p. 17. The "Sakai memo" in ibid., p. 102 dates the appointment of *kanjiyaku* in September 1939.
79. Shōwa kenkyūkai, *Burokku keizai*, pp. 288–89.
80. Ibid., p. 239; Takahashi, "Nihon keizai 1930 nendai," p. 179; Shōwa kenkyūkai jimukyoku, "Tōa burokku keizai kenkyū oboegaki" [Research notes on an East Asian bloc economy], December 1938, *SKKS*, item 147, pp. 9–11.
81. Ibid., pp. 13–15.
82. Shōwa kenkyūkai, *Burokku keizai*, pp. 311–21.
83. Ryū, "Ajia ni okeru," p. 4.
84. Ibid., p. 17.
85. "Shōwa 14 nendo Shōwa kenkyūkai kenkyū taikō (fu shōwa 13 nendo jigyō hōkoku)," p. 22.
86. See Kimura, "Financial Control," pp. 102–8.
87. A concise summary of the activity of this clique of civil servants is Miyaji,

"Kikakuin jiken," pp. 372–418. The Harmonization Society was a governmental body that mediated labor disputes.

88. Ibid., p. 385. See also Naimushō keihōkyoku hōanka, *Tokkō geppō*, February 1942, pp. 24–25 (hereafter referred to as *Tokkō geppō*).

89. For a list of the members of Ryū's economics committee in 1939, see Shōwa dōjinkai, *Shōwa kenkyūkai*, appendix, pp. 38–39.

90. Interview with Wada Kōsaku by the author on November 5, 1973, in Tokyo. Masaki Chifuyu states that Ryū's theories had a great influence on the bureaucrats from the Cabinet Planning Board. Interview with Masaki Chifuyu by the author on July 19, 1974, in Kamakura, Japan. See also *Shōwa shi no tennō*, 18:150–54.

91. Ryū, "Bukka mondai no shinten to konponteki taisaku no kyūmu—kokumin no kakugo ni tsuite" [The development of the price problem and the urgency of basic policies—About national awareness], *Kokkenkai hō*, April 10, 1939, *SKKS*, item 209, pp. 1–6.

92. Ibid., pp. 5–6.

93. Shōwa kenkyūkai jimukyoku, "Keizai saihensei no kihon hōkō—Saimoku kenkyū no puran sakusei no tame no sankō iken" [The basic direction of economic reorganization—A reference opinion for making plans for detailed research], September 27, 1939, *SKKS*, item 181, pp. 4–12.

94. Ibid., pp. 12–19.

95. Ibid., p. 26.

96. Ibid., pp. 30–31.

97. Ibid., p. 3; Shōwa dōjinkai, *Shōwa kenkyūkai*, pp. 125–26; Wada, *Watakushi no shōwa shi*, pp. 40–41.

98. "Kakushin ha no hitobito," *Yomiuri shimbun*, July 25, 1940. I am indebted to Ebata Kiyoshi for bringing this article to my attention.

99. Shimizu, "Miki Kiyoshi to Shōwa kenkyūkai," p. 59, and Ryū, "Zunō to jōnetsu," pp. 504–6.

100. Ryū, *Nihon keizai no saihensei*, p. 153.

101. Ibid., pp. 174–77.

102. Ibid., pp. 158–65.

103. Ibid., pp. 148–49, 166.

104. Ibid., pp. 165–72.

105. Ibid., pp. 74–76.

106. Ibid., pp. 128–29, 146–47.

107. Yamamoto, *Keikaku keizai hihan*, pp. 169–70.

108. Ryū, *Nihon keizai no saihensei*, appendix, pp. 198, 218–19.

109. Ibid., pp. 236–43.

110. Ishihama, "Book Review," pp. 1057–59.

111. Toda, "Keizai rinri," p. 291.

112. Shōwa kenkyūkai jimukyoku, *Nihon keizai saihensei shikian*. Professors Nakamura Takafusa and Hara Akira have estimated that the first copy of this draft was composed in August 1939. See Nakamura and Hara, "Keizai shintaisei," pp. 105–6, fn. 3.

There is some dispute about the precise authorship of this plan. Kawai Tetsu, a member of the administrative bureau from 1939 to 1940, said that Ryū wrote it. See "Kenkyū shiryō" [Research materials], *Tokkō geppō*, February 1942, p. 116. Arakawa Ikuo, too, is convinced that Ryū was responsible for the draft (Arakawa, *1930 nendai-Shōwa shisō shi*, p. 230). Ōyama Iwao, also a former member of the administrative bureau, has asserted, on the other hand, that Professor Arisawa Hiromi was the author (Taira Teizō et al., "Shōwa kenkyūkai no rekishiteki yakuwari," third article, p. 25). Nakamura and Hara, on page 84 of their article cited above, suggest that Ryū or a member of his committee penned the draft. Professor Nakamura has also speculated that Ōyama's influence can be detected in the document (Nakamura, "Ryū Shintarō to tōsei keizai," p. 72).

In this later article, Nakamura de-emphasizes Ryū's influence on the draft because Nakamura argues that the phrase "separation of management and capital" (*keiei to shihon no bunri*) appears in the draft but not in Ryū's *Reorganization of the Japanese Economy*. Ryū, however, did state that the "function of industrialists and the position of capitalists are separating [*kigyōka to iu shokunō to shihonka to iu chii to ga bunri shite kuru*]" (*Nihon keizai no saihensei*, p. 153). Thus, it is probable that Ryū did guide the final composition of the draft.

Most recently, Sakai Saburō has written that Professor Arisawa composed the first draft of this plan, which Ryū later used as a basis for discussions of his study group (*Shōwa kenkyūkai*, pp. 130–31).

113. Ryū, *Nihon keizai no saihensei*, appendix, pp. 240–43.

114. Some scholars believe that the theory of the *kyōdōtai* evolved naturally into the ideal of the Greater East Asian Coprosperity Sphere. See Kishi Kōichi, "Taiheiyō sensō e no michi," pp. 27–34. Others argue that the *kyōdōtai* theory made concessions to Chinese nationalism and that the army twisted the theory to fit the army's own needs. See Hashikawa, "Tōa shinchitsujo no shinwa," pp. 364–66, and Hashikawa, "Japanese Perspectives on Asia," pp. 349–50.

115. Miki and Chou, "Minzokushugi no mondai," pp. 82–85. Chou Fo-hai collaborated with the Japanese to establish a Chinese government separate from the Nationalist government. See Marsh, "Chou Fo-hai."

116. Hashikawa, "Shinchitsujo no shinwa," p. 357.

117. For an analysis of the writings of Tachibana and Gondō, see Havens, *Farm and Nation*, chaps. 7–11.

Chapter 8

1. Berger, *Parties out of Power*, p. 167; "Jūyō sangyō gokanen keikaku yōkō jisshi ni kansuru seisaku taikō," p. 744; Miyazaki, *Tōa renmei ron*, pp. 78–79.

2. For example, see Sakai, *Shōwa kenkyūkai*, pp. 123–26; and "Naikaku seido kaikaku yōkō" [An outline of reforms of the cabinet system], August 1938, *SKKS* (unpublished documents collected by the Shōwa dōjinkai and kept at the University of Tokyo), item 43.

3. Seiji dōkō no iinkai, "Nihon no seiji taisei saihensei e no ippanteki genin" [The general causes for the reorganization of Japan's political system], May 23, 1938, *SKKS*, item 69, p. 3.

4. Shōwa dōjinkai, *Shōwa kenkyūkai*, pp. 94–95.

5. Sassa, "Kokumin soshiki," pp. 30–40.

Rōyama and Sassa were both members of the East Asian Politics Committee and the

Political Trends Committee. Miki Kiyoshi and Ryū Shintarō participated in the latter group, whose roster also included Itō Nobushi, Ichikawa Seibin, Inaba Hidezō, Katsumata Seiichi, Kirihara Shigemi, Gotō Fumio, Gotō Ryūnosuke, Taira Teizō, Teruoka Gitō, Hashimoto Seinosuke, Hayashi Hirokichi, Hirai Yōzō, Furuno Inosuke, Yamazaki Seijun, Miwa Jusō, and Yoshida Shigeru. See Shōwa dōjinkai, *Shōwa kenkyūkai*, appendix, pp. 37–38.

6. For information on the Shōwa dōjinkai, see Baba, "1930 nendai ni okeru nihon chishikijin," pp. 131–34. A membership list is included in "Shōwa dōjinkai kiyaku to meibo" [The roster and regulations of the Shōwa Brotherhood], *SKKS*, item 18.

7. For recollections about the Shōwa juku, see Taira, "Shōwa juku kaisō," p. 29, and Shōwa dōjinkai, *Shōwa kenkyūkai*, pp. 117–30. Regulations for the operation of the academy are presented in "Jukusoku an" [A draft of regulations for the academy], *SKKS*, item 20; a police report on the founding of the academy appears in Naimushō keihōkyoku hōanka, *Tokkō geppō*, November 1938, pp. 54–57 (hereafter cited as *Tokkō geppō*). A recent study of the academy by a former student is Muroga, *Shōwa juku*, which contains a list of students from 1938 to 1941 on pp. 198–203. In all, 213 students attended the academy, and many of them became prominent in postwar Japan. The most famous alumnus is probably Okita Saburō, an economist who helped direct Japan's postwar economic development and has served as foreign minister of Japan.

8. For more information on the Kokumin undō kenkyūkai, see Imai and Itō, *Kokumin sōdōin*, 2, pp. xxxiv–vii; Shōwa dōjinkai, *Shōwa kenkyūkai*, pp. 107–10; Hanyū, "Kokumin undō kenkyūkai," pp. 387–90; Kinoshita, *Shintaisei jiten*, pp. 64–65; and *Tokkō geppō*, August 1939, pp. 36–38.

The main organizers were Nemoto Akira, a medical doctor, and two members of the Shōwa Research Association: Hayashi Hirokichi, a former *Asahi* correspondent, and Hanyū Shinshichi, a member of the Nagano Prefectural Assembly. Ryū Shintarō's economic section—Ryū, Wada Kōsaku, Katsumata Seiichi, and Inaba Hidezō—was also active in this organization.

9. Rōyama, "Tōa kyōdōtai no riron," pp. 3–40, especially p. 28. Within the Shōwa Research Association, Rōyama was recognized, along with Miki and Ryū, as one of the three main theorists of the cooperative body. Rōyama's main contribution was relating the concept of the *kyōdōtai* to political issues and to Japan's policy toward China (Muroga, *Shōwa juku*, pp. 21–22 and 83).

10. Rōyama, "Tōa kyōdōtai no riron," pp. 34–40.

11. Rōyama, "Kokumin kyōdōtai no keisei," p. 6.

12. Ibid., p. 24.

13. Ibid., pp. 24–25.

14. Rōyama, *Sekai no henkyoku*, pp. 307–9.

15. Rōyama, "Jimu no honshitsu," pp. 15–18.

16. Rōyama, "Kokumin kyōdōtai no keisei," pp. 25–27.

17. For example, see Baba, "Hostilities and Parliament," pp. 590–600, and Rōyama, *Gendai shakai shisō kōwa*, pp. 317–19.

18. Rōyama, "Kokumin kyōdōtai no keisei," pp. 16–17.

19. Ibid., p. 28. Ishida Takeshi notes Rōyama's increasingly mystical views on the Meiji Constitution in Ishida, *Nihon kindai shisō*, pp. 229–30.

20. Rōyama, *Sekai no henkyoku*, pp. 284–89, and Rōyama, "Kokumin kyōdōtai no keisei," p. 7.

21. Sakai, *Shōwa kenkyūkai*, pp. 193–96.
22. Rōyama, "Ōshū taisen to futatsu no teikokushugi," pp. 270–72.
23. Ibid., p. 273.
24. Shōwa kenkyūkai jimukyoku, "Seiji kikō kaishin taikō" [An outline for reform of the political structure] (Tokyo: Sakano insatsujo, June 1940), reprinted in Imai and Itō, *Kokka sōdōin*, 2, pp. 161–73. Yabe claims to have composed this report in Yabe Teiji nikki kankōkai, *Yabe Teiji nikki*, p. 339.

Participants in the political study groups of the Shōwa Research Association included officials Gotō Fumio, Yoshida Shigeru, Karazawa Toshiki, Katsumata Seiichi, Inaba Hidezō, and Aoki Kazuo; journalists Maeda Tamon and Ryū Shintarō; Youth Association leader Tazawa Yoshiharu; philosopher Miki Kiyoshi; and political scientist Yabe Teiji.

25. Shōwa kenkyūkai jimukyoku, "Seiji kikō kaishin taikō," p. 162.
26. The description of the outline in the next four paragraphs is based on ibid., pp. 163–67.
27. "Seiji dōkō no sōtei" [An estimate of political trends], *SKKS*, item 94. Also reprinted in Imai and Itō, *Kokka sōdōin*, 2, pp. 346–48.
28. Arima's diary is quoted in Kisaka, "Taisei yokusankai no seiritsu," p. 289.
29. Tannenbaum, *The Fascist Experience*, pp. 91–92. "Royal Decree of September 20, 1934, No. 2011," cited in Field, *Syndical and Corporative Institutions*, p. 139; see also pp. 137–203.
30. Imai and Itō, *Kokka sōdōin*, 2, pp. 1–li, and Shōwa dōjinkai, *Shōwa kenkyūkai*, p. 102.
31. Berger, *Parties out of Power*, p. 257.
32. Hanyū, "Kokumin undō kenkyūkai," p. 388.
33. Ibid.; Tomita, *Haisen nihon no uchigawa*, pp. 46–47.
34. *Yabe Teiji nikki*, pp. 314–15.
35. Cited in Baba, "1930 nendai ni okeru nihon chishikijin," p. 169.
36. *Yabe Teiji nikki*, p. 323, and Shōwa dōjinkai, *Shōwa kenkyūkai*, p. 277.
37. *Yabe Teiji nikki*, pp. 328–29.
38. "Seiji dōkō no sōtei."
39. Tōyama, Imai, and Fujiwara, *Shōwa shi*, p. 179.
40. Gotō Ryūnosuke has argued that Konoe was disheartened by the precipitous fall of the Yonai cabinet and the rapid breakup of the political parties within a month because these events prevented the orderly implementation of a new political movement (Shōwa dōjinkai, *Shōwa kenkyūkai*, pp. 280–81).

There is, however, little reason to believe that Konoe was surprised by the fall of the Yonai cabinet or by the dissolution of the parties. Konoe's resignation from the Privy Council signaled publicly his intention to form a cabinet soon. Major leaders of the parties had conferred with him throughout the spring, and his associates had adopted a timetable for rapid implementation of a new political order.

41. For a description of how Konoe formed his cabinet, see Yabe, *Konoe Fumimaro*, 2:121–28.
42. For an assessment of Matsuoka Yōsuke's career, see Barbara S. Teters, "Matsuoka Yōsuke," pp. 275–96.
43. For contemporary analyses of Konoe's groups of advisers, see Suzuki, "Kakushin seinensō no taitō," pp. 93–95, and Furuta, "A New Political Structure," pp. 10–

12. Arima favored the creation of both a new political party and a national organization based on occupational groups, what he called a "dual system" (Arima Yoriyasu and Miki Kiyoshi, "Shin seiji taisei taidan bassui" [Extracts from a discussion of the new political order], *Kaizō*, August [1940], jikyoku han, no. 9, collected in Zenkoku daigaku kyōjū renmei shintaisei kenkyūkai, *Shintaisei shiryō* [Materials relating to the new order], *SKKS*, item 81. Reprinted in Imai and Itō, *Kokka sōdōin*, 2, pp. 259–61).

See also Yabe, "Shintaisei no kihon kōsō" [The basic concepts of the new order], August 28, 1940, reprinted in Imai and Itō, *Kokka sōdōin*, 2, pp. 311–16, and "Sassa Hiroo shi shoken yōroku" [A digest of the opinions of Sassa Hiroo], July 30, 1940, collected in Zenkoku daigaku kyōjū renmei shintaisei kenkyūkai, *Shintaisei shiryō*, *SKKS*, item 81. This document is also reprinted in Imai and Itō, *Kokka sōdōin*, 2, p. 263.

44. Arima and Miki, "Shin seiji taisei taidan bassui"; Miki, "Kokuminsei no kaizō," pp. 412–20.

45. Rōyama, "Gaikō sasshin to kokunai shintaisei," pp. 312, 314–15.

46. Ibid., pp. 307–8, 301, 309–10.

47. Shōwa kenkyūkai, "Shintaisei kensetsu yōkō" [Principles for constructing the new order], August 1940, reprinted in Imai and Itō, *Kokka sōdōin*, 2, p. 326.

48. *Yabe Teiji nikki*, p. 340. Yabe said he was too busy and wanted to remain a shadow (*kagemusha*) for Gotō Ryūnosuke.

49. Yokusan undō shi kankōkai, *Yokusan kokumin undō shi*, pp. 101–5 (hereafter cited as *Yokusan kokumin undō shi*). Fearful that the term *party* connoted a partisan political body, the secretariat stated that the new organization would not be a national party.

50. Some scholars have argued that Konoe's aim was to organize a mass movement to control the military. See Rekishigaku kenkyūkai, *Nitchū sensō, 2, 1937–1945*, pp. 207–8; Hayashi, *Taiheiyō sensō*, p. 150; Yabe, *Konoe Fumimaro*, 2:75; Otani, *Gunbatsu*, pp. 20–21. Gordon Berger argues that Konoe wanted to expand the powers of the premier through radical reforms and also anticipated a successful conclusion to secret peace negotiations with the Chinese Nationalist government (*Parties out of Power*, pp. 253–58).

51. "Address by Prince Fumimaro Konoye [sic] at the First Session of the Preparatory Committee for the New National Structure, August 29, 1940," pp. 1366–69. For a description of how the speech was drafted, see Oka, *Konoe Fumimaro*, pp. 132–33.

52. Ryū et al., " 'Nihon keizai no saihensei' tōronkai," pp. 236–37.

53. "Kenkyū shiryō" [Materials for research], *Tokkō geppō*, February 1942, p. 125.

54. Cited in "March of Events," *Contemporary Japan* 9 (September 1940): 1086–89.

55. Ōmichi, "Keizai shintaisei no butai ura," p. 187, and Kitagawa, "Zaikai to kakushin kanryō," pp. 156–57.

56. Minobe, et al., "Zadankai: Kokubō kokka o kataru," pp. 184–85. Unfortunately, records of discussions in the council do not remain.

57. This plan, "Keizai shintaisei setsuritsu yōkō" [Outline for creating the economic new order], is reprinted in Nakamura and Hara, "Keizai shintaisei," pp. 121–26.

58. Ibid., p. 92, argues that Ryū's ideas were not authoritarian and that the Cabinet Planning Board changed his ideas to extend its bureaucratic control. For Ryū's expec-

tations for an appointment, see Muroga, *Shōwa juku*, p. 103.

59. See "Shin keizai taisei no zenshin," *Asahi shimbun*, September 10, 1940, p. 3. For the personal views of Kishi Nobusuke, see Kishi, *Nihon senji keizai*.

60. Cited in Cohen, *Japan's Economy in War and Reconstruction*, p. 29.

61. For examples of vitriolic criticism of the Shōwa Research Association's influence on the New Order Movement, see the magazine *Genri Nihon*, September and October issues, 1940. In particular, see Minoda, "Shōwa kenkyūkai no gengo majutsu," and Mitsui, "Shōwa kenkyūkai kyōgaku shisō." For a sample of the criticism of the new political order as originally proposed by the secretariat within the preparation committee, see *Yokusan kokumin undō shi*, pp. 109–10.

62. Cited in Tōyama, Imai, and Fujiwara, *Shōwa shi*, p. 183.

63. Shōwa dōjinkai, *Shōwa kenkyūkai*, pp. 121–25; Miki Kiyoshi, letter of November 9, 1940, in Miki Kiyoshi, *Zenshū* 19:412.

64. Berger, *Parties out of Power*, p. 324.

65. Interview with Gotō Ryūnosuke by author in Tokyo on December 12, 1973.

66. Tōyama, Imai, and Fujiwara, *Shōwa shi*, p. 185, and Berger, *Parties out of Power*, p. 342.

67. Berger, "Changing Historiographical Perspectives on Early Shōwa Politics," pp. 480–81.

68. For an outline of the struggle between the bureaucracy and the business world, see Nakamura and Hara, "Keizai shintaisei," pp. 92–104.

69. Hoashi, "Shin keizai taisei e no tenbō," pp. 37–38.

70. The petition of the Japan Economic League is printed in Minobe, "Keizai shintaisei kanken," pp. 12–15.

71. "March of Events," *Contemporary Japan* 10 (January 1941): 6.

72. Nakamura and Hara, "Keizai shintaisei," p. 102.

73. A copy of "Keizai shintaisei kakuritsu yōkō" [Principles for creating the economic new order] is reprinted in Nakamura and Hara, *Kokka sōdōin, 1*, pp. 169–71.

74. Minobe, "The Principles of the New Economic Structure," p. 182.

75. Ugaki, *Ugaki Kazushige nikki*, p. 1436.

76. Miyaji, "Kikakuin jiken," p. 404.

77. Shōwa dōjinkai, *Shōwa kenkyūkai*, pp. 22–23; Sakai, *Shōwa kenkyūkai*, pp. 220–21.

Chapter 9

1. For a contrasting view, see Sakai, *Shōwa kenkyūkai*, pp. 289–99. Sakai argues that the aim of the association was to harness the military and that the association was to some extent the victim of the mood and "trends" of the 1930s.

Kaji Ryūichi, a member of the Social Thought Association in the 1920s and of the *Asahi* editorial board in the 1930s, recalls warning that the "sweet dreams" of the New Order Movement would only "smooth the path to military dictatorship" (*Ogata Taketora*, pp. 178–79).

2. For general treatments of this issue, see Bourne, *War and the Intellectuals*, pp. 3–14; Hofstadter, *Anti-Intellectualism in American Life*, pp. 428–29; Coser, *Men of Ideas*, pp. 138–40; and Chomsky, *American Power and the New Mandarins*, pp. 23–28.

3. Former members of the association have stated that its proposals contained fascist ideas. See Shōwa dōjinkai, *Shōwa kenkyūkai*, p. 126, and Ōyama et al., "Shōwa kenkyūkai no rekishiteki yakuwari," pp. 4, 6.
4. Mosse, "Towards a General Theory of Fascism," pp. 6-8.
5. Ibid., pp. 29-30.
6. Ryū, *Nihon keizai no saihensei*, p. 177.
7. Sakai and Gotō, "Shōwa shi no gekiryū no naka de," p. 16.
8. Mosse, "Towards a General Theory of Fascism," pp. 26-30, and Sternhell, "Fascist Ideology," pp. 339-41.
9. Ibid., p. 350, and Roberts, *The Syndicalist Tradition and Italian Fascism*, p. 252.
10. According to Soucy, *Fascist Intellectual*, Drieu La Rochelle remained a committed fascist through the Petain regime in France; according to Roberts, *The Syndicalist Tradition and Italian Fascism*, Sergio Panunzio retained his belief in fascism until his death in 1944. Von Klemperer, *Germany's New Conservatism*, pp. 129-34, 225-26, describes the circle of intellectuals associated with the magazine *Tat*; they were at first attracted by the revolutionary potential of Nazism, but were disillusioned soon after Hitler's assumption of power. (Professor Michael S. Steinberg brought the *Tat* group to my attention.)

The attraction of fascism to intellectuals and white-collar workers is indicated in Seton-Watson "The Age of Fascism," p. 360, and Winkler, "Hitler and the Illusion of Restoration," p. 145.

11. Soucy, *Fascist Intellectual*, p. 19, raises this issue.
12. The debate over the promodern or antimodern character of fascism is outlined in chap. 1, fn. 2.
13. For a recent statement of this type of interpretation, see Yamaguchi, *Fuashizumu*, pp. 192-96.
14. Ryū, "Japanese Thought."
15. Sakai, *Shōwa kenkyūkai*, pp. 290-92.
16. In contrast, many scholars have labeled these writers as liberals. See Matsuzawa, "Minshū shakaishugi no hitobito," pp. 251-52, 302; Tsurumi, "Yokusan undō no gakumon ron," pp. 182-83; and Johnson, *An Instance of Treason*, pp. 114, 118-19.

Selected Bibliography

Unpublished Materials

Shōwa kenkyūkai kankei shiryō [Materials related to the Shōwa Research Association]. Compiled by the Shōwa Brotherhood (*Shōwa dōjinkai*) and kept at the University of Tokyo in Tokyo, Japan. Microfilm copies of these materials are available at the Sterling Memorial Library at Yale University, New Haven, Connecticut, and the Wilson Library at the University of North Carolina at Chapel Hill.

Shōwa kenkyūkai jimukyoku. "Nihon keizai no saihensei ni tsuite—R shi kenkyū hōkoku ni yoru" [About the reorganization of Japan's economy—Based on a research report by Mr. R.]. December 22, 1938. Nōgyō mondai kenkyūkai shiryō, 2. A copy was given to the author by Professor Amari Chōzō.

Japanese Foreign Ministry Archives. Library of Congress.

Selected Archives of the Japanese Army, Navy, and other Government Agencies, 1868–1945. Library of Congress.

Periodicals

Bungei shunjū, 1940–41.
Chūō kōron, 1930–41.
Contemporary Japan, 1935–41.
Contemporary Opinions, 1935–41.
Genri nihon, 1940
Kaizō, 1930–41.
Nihon hyōron, 1940–41.
Shakai seisaku jihō, monthly journal of Kyōchō kai, English supplement, 1928–35.
Shakai shisō, 1922–28.

Interviews

The following interviews were conducted by the author in Tokyo, Japan:
Matsumoto Shigeharu, January 18, 1973
Ogata Shijurō and Mrs. Ogata Sadako, January 1973
Ebata Kiyoshi, July 7, 1973
Sawamura Katsundo, August 2, 1973
Danno Nobuo, August 14, 1973, and July 9, 1974
Amari Chōzō, August 20, 1973
Mrs. Ryū Hatsue, August 23, 1973
Okada Takao, September 3, 1973
Wada Kōsaku, November 5, 1973
Doi Akira, November 11, 1973
Gotō Ryūnosuke, December 12, 1973

Sakai Saburō, December 14, 1973
Nakayama Ichirō, May 31, 1974
Inoue Ryōji, June 6, 1974
Aochi Shin, July 3, 1974
In Kamakura, Japan:
Masaki Chifuyu, July 19, 1974

I was also fortunate to participate in a group interview with Hotsumi Shichirō in Tokyo on April 20, 1974.

Published Books, Reports, and Yearbooks
Japanese Language

Arakawa Ikuo. *1930 nendai—shōwa shisō shi* [The 1930s—Shōwa thought]. Gendai nihon shisō shi [A history of modern Japanese thought], vol. 5. Tokyo: Aoki shoten, 1971 .

———. *Miki Kiyoshi*. Tokyo: Kinokuniya shoten, 1968.

——— and Ikimatsu Keizō. *Kindai nihon shisō shi* [A history of modern Japanese thought]. Tokyo: Yuikaku, 1973.

Aritake Shūji. *Shōwa keizai sokumen shi* [A history of aspects of the Shōwa economy]. Tokyo: Kawashutsu shobō, 1952.

Asahi shimbunsha shashi henshūshitsu, ed. *Asahi shimbun no kyūjū nen* [Ninety years of the Asahi newspaper]. Tokyo: Asahi shimbunsha, 1969.

Chō Yukio. *Shōwa kyōkō* [The depression of Shōwa]. Tokyo: Iwanami shoten, 1973.

Ebata Kiyoshi, ed. *Kaisō Ryū Shintarō* [Remembrances of Ryū Shintarō]. Tokyo: Asahi shimbunsha, 1969.

Funayama Shinshichi. *Shōwa yuibutsuron shi* [A history of dialectical materialism in the Shōwa period]. Tokyo: Fukumura shuppansha, 1967.

Hata Ikuhiko and Usui Katsumi, eds. *Nitchū sensō, 2* [The Sino-Japanese War, 2]. Edited by Nihon kokusai seiji gakkai. Taiheiyō sensō e no michi [The road to the Pacific war], vol. 8. Tokyo: Asahi shimbunsha, 1963.

Hayashi Shigeru. *Taiheiyō sensō* [The Pacific war]. Nihon no rekishi [The history of Japan], vol. 25. Tokyo: Chūō kōronsha, 1971.

Hirota Kōki denki kankōkai, ed. *Hirota Kōki*. Tokyo: Chūō kōron jitsugyō shuppan, 1966.

Honda Jotarō, ed. *Asahi shimbun nanajū nen shōshi* [A short history of seventy years of the Asahi newspaper]. Ōsaka: Asahi shimbunsha, 1949.

Ikimatsu Keizō. *Taishōki no shisō to bunka* [Thought and culture of the Taishō period]. Gendai nihon shisō shi [A history of modern Japanese thought], vol. 4. Tokyo: Aoki shoten, 1971.

Imai Seiichi. *Taishō demokurashii* [Taishō democracy]. Nihon no rekishi [History of Japan], vol. 23. Tokyo: Chūō kōronsha, 1967.

Imai Seiichi and Itō Takashi, eds. *Kokka sōdōin, 2* [National mobilization, 2]. Gendai shi shiryō [Materials for modern history], vol. 44. Tokyo: Misuzu shobō, 1974.

Ishida Takeshi. *Nihon kindai shisō shi ni okeru hō to seiji* [Politics and law in the history of Japan's modern thought]. Tokyo: Iwanami shoten, 1976.

Ishikawa Junkichi. *Sōgō kokusaku to kyōiku kaikaku an—Naikaku shingikai, naikaku chōsakyoku kiroku* [Comprehensive national policies and plans for educational reform—Records of the cabinet council and investigation bureau]. Tokyo: Kiyomizu shoin, 1964.
Itō Takashi. *Gojū nen sensō* [The fifteen-year war]. Tokyo: Shōgakkan, 1976.
———. *Shōwa shoki seiji shi kenkyū* [Research in the political history of the early Shōwa period]. Tokyo: Tokyo daigaku shuppankai, 1969.
Jinji kōshinroku [Personnel directory]. Tokyo: Jinji kōshinjo.
Kaji Ryūichi. *Ogata Taketora*. Tokyo: Jiji tsūshinsha, 1962.
Kano Masanao. *Taishō demokurashii no teiryū: "Dochaku" teki seishin e no kaiki* [The basic currents of Taisho democracy: A return to a "native" spirit]. Tokyo: NHK bokkusu, 1973.
Kazami Akira. *Konoe naikaku* [Konoe's cabinet]. Tokyo: Nihon shuppan kyōdō kabushiki kaisha, 1951.
Kido Kōichi nikki kenkyūkai. *Kido Kōichi kankei monjo* [Documents relating to Kido Kōichi]. Tokyo: Tokyo daigaku shuppankai, 1966.
Kinoshita Hanji. *Shintaisei jiten* [A dictionary of the new order]. Tokyo: Asahi shimbunsha, 1941.
Kishi Nobusuke. *Nihon senji keizai no susumu michi* [The road for the advance of Japan's wartime economy]. Tokyo: Kenshinsha, 1942.
Konoe Fumimaro. *Konoe kō seidanroku* [Records of the political talks of Prince Konoe]. Edited by Ito Takeshi. Tokyo: Chikura shobō, 1937.
Manshū mondai kaiketsu an [A draft for resolving the Manchurian problem]. Tokyo: 1932.
Maruyama Masao. *Gendai seiji no shisō to kōdō* [Thought and behavior in modern politics]. Rev. ed. Tokyo: Miraisha, 1973.
———. *Nihon no shisō* [Japanese thought]. Tokyo: Iwanami shoten, 1961.
Maruyama Tsurukichi. *Nanajū nen tokoro dokoro* [Here and there for seventy years]. Tokyo: Maruyama Tsurukichi tokoro dokoro kankōkai, 1955.
Matsumoto Shigeharu. *Shanhai jidai* [The Shanghai era]. Vol. 1. Tokyo: Chūō kōronsha, 1974.
Matsuzawa Hiroaki. *Nihon shakaishugi no shisō* [The thought of Japanese socialism]. Tokyo: Chikuma shobō, 1973.
Miki Kiyoshi. *Chosakushū* [Collected works]. 16 vols. Tokyo: Iwanami shoten, 1946–51.
———. *Kōsōryoku no ronri* [The logic of imagination] (1937–43). In Miki Kiyoshi, *Chosakushū* [Collected Works], vol. 8, pp. 3–497. Tokyo: Iwanami shoten, 1948.
———. *Zenshū* [Complete works]. 19 vols. Tokyo: Iwanami shoten, 1966–68.
Mitamura Takeo. *Sensō to kyōsanshugi* [Communism and the war]. Tokyo: Minshū seido fukyūkai, 1950.
Mitani Taichirō. *Taishō demokurashii ron* [About Taishō democracy]. Tokyo: Chūō kōronsha, 1974.
Miyakawa Tōru. *Miki Kiyoshi*. Tokyo: Tokyo daigaku shuppankai, 1970.
———. *Nishida, Miki, Tosaka no tetsugaku* [The Philosophy of Nishida, Miki, and Tosaka]. Tokyo: Kōdansha, 1967.
Miyazaki Masayoshi. *Tōa renmei ron* [A discussion of the East Asian League]. Tokyo: Kaizōsha, 1938.

Monbushō. *Kokutai no hongi* [The fundamental principles of the national polity]. Tokyo: Naikaku insatsukyoku, 1937.
Muroga Sadanobu. *Shōwa juku* [The Shōwa Academy]. Tokyo: Nihon keizai shimbun, 1978.
Naimushō keihōkyoku hōanka. *Tokkō geppō* [Monthly reports of the higher police], 1937-42.
Nakajima Tarō. *Kindai nihon kyōiku seido shi* [A history of the system of modern Japanese education]. Tokyo: Iwasaki shoten, 1966.
Nakamura Hideo. *Saikin no shakai undō* [Recent social movements]. Tokyo: Kyōchōkai, 1929.
Nakamura Takafusa. *Nihon keizai seichō no bunseki* [An analysis of Japanese economic growth]. Tokyo: Iwanami shoten, 1971.
―――― and Hara Akira, eds. *Kokka sōdōin, 1* [National mobilization,1]. Gendai shi shiryō [Materials for modern history], vol. 43. Tokyo: Misuzu shobō, 1970.
Nihon rōdō nenkan [Japan labor yearbook]. Tokyo: Dōjinsha, 1928-33; Kurita shoten, 1934-35.
Nihon shinshiroku [Who's who in Japan]. Tokyo: Kōjunsha, 1937-77.
Ogata Taketora denki kankōkai. *Ogata Taketora*. Tokyo: Asahi shimbunsha, 1963.
Ohara shakai mondai kenkyūjo. *Ohara shakai mondai kenkyūjo sanjū nen shi* [A history of thirty years of the Ohara Social Problems Research Institute]. Tokyo: Hōsei daigaku Ohara kenkyūjo, 1954.
Oka Yoshitake. *Konoe Fumimaro*. Tokyo: Iwanami shoten, 1972.
Ōsaka rōdō gakkō jū nen shi hensan iinkai. *Ōsaka rōdō gakkō jū nen shi* [A history of ten years of the Ōsaka Labor School]. Ōsaka: Ōsaka rōdō gakkō, 1931.
Ōshima Kiyoshi et al., eds. *Takano Iwasaburō den* [A biography of Takano Iwasaburō]. Tokyo: Iwanami shoten, 1967.
Ōtani Keijirō. *Gunbatsu* [Military cliques]. Tokyo: Tosho shuppansha, 1966.
Ōuchi Hyōe. *Keizaigaku gojū nen* [Fifty years of economics]. Tokyo: Tokyo daigaku shuppankai, 1959.
Ōuchi Tsutomu. *Fuashizumu e no michi* [The road to fascism]. Nihon no rekishi [History of Japan], vol. 24. Tokyo: Chūō kōronsha, 1967.
Rekishigaku kenkyūkai, ed. *Nitchū sensō 1, 1932-1937* [The Sino-Japanese War, 1932-1937]. Taiheiyō sensō shi [A history of the Pacific war], vol. 2. Tokyo: Aoki shoten, 1972.
――――. *Nitchū sensō 2, 1937-1945* [The Sino-Japanese War, 1937-1945]. Taiheiyō sensō shi [A history of the Pacific war], vol. 3. Tokyo: Aoki shoten, 1973.
Rōyama Masamichi. *Gendai no shakai shisō* [Modern social thought]. Tokyo: Kōyō shoin, 1934.
――――. *Gendai shakai shisō kōwa* [Lectures on modern social thought]. Tokyo: Kōyō shoin, 1937.
――――. *Gikai, seitō, senkyo* [The Diet, political parties, and elections]. Tokyo: Nihon hyōronsha, 1935.
――――. *Kōmin seiji ron* [A discussion of citizen politics]. Tokyo: Yūfūkan shobō, 1931.
――――. *Nihon seiji dōkō ron* [A discussion of political trends in Japan]. Tokyo: Kōyō shoin, 1933.
――――. *Seijigaku no ninmu to taishō* [The objects and responsibilities of political

science]. Tokyo: Genmatsudō shoten, 1925.

———. *Sekai no henkyoku to nihon no sekai seisaku* [World changes and Japan's world policies]. Tokyo: Genmatsudō shoten, 1938.

Ryū Shintarō. *Beikoku kanzei chōsa* [An investigation of tariffs on rice] (1930). In Ryū Shintarō, *Zenshū* [Complete works], vol. 8, pp. 219–365. Tokyo: Asahi shimbunsha, 1969.

———. *Junsenji tōsei keizai* [The quasi-wartime controlled economy] (1937). In Ryū Shintarō, *Zenshū* [Complete works], vol. 2, pp. 273–513. Tokyo: Asahi shimbunsha, 1969.

———. *Nihon keizai no saihensei* [The reorganization of the Japanese economy]. Tokyo: Chūō kōronsha, 1940.

———. *Shupengurā no rekishishugiteki tachiba* [The historicist position of Spengler] (1928). In Ryū Shintarō, *Zenshū* [Complete works], vol. 8, pp. 1–190. Tokyo: Asahi shimbunsha, 1969.

———. *Tsūka shinyō tōsei hihan* [A critique of the control of currency and credit] (1934). In Ryū Shintarō, *Zenshū* [Complete works], vol. 2, pp. 3–272. Tokyo: Asahi shimbunsha, 1969.

———. *Zenshū* [Complete works]. 8 vols. Tokyo: Asahi shimbunsha, 1968–69.

Ryū Shintarō Zenshū geppō [Monthly bulletins of the complete works of Ryū Shintarō]. Tokyo: Asahi shimbunsha, 1968–69.

Sakai Saburō. *Shōwa kenkyūkai—Aru chishikijin shūdan no kiseki* [The Shōwa Research Association—The course of one group of intellectuals] Tokyo: TBS Brittanica, 1979.

Sassa Hiroo. *Nihon fuashizumu no hatten katei* [The process of the development of Japanese fascism]. Tokyo: Asano shoten, 1932.

———. *Seiji no hinkon* [The poverty of politics]. Tokyo: Chikura shobō, 1931.

———. *Zoku: Jimbutsu shunjū* [Continued: A variety of personalities]. Tokyo: Kaizōsha, 1935.

Senkyo shukusei undō dōrenmei, ed. *Senkyo shukusei chūō renmei jigyō gaiyō* [An outline of activity of the Central League for Election Purification]. Tokyo: Senkyo shukusei chūō renmei, 1936.

Shimada Toshihiko and Inaba Masao, eds. *Nitchū sensō, 1* [The Sino-Japanese War, 1]. Gendai shi shiryō [Materials for modern history], vol. 8. Tokyo: Misuzu shobō, 1964.

Shinobu Seisaburō. *Taishō seiji shi* [A history of Taishō politics]. Tokyo: Keisō shobō, 1968.

Shisō no kagaku kenkyūkai, ed. *Tenkō* [Apostasy]. 3 vols., with a foreword by Tsurumi Shunsuke. Rev. ed. Tokyo: Heibonsha, 1967.

Shōwa dōjinkai, ed. *Shōwa kenkyūkai* [The Shōwa Research Association]. Tokyo: Keizai ōraisha, 1968.

Shōwa kenkyūkai, ed. *Burokku keizai ni kansuru kenkyū* [Research on the bloc economy]. Tokyo: Seikatsusha, 1939.

———. *Kyōdōshugi no keizai rinri* [The Economic Ethics of Cooperativism] (1940). Reprinted in Sakai Saburō, *Shōwa kenkyūkai—Aru chishikijin shūdan no kiseki* [The Shōwa Research Association—The course of one group of intellectuals], pp. 342–56. Tokyo: TBS Brittanica, 1979.

———. *Minkan keizai chūsū kikan shikian* [A draft for a civilian economic central body]. Tokyo: Shōwa kenkyūkai, reprint, 1939.

──────. *Nihon keizai saihensei shikian* [A draft for the reorganization of the Japanese economy]. Tokyo: Sakano insatsujo, 1940.

──────. *Shinnihon no shisō genri* [Principles of thought for a new Japan]. Tokyo: 1939.

──────. *Shinnihon no shisō genri, zokuhen—Kyōdōshugi no tetsugakuteki kiso* [Principles of thought for a new Japan—The philosophical basis of cooperativism]. In Miki Kiyoshi, *Zenshū* [Collected works], vol. 17, pp. 534–88. Tokyo: Iwanami shoten, 1968.

Shōwa shi no tennō [The Emperor of Shōwa History]. Vol. 18. Tokyo: Yomiuri shimbunsha, 1974.

Soma Masao. *Nihon senkyo keihatsu shi* [A history of the initial development of Japanese elections]. Tokyo: 1972.

Takeyama Michio. *Shōwa seishin shi* [A spiritual history of Shōwa]. Tokyo: Shinchōsha, 1956.

Tazawa Yoshiharu. *Seinendan no shimei* [The mission of the Youth Association]. Tokyo: Seinenkan, 1930.

Tazawa Yoshiharu kinenkai. *Tazawa Yoshiharu*. Tokyo: Tazawa Yoshiharu kinenkai, 1954.

Tōhata Seiichi and Tanigawa Teizō, eds. *Kaisō Miki Kiyoshi* [Remembrances of Miki Kiyoshi]. Tokyo: Bunka shoin, 1948.

Tomita Kenji. *Haisen nihon no uchigawa—Konoe kō omoide* [Inside defeated Japan—Remembering Prince Konoe]. Tokyo: Kokon shoin, 1962.

Tōyama Shigeki, Fujiwara Akira, and Imai Seiichi. *Shōwa shi* [A History of Shōwa]. Tokyo: Iwanami shoten, 1955; rev. ed., 1972.

Tsurumi Shunsuke and Kuno Osamu. *Gendai nihon no shisō* [Modern Japanese thought]. Tokyo: Iwanami shoten, 1970.

Ugaki Kazushige. *Ugaki Kazushige nikki* [The diary of Ugaki Kazushige]. Tokyo: Misuzu shobō, 1971.

Wada Kōsaku. *Watakushi no shōwa shi* [My history of Shōwa]. Tokyo: Shinseiki shuppansha, 1964.

Yabe Teiji. *Konoe Fumimaro*. 2 vols. Tokyo: Kōbundo, 1952.

Yabe Teiji nikki kankōkai, ed. *Yabe Teiji nikki* [The diary of Yabe Teiji]. Tokyo: Yomiuri shimbunsha, 1974.

Yamaguchi Yasushi. *Fuashizumu* [Fascism]. Tokyo: Yuikaku, 1979.

Yamamoto Katsuichi. *Keikaku keizai hihan* [A critique of the planned economy]. Tokyo: Risōsha shuppanbu, 1941.

Yatsugi Kazuo. *Shōwa dōran shishi* [A private history of the tumult of the Shōwa era]. 2 vols. Tokyo: Keizai ōraisha, 1971.

Yokusan undō shi kankōkai, ed. *Yokusan kokumin undō shi* [A history of the national Imperial Rule Assistance Movement]. Tokyo: Yokusan undō shi kankōkai, 1954.

Yoshida Shigeru denki kankō henshū iinkai. *Yoshida Shigeru*. Tokyo: Meikōsha, 1959.

Articles
Japanese Language

Abe Hirozumi. "Kyūshin fuashizumu undō ron" [Radical fascist movements]. In

Eguchi Teiichi, ed., *Nihon fuashizumu keisei* [The formation of Japanese fascism], Taikei nihon gendai shi [A series in the modern history of Japan], vol. 1. Tokyo: Nihon hyōronsha, 1978, pp. 125-66.
Anagaki Hideo. "Ningen Ryū san" [The person Ryū]. In *Kaisō Ryū Shintarō* [Remembrances of Ryū Shintarō], edited by Ebata Kiyoshi, pp. 207-13. Tokyo: Asahi shimbunsha, 1969.
Arakawa Ikuo. "1930 nendai to chishikijin no mondai" [The problems of intellectuals and the 1930s]. *Shisō*, no. 624 (June 1976):2-14.
Baba Shūichi. "1930 nendai ni okeru Nihon chishikijin no dōkō" [The trends of Japanese intellectuals in the 1930s]. *Shakai kagaku kiyō* (1969): 67-207.
──────. "1930 nendai to Nihon chishikijin" [Japanese intellectuals and the 1930s]. *Shakai shisō*, no. 1 (1971): 4-47.
Baba Tsunego. "Kanryō seiji ron" [Bureaucratic politics]. *Chūō kōron* 52 (January 1937): 155-62.
Doihara Kenji. "Taishi kokumin kōryō no konkan" [The basis of a national plan for China]. *Chūō kōron* 53 (November 1938): 116-24.
Eguchi Teiichi. "Manshū jihen to taishimbun" [The large newspapers and the Manchurian Incident]. *Shisō*, January 1973, pp. 98-113.
──────. "Nitchū sensō no zenmenka" [The spread of the Sino-Japanese War]. In *Iwanami kōza: Nihon rekishi* [Iwanami lectures: Japanese history], vol. 20, pp. 127-70. Tokyo: Iwanami shoten, 1976.
──────. "Shinryaku sensō to fuashizumu no keisei" [The war of aggression and the formation of fascism]. In *Kōza Nihon shi* [Lectures on Japanese history], edited by the Rekishigaku kenkyūkai, Nihon shi kenkyūkai, vol. 7, pp. 231-52. Tokyo: Tokyo daigaku shuppankai, 1971.
Endō Shokichi. "Shokugyōteki chishikijin—Sono ishiki to yakuwari" [Professional Intellectuals—Their Consciousness and Role]. In *Kindai Nihon shisō shi kōza* [Lectures on the history of modern Japanese thought], vol. 4, pp. 283-322. Tokyo: Chikuma shobō, 1972.
Fujimura, Tōru. "Shōwa kenkyūkai no keizai seisaku" [The economic policies of the Shōwa Research Association]. (1) *Shōwa dōjin* 13 (November 1967): 14-19; (2) 13 (December 1967): 15-31; (3) 14 (January 1968): 12-18; (4) 14 (February 1968): 22-31.
Fukumoto Kazuo. "Shakai no kōsei naranni henkaku no katei—Yuibutsu shikan no hōhōronteki kenkyū" [The structure of society and the process of change—Methodological research of historical materialism]. In Fukumoto Kazuo, *Shoki chosakushū* [Collected early works], vol. 1, pp. 41-216. Tokyo: Kobushi shobō, 1971.
Furuya Tetsuo. "Nihon fuashizumu ron" [Japanese fascism]. In *Iwanami kōza: Nihon rekishi* [Iwanami lectures: Japanese history], vol. 20, pp. 79-126. Tokyo: Iwanami shoten, 1976.
Hanyū Shinshichi. "Kokumin undō kenkyūkai no koro" [At the time of the Research Association for a National Movement]. In *Kaisō Ryū Shintarō* [Remembrances of Ryū Shintarō], edited by Ebata Kiyoshi, pp. 387-400. Tokyo: Asahi Shimbunsha, 1969.
Hashikawa Bunsō. "Nihon fuashizumu no shisōteki tokushitsu" [The special quality of the thought of Japanese fascism]. In *Kōza Nihon shi* [Lectures on Japanese

history], edited by the Rekishigaku kenkyūkai, Nihon shi kenkyūkai, vol. 7, pp. 329–51. Tokyo: Tokyo daigaku shuppankai, 1971.

———. "Shinkanryō no seiji shisō" [The political thought of the new bureaucrats]. In Hashikawa Bunsō, *Kindai Nihon seiji shisō no shosō* [Aspects of political thought in modern Japan], pp. 279–304. Tokyo: Miraisha, 1968.

———. "Teikōsha no seiji shisō" [The political thought of resisters]. In *Kindai Nihon seiji shisō shi* [A history of modern Japanese political thought], edited by Hashikawa Bunsō and Matsumoto Sannosuke, vol. 2, pp. 399–411. Tokyo: Yuikaku, 1968.

———. "Tōa shinchitsujo no shinwa" [The myth of an East Asian new order]. In *Kindai Nihon seiji shisō shi* [A history of modern Japanese political thought], edited by Hashikawa Bunsō and Matsumoto Sannosuke, vol. 2, pp. 352–67. Tokyo: Yuikaku, 1968.

Hirakawa Rokurō. "Eikoku ni okeru nidai rōdōsha kyōiku kikan" [Two large agencies for labor education in England]. *Shakai shisō* 2 (February 1923): 63–73.

Hoashi Kei. "Shin keizai taisei e no tenbō" [Prospects for a new economic order]. *Chūō kōron* 55 (October 1940): 34–44.

Imai Seiichi. "Nihon fuashizumu ni tsuite no dansō" [Some thoughts on Japanese fascism]. *Rekishigaku kenkyū*, no. 399 (August 1973): 41–43.

Ishizeki Keizō. "Chishikijin no kokka ishiki" [The national consciousness of intellectuals]. In *Nihon no fuashizumu 2: Sensō to kokumin* [Japanese fascism, 2: War and the people], edited by the Waseda daigaku shakai kagaku kenkyūjo, pp. 3–44. Tokyo: Waseda daigaku shuppanbu, 1974.

———. "Dainiji taisenka ni okeru chishikijin no kokka ishiki" [The national consciousness of intellectuals during World War II]. *Shakai kagaku tōkyū*, no. 53 (March 1973): 411–48.

Itō Takashi. "'Kyokoku itchi' naikaku no seikai saihensei mondai" [The problems of political reorganization during the period of national unity cabinets]. *Shakai kagaku kenkyū* 24 (February 1974): 59–147.

———. "Shōwa seiji shi kenkyū e no ichi shikaku" [One perspective on research on the political history of shōwa]. *Shisō*, no. 624 (June 1976): 215–28.

"Kakushin ha no hitobito" [The radical reform group]. *Yomiuri shimbun* (July 25, 1940).

Kanda Fuhito. "Shōwa kyōkōki no shakai undō" [Social movements during the Shōwa Depression]. In *Shōwa kyōkō: Fuashizumuki no kokka to shakai 1* [The Shōwa Depression: The nation and society in the age of fascism 1], edited by the Tokyo daigaku shakai kagaku kenkyūjo, pp. 295–318. Tokyo: Tokyo daigaku shuppankai, 1979.

Kawano Takeshi. "Rōdō nenkan o buntan shite" [Sharing the editorship of the labor yearbook]. In *Kaisō Ryū Shintarō* [Remembrances of Ryū Shintarō], edited by Ebata Kiyoshi, pp. 67–70. Tokyo: Asahi shimbunsha, 1969.

Kaya Okinori et al. "Shōwa no katsukazan—Gekidō no shōwa jū nendai to Shōwa kenkyūkai" [The active volcano of Shōwa—The turbulent 1930s and the Shōwa Research Association]. *Keizai ōrai* 20 (May 1968): 350–70.

Kimura, Sadamu. "Wasurenokori no ki" [A record of things forgotten and remembered]. In *Ryū Shintarō zenshū geppō* [Monthly reports of the collected works of Ryū Shintarō], no. 8, pp. 3–5. Tokyo: Asahi shimbunsha, 1969.

Kisaka Junichirō. "Taisei yokusankai no seiritsu" [The creation of the IRAA]. In

Iwanami kōza: Nihon rekishi [Iwanami lectures: Japanese history], vol. 20, pp. 269–314. Tokyo: Iwanami shoten, 1976.

Kishi Kōichi. "Taiheiyō sensō e no michi to shite no nanpō seisaku kettei to Shōwa kenkyūkai" [The Shōwa Research Association and the decision on the southern policy as the road to the Pacific war]. *Tōyō kenkyū* 7 (February 1964): 27–34.

Kitagawa Kazuo. "Zaikai to kakushin kanryō" [The financial world and the reform bureaucrats]. *Kaizō* 24 (January 1941): 156–63.

Kurihara Takeo, Katō Hideo, and Yamada Minoru. "Jānarizumu no shisōteki yakuwari" [The intellectual role of journalism]. In *Kindai Nihon shisō shi kōza* [Lectures on the history of modern Japanese thought], vol. 5, pp. 141–83. Tokyo: Chikuma shobō, 1972.

Kushida Tamizō. "Marukusugaku ni okeru yuibutsu shikan no chii" [The place of historical materialism in Marxism]. *Warera* 2 (July 1920): pp. 6–18.

Masubuchi Tatsuo. "Miura Shinshichi sensei nenpu" [A chronology of the life of Professor Miura Shinshichi]. In Miura Shinshichi, *Tōsei bunmei shi* [A history of eastern and western civilizations], pp. 483–92. Tokyo: Iwanami shoten, 1950.

Matsuzawa Hiroaki. "Minshū shakaishugi no hitobito: Rōyama Masamichi hoka" [Democratic Socialists: Rōyama Masamichi and others]. In *Tenkō* [Apostasy], vol. 3, edited by the Shisō no kagaku kenkyūkai, pp. 249–307. Tokyo: Heibonsha, 1967.

Miki Kiyoshi. "Benshōhō no riron to rekishi" [The theory of the dialectic and history] (date uncertain). In Miki Kiyoshi, *Zenshū* [Complete works], vol. 19, pp. 505–20. Tokyo: Iwanami shoten, 1968.

———. "Chishiki kaikyū ni atae" [To the intellectual class] (1938). In Miki Kiyoshi, *Zenshū* [Complete works], vol. 19, pp. 710–11. Tokyo: Iwanami shoten, 1968.

———. "Chishiki kaikyū to dentō no mondai" [The intellectual class and the problem of tradition] (1937). In Miki Kiyoshi, *Chosakushū* [Collected works], vol. 12, pp. 195–215. Tokyo: Iwanami shoten, 1948.

———. "Fuan no shisō to sono chōkoku" [The thought of Anguish and overcoming It] (1933). Miki Kiyoshi, *Chosakushū* [Collected works], vol. 13, pp. 133–57. Tokyo: Iwanami shoten, 1950.

———. "Haidegga no sonzairon" [The ontology of Heidegger] (1930). In Miki Kiyoshi, *Chosakushū* [Collected works], vol. 11, pp. 70–77. Tokyo: Iwanami shoten, 1950.

———. "Higorishugi keikō ni tsuite" [About the trend toward irrationality] (1935). In Miki Kiyoshi, *Chosakushū* [Collected works], vol. 11, pp. 377–94. Tokyo: Iwanami shoten, 1950.

———. "Hyūmanizumu no gendaiteki igi—Nishida Kitarō hakase ni kiku" [The modern meaning of humanism—A discussion with Doctor Nishida Kitarō] (1936). In Miki Kiyoshi, *Zenshū* [Complete works], vol. 17, pp. 492–504. Tokyo: Iwanami shoten, 1968.

———. "Jikyoku to shisō no dōkō" [The general situation and trends in thought] (1936). In Miki Kiyoshi, *Chosakushū* [Collected works], vol. 14, pp. 62–72. Tokyo: Iwanami shoten, 1950.

———. "Jiyūshugi igo" [After liberalism] (1935). In Miki Kiyoshi, *Chosakushū* [Collected works], vol. 12, pp. 68–75. Tokyo: Iwanami shoten, 1950.

———. "Jiyūshugi kannen hitei e no kaigi" [Skepticism toward the denial of the concept of liberalism] (1936). In Miki Kiyoshi, *Zenshū* [Complete works], vol. 19, pp. 682–85. Tokyo: Iwanami shoten, 1968.

———. "Kiki ni okeru rironteki imi" [The theoretical meaning of the crisis] (1929). In Miki Kiyoshi, *Chosakushū* [Collected works], vol. 12, pp. 3–16. Tokyo: Iwanami shoten, 1950.

———. "Kokuminsei no kaizō" [The reform of national character]. *Chūō kōron* 55 (June 1940): 412–20.

———. "Marukusushugi to yuibutsuron" [Marxism and materialism] (1927). In Miki Kiyoshi, *Chosakushū* [Collected works], vol. 3, pp. 39–74. Tokyo: Iwanami shoten, 1947.

———. "Nihon bunka no tokushitsu—Nishida Kitarō hakase to no ichimon ittō" [The special characteristics of Japanese culture—A dialogue with Doctor Nishida Kitarō] (1935). In Miki Kiyoshi, *Zenshū* [Complete works], vol. 17, pp. 475–91. Tokyo: Iwanami shoten, 1968.

———. "Nihonteki seikaku to fuashizumu" [Japanese character and fascism] (1936). In Miki Kiyoshi, *Chosakushū* [Collected works], vol. 12, pp. 118–44. Tokyo: Iwanami shoten, 1950.

———. "Ningen saisei to bunka no kadai" [The regeneration of man and the topic of culture] (1935). In Miki Kiyoshi, *Chosakushū* [Collected works], vol. 12, pp. 76–90. Tokyo: Iwanami shoten, 1948.

———. "Ningengaku no marukusuteki keitai" [The Marxist form of anthropology] (1928). In Miki Kiyoshi, *Chosakushū* [Collected works], vol. 3, pp. 1–38. Tokyo: Iwanami shoten, 1947.

———. "Nishida tetsugaku no seikaku ni tsuite" [About the character of Nishida's Philosophy] (1936). In *Nishida Kitarō shū* [Collected Essays of Nishida Kitarō], edited by Takeuchi Yoshitomo, pp. 423–35. Tokyo: Chikuma shobō, 1974.

———. "Nisshi shisō mondai" [The problem of an ideology for Japan and China] (1935). In Miki Kiyoshi, *Chosakushū* [Collected works], vol. 14, pp. 16–23. Tokyo: Iwanami shoten, 1950.

———. "Puragumachizumu no tetsugaku" [The philosophy of pragmatism] (1927). In Miki Kiyoshi, *Chosakushū* [Collected works], vol. 3, pp. 74–116. Tokyo: Iwanami shoten, 1947.

———. "Seiji no hinkon" [The Poverty of Politics] (1939). In Miki Kiyoshi, *Chosakushū* [Collected works], vol. 14, pp. 170–81. Tokyo: Iwanami shoten, 1950.

———. "Seiji to bunka" [Politics and culture]. In *Seiji taisei kōza: Sekai to shintairiku* [Lectures on the political system: The world and the new continent], edited by the Nihon seinen gaikō kyōkai. Tokyo: 1939.

———. "Sekaiteki shisō no yōbō" [Hopes for a world thought] (1938). In Miki Kiyoshi, *Zenshū* [Complete works], vol. 19, pp. 708–9. Tokyo: Iwanami shoten, 1968.

———. "Setcho hihyō ni kotau" [Responding to criticism of my work] (1932). In Miki Kiyoshi, *Chosakushū* [Collected works], vol. 11, pp. 199–224. Tokyo: Iwanami shoten, 1950.

———. "Shakai jihyō" [Comments on society] (1936). In Miki Kiyoshi, *Chosakushū* [Collected works], vol. 14, pp. 48–61. Tokyo: Iwanami shoten, 1950.

———. "Zentaishugi hihan" [A Critique of Totalitarianism] (1935). In Miki Kiyoshi,

Zenshū [Complete works], vol. 19, pp. 665-72. Tokyo: Iwanami shoten, 1968.
―――― and Chou Fo-hai. "Minzokushugi no mondai" [The problem of nationalism]. *Chūō kōron* 55 (May 1940): 82-85.
Minobe Yōji. "Keizai shintaisei kanken" [A view of the economic new order]. *Nihon hyōron* 16 (March 1941): 12-21.
―――― et al. "Zadankai: Kokubō kokka o kataru" [Discussing the national defense state]. *Nihon hyōron* 15 (November 1940): 175-201.
Minoda Muneki. "Shōwa kenkyūkai no gengo majutsu" [The magic of the language of the Shōwa Research Association]. *Genri nihon*, September 1940, pp. 2-18.
Mitsui Katsushi. "Shōwa kenkyūkai kyōgyaku shisō o shōri subeshi" [The need to control the alarming thought of the Shōwa Research Association]. *Genri nihon*, October 1940, pp. 2-35.
Miyaji Masato. "Kikakuin jiken—Senji keikaku keizai o meguru kōsō no gisei" [The cabinet planning board incident—Victims of the struggles surrounding the wartime planned economy]. In *Nihon seiji saiban shi roku* [A record of the history of political trials in Japan], vol. 5, pp. 372-418. Tokyo: Daiichi hōki shuppan kabushiki kaisha, 1970.
Murata Katsumi. "Shōwa kenkyūkai ni taisuru hyōka" [Evaluations of the Shōwa Research Association]. *Tōyō kenkyū* 9 (October 1964): 59-72.
Nakamura Takafusa. "Ryū Shintarō to tōsei keizai" [Ryū Shintarō and the controlled economy]. *Rekishi to jimbutsu*, no. 32 (April 1974): 66-74.
―――― and Hara Akira. "Keizai shintaisei" [The economic new order]. In *"Konoe shintaisei" no kenkyū* [Research on "Konoe's New Order"], edited by the Nihon seiji gakkai, pp. 71-133. Tokyo: Iwanami shoten, 1972.
Ōmichi Meisuke. "Keizai shintaisei no butai ura" [Behind the stage of the economic new order]. *Chūō kōron* 56 (January 1941): 186-92.
Ōuchi Hyōe. "Kushida Tamizō: Marukusugaku no kakuritsusha" [Kushida Tamizō: A founder of Marxist studies]. In *Nihon no shisōka* [Thinkers of Japan], vol. 3, edited by the *Asahi Jānaru*, pp. 150-67. Tokyo: Asahi shimbunsha, 1973.
――――. "Ohara shaken nyūjo no koro" [When Ryū entered the Ohara Institute]. In *Kaisō Ryū Shintarō* [Remembrances of Ryū Shintarō], edited by Ebata Kiyoshi, pp. 305-10. Tokyo: Asahi shimbunsha, 1969.
Ōyama Iwao et al. "Shōwa kenkyūkai no rekishiteki yakuwari" [The historical role of the Shōwa Research Association]. *Shōwa dōjin* 7 (February 1961): 1-15.
Rōyama Masamichi. "Doitsu musanseitō undō no genjō to nihon" [Japan and the current situation of the German proletarian party movement]. *Shakai shisō* 6 (February 1927): 29-37.
――――. "Gaikō sasshin to kokunai shintaisei" [The reform of foreign policy and the domestic new order] (1940). In Rōyama Masamichi, *Tōa to sekai* [East Asia and the world], pp. 299-316. Tokyo: Kaizōsha, 1941.
――――. "Gikai no sasshin" [Reform of the Diet]. *Chūō kōron* 51 (March 1936): 33-44.
――――. "Gyōsei kikō kaikaku no mondaisei" [The problem of reforming the structure of administration]. *Kaizō* 18 (November 1936): 56-62.
――――. "Gyōsei seiri no shakaiteki igi" [The social meaning of administrative management]. *Shakai shisō* 3 (September 1924): 2-5.

―――. "Jimu no honshitsu to kakushin no dōkō" [The basic character of affairs and trends of reform]. *Chūō kōron* 53 (April 1938): 4–18.

―――. "Kaku kuni ni okeru keizai kaigi no hikaku seido kenkyū" [Comparative research on systems of economic councils in each nation] (1934). In Rōyama Masamichi, *Gyōseigaku kenkyū ronbunshū* [Collected articles on research in administrative science], pp. 82–96. Tokyo: Keisō shobō, 1965.

―――. "Kaku kuni rōdō kaikyū futsu senkyo: Fusen ni yoru waga seikyoku no shintenkai to rōdō kaikyū" [The working class in each nation and universal suffrage: The working class and new developments in our political situation based on universal suffrage]. *Shakai shisō* 3 (March 1924): 9–18.

―――. "Kiki no shihai to jiyū no mondai" [The dominance of crisis and the problem of liberty]. *Kaizō* 15 (July 1933): 139–45.

―――. "Kokumin kyōdōtai no keisei" [The formation of a national cooperative body]. *Kaizō* 21 (May 1939): 4–29.

―――. "Kokumin no kakuzame ga hitsuyō" [The necessity for a national awakening]. *Kaizō* 14 (June 1932): 99–102.

―――. "Nōchi no shoyū to kōsaku jōtai" [The possession of farm land and the situation of farming]. *Shakai shisō* 7 (May 1928): 74–80.

―――. "Ōshū taisen to futatsu no teikokushugi" [The great European war and two kinds of imperialism] (1939). In Rōyama Masamichi, *Tōa to sekai* [East Asia and the world], pp. 260–74. Tokyo: Kaizōsha, 1941.

―――. "Rikken seido shinka no ichi dankai: Iaku jōhō mondai no seijigakuteki kōsatsu" [One stage in the advance of the constitutional system: A consideration of the problem of direct appeal to the Emperor from the view of political science]. *Shakai shisō* 1 (April 1922): 13–18.

―――. "Sengo shinkenpō ni okeru shomondai" [Various problems in the new postwar constitutions]. *Shakai shisō* 1 (August 1922): 165–75.

―――. "Shinjoteki nashionarisuto" [An emotional nationalist]. In *Kaisō—Ryū Shintarō* [Remembrances of Ryū Shintarō], edited by Ebata Kiyoshi, pp. 139–42. Tokyo: Asahi shimbunsha, 1969.

―――. "Tōa kyōdōtai no riron" [The theory of the East Asian cooperative body] (1939). In Rōyama Masamichi, *Tōa to sekai* [East Asia and the world], pp. 3–40. Tokyo: Kaizōsha, 1941.

―――. "Tokyo shisei kaizen mondai to musanseitō" [The proletarian parties and the problems of reforming the municipal politics of Tokyo]. *Shakai shisō* 7 (November 1928): 8–11.

―――. "Toshi keikaku to rōdōsha kaikyū" [City planning and the working class]. *Shakai shisō* 3 (January 1924): 27–32.

――― and Masui Mitsuzō. "Sekai kyōkō to burokku keizai" [The world depression and the bloc economy]. In *Gendai keizaigaku zenshū* [Collected works on modern Economics], vol. 29. Tokyo: Nihon hyōronsha, 1932.

―――, Sassa Hiroo, and Akamatsu Katsumaro. "Fuashizumu hihan" [Criticism of fascism]. *Keizai ōrai* 7 (January 1932): 37–65.

Ryū Shintarō. "Ajia ni okeru nihon no keizaiteki chii" [Japan's economic position in Asia]. In *Ajia mondai kōza* [Lectures on Asian problems], pp. 3–17. Tokyo: Sōgensha, 1939.

―――. "Denryoku mondai to kokuei mondai" [The problem of electrical power and the problem of national management]. *Chūō kōron* 51 (October 1936): 67–81.

―――. "Ginkō kyōkō no haigo" [The background of the bank Panic]. *Warera*, June 1927, pp. 23–34.

―――. "Infureshonka no shihon to rōdō" [Capital and labor in a period of inflation] (1932). In Ryū Shintarō, *Zenshū* [Complete works], vol. 8, pp. 414–24. Tokyo: Asahi shimbunsha, 1969.

―――. "Kahei ni okeru burujoa ideorogii" [The bourgeois ideology in currency] (1931). In Ryū Shintarō, *Zenshū* [Complete works], vol. 8, pp. 441–63. Tokyo: Asahi shimbunsha, 1969.

―――. "Kaigai de no hachigatsu jūgo nichi" [August 15 Overseas] (1951). In Ryū Shintarō, *Zenshū* [Complete works], vol. 6, pp. 215–22. Tokyo: Asahi shimbunsha, 1969.

―――. "Kin yushutsu saikinshi 'ron' to kin yushutsu saikinshi" [The reembargo on gold and "discussion" in favor of it]. *Chūō kōron* 46 (November 1931): 83–94.

―――. " 'Kokusai' no taijō to 'kokusai' no tōjō" [The fall and rise of "internationalism"]. *Ekonomisuto* 13 (February 1935): 11–13.

―――. "Konoe kō no jidai" [The era of Prince Konoe] (1966). In Ryū Shintarō, *Zenshū* [Complete works], vol. 1, pp. 602–13. Tokyo: Asahi shimbunsha, 1969.

―――. "Kyōkō ni arawareta gendankai" [The current stage shown in the depression]. *Taiyō* 34 (January 1928): 39–52.

―――. "Miura Shinshichi hakase" [Doctor Miura Shinshichi] (1958). In Ryū Shintarō, *Zenshū* [Complete works], vol. 5, pp. 400–418. Tokyo: Asahi shimbunsha, 1969.

―――. "Nihon keizai no saihensei" [The reorganization of Japan's economy]. *Chūō kōron* 53 (December 1938): 4–18.

―――. "Shiteki yuibutsuron" [Historical materialism]. *Chūō kōron* 46 (January 1931): 123–26.

―――. "Supengurā no keizai kan" [The economic view of Spengler]. *Shōgaku kenkyū*, 1924, pp. 137–87.

―――. "Zunō to jōnetsu no hito—Miki Kiyoshi kun" [A person of intelligence and enthusiasm—Miki Kiyoshi] (1967). In Ryū Shintarō, *Zenshū* [Complete works], vol. 5, pp. 501–6. Tokyo: Asahi shimbunsha, 1969.

――― and Aochi Shin. "Jijitsu o miru: Taiwa ni yoru kaisetsu" [Viewing reality: An explanation based on a conversation]. In Ryū Shintarō, *Jijitsu o miru* [Viewing reality], pp. 393–430. Tokyo: Kōdansha, 1968.

――― et al. " 'Nihon keizai no saihensei' tōronkai" [A discussion on the reorganization of the Japanese economy]. *Chūō kōron* 55 (May 1940): 226–55.

Sakai Saburō and Gotō Ryūnosuke. "Shōwa shi no gekiryū no naka de: Taidan" [In the swift currents of Shōwa history: A conversation]. In Sakai Saburō, *Shōwa kenkyūkai—Aru chishikijin shūdan no kiseki* [The Shōwa Research Association—The course of one group of intellectuals], appendix, pp. 1–14. Tokyo: TBS Brittanica, 1979.

Sakai Saburō, Iwasaki Eikyō, and Gotō Ryūnosuke. "Shōwa shi no katsukazan—Shōwa kenkyūkai" [The active volcano of Shōwa history—The Shōwa Research Association]. *Keizai ōrai* 19 (October 1967): 192–207.

Sassa Hiroo. "Eikoku kindai shakaishugi undō" [The modern socialist movement in England]. *Shakai shisō* 1 (July 1922): 143–44.

———. "Kokumin soshiki mondai no kentō" [An investigation of the problems of a national organization]. *Chūō kōron* 54 (January 1939): 30–40.

———. "Seiyūkai hōkai to shinseitō no mondai" [The destruction of the Seiyūkai and the problem of a new party]. *Kaizō* 17 (June 1935): 322–28.

———. "Shinkanryō no botsuraku" [The fall of the new bureaucrats]. *Chūō kōron* 50 (January 1935): 254–65.

———. "Shintō keikaku o meguru seikyoku no gendankai" [The current stage of the political situation concerning plans for a new party]. *Kaizō* 17 (October 1935): 306–13.

Shimizu Ikutarō. "Miki Kiyoshi to Shōwa kenkyūkai" [Miki Kiyoshi and the Shōwa Research Association]. *Rekishi to jimbutsu*, no. 32 (April 1974): 57–65.

"Shin keizai taisei no zenshin" [The progress of the new economic order]. *Asahi shimbun*, September 10, 1940, p. 3.

Suzuki Naoto. "Kakushin seinensō no taitō" [The rise of a class of radical reform youth]. *Bungei shunjū* 18 (September 1940): 92–103.

Taira Teizō. "Shakai shisōsha kessei no koro" [When the Social Thought Association formed]. In *Miwa Jusō no seichō* [The life of Miwa Jusō], edited by the Miwa Jusō denki kankōkai, pp. 195–209. Tokyo: Chūō kōron jitsugyō shuppan, 1966.

———. "Shakai shisōsha no koro" [At the time of the Social Thought Association]. In *Kaisō Ryū Shintarō* [Remembrances of Ryū Shintarō], edited by Ebata Kiyoshi, pp. 148–57. Tokyo: Asahi shimbunsha, 1969.

———. "Shōwa juku kaisō" [Remembrances of the Shōwa Academy]. *Shōwa dōjin* 6 (November 1960): 29–30.

——— et al. "Shōwa kenkyūkai no rekishiteki yakuwari" [The Historical Role of the Shōwa Research Association]. *Shōwa dōjin* 7 (April 1961): 18–28.

Takagaki Enjirō. "Ryū kun no omoishutsu" [Memories of Ryū]. In *Kaisō Ryū Shintarō* [Remembrances of Ryū Shintarō], edited by Ebata Kiyoshi, pp. 75–82. Tokyo: Asahi shimbunsha, 1969.

Takahashi Kamekichi. "Nihon keizai 1930 nendai" [The Japanese economy and the 1930s]. *Shisō*, June 1976, pp. 174–84.

Tanigawa Teizō. "Tetsugakusha to shite no Miki Kiyoshi" [Miki Kiyoshi as a philosopher]. In *Kaisō no Miki Kiyoshi* [Remembrances of Miki Kiyoshi], edited by Tanigawa Teizō and Tōhata Seiichi, pp. 128–45. Tokyo: Bunka shoin, 1948.

Toda Takeo. "Keizai rinri no mondai" [The problem of economic ethics]. *Nihon hyōron* 15 (May 1940): 289–92.

Tosaka Jun. "Shimbun genshō no bunseki" [An analysis of the phenomenon of newspapers]. In *Jānarizumu no shisō* [The thought of journalism], Gendai Nihon shisō taikei [A series in modern Japanese thought], vol. 12, edited by Tsurumi Shunsuke, pp. 236–72. Tokyo: Chikuma shobō, 1973.

Tsurumi Shunsuke. "Tenkō no kyōdō kenkyū ni tsuite" [About cooperative research on apostasy]. In *Tenkō* [Apostasy], edited by the Shisō no kagaku kenkyūkai, vol. 1, pp. 1–27. Tokyo: Heibonsha, 1967.

———. "Yokusan undō no gakumon ron" [The scholarship supporting the Imperial Rule Assistance Movement]. In *Tenkō* [Apostasy], edited by the Shisō no kagaku kenkyūkai, vol. 2, pp. 152–200. Tokyo: Heibonsha, 1967.

———. "Yokusan undō no sekkeisha—Konoe Fumimaro" [The planner of the Imperial Rule Assistance Movement—Konoe Fumimaro]. In *Tenkō* [Apostasy], edited

by the Shisō no kagaku kenkyūkai, vol. 2, pp. 53-120. Tokyo: Heibonsha, 1967.
Uotsu Ikuo. "Aru jiyūshugi saha no chishikijin Miki Kiyoshi" [An intellectual of the leftist group of liberals: Miki Kiyoshi]. In *Tenkō* [Apostasy], edited by the Shisō no kagaku kenkyūkai, vol. 1, pp. 366-82. Tokyo: Heibonsha, 1967.
Watanabe Tōru. "Nihon no marukusushugi undō" [Marxist movements in Japan]. In *Nihon, Kōza marukusushugi* [Lectures on Marxism, Japan], vol. 12, edited by Yamazaki Harunari, pp. 137-250. Tokyo: Nihon hyōronsha, 1968.
XYZ. "Shōwajuku, Shōwa kenkyūkai no tanbō" [A report on the Shōwa Academy and the Shōwa Research Association]. *Chūō kōron* 53 (December 1938): 277-81.
Yamada Munemutsu. "Miki Kiyoshi." In *Nihon no shisōka* [Thinkers of Japan], edited by the Asahi Jānaru, vol. 3, pp. 302-17. Tokyo: Asahi shimbunsha, 1963.
Yanaihara Tadao. "Shina mondai no shozai" [The present situation of the China problem]. *Chūō kōron* 52 (February 1937): 4-17.

Books and Dissertations
English Language

Allinson, Gary D. *Japanese Urbanism: Industry and Politics in Kariya, 1872-1972*. Berkeley: University of California Press, 1975.
Arima Tatsuo. *The Failure of Freedom*. Cambridge: Harvard University Press, 1969.
Bank of Japan, Investigation Bureau. *Economic Statistics of Japan*. Tokyo: Bank of Japan, 1937.
Beckmann, George M., and Okubo Genji. *The Japanese Communist Party, 1922-1945*. Stanford: Stanford University Press, 1969.
Benians, E. A., et al., eds. *The Empire-Commonwealth, 1870-1919*. The Cambridge History of the British Empire, vol. 3. Cambridge: Cambridge University Press, 1959.
Berger, Gordon M. *Parties out of Power in Japan*. Princeton: Princeton University Press, 1976.
Berlin, Isaiah. *Four Essays on Liberty*. New York: Oxford University Press, 1969.
Bernstein, Gail Lee. *Japanese Marxist: A Portrait of Kawakami Hajime, 1879-1946*. Cambridge: Harvard University Press, 1976.
Bikle, George B. *The New Jerusalem: Aspects of Utopianism in the Thought of Kagawa Toyohiko*. Tuscon: University of Arizona Press, 1976.
Borg, Dorothy, and Shumpei Okamoto, eds. *Pearl Harbor as History: Japanese-American Relations, 1931-1941*. New York: Columbia University Press, 1973.
Bottomore, T. B., and Maximilien Rubel, eds. *Karl Marx: Selected Writings in Sociology and Social Philosophy*. Middlesex: Penguin Books, 1970.
Bourne, Randolph S. *War and the Intellectuals: Essays*. Edited by Carl Resek. New York: Harper and Row, 1964.
Bowen, Ralph H. *German Theories of the Corporative State, with Special Reference to the Period 1870-1918*. New York: McGraw-Hill, 1947.
Boyle, John Hunter. *China and Japan at War, 1937-1945: The Politics of Collaboration*. Stanford: Stanford University Press, 1972.
Bunker, Gerald E. *The Peace Conspiracy: Wang Ching-wei and the China War, 1937-1941*. Cambridge: Harvard University Press, 1972.
Byas, Hugh. *Government by Assassination*. New York: Knopf, 1942.

Carpenter, L. P. *G. D. H. Cole*. New York: Cambridge University Press, 1973.
Carroll, Bernice A. *Design for Total War: Arms and Economics in the Third Reich*. The Hague: Mouton, 1968.
Chomsky, Noam. *American Power and the New Mandarins*. New York: Pantheon Books, 1969.
Cohen, Jerome. *Japan's Economy in War and Reconstruction*. New York: Institute of Pacific Relations, 1949.
Cole, George Douglas Howard. *Self Government in Industry*. London: G. Bell and Sons, 1918.
Coser, Lewis A. *Men of Ideas: A Sociologist's View*. New York: Free Press, 1965.
Crowley, James B. *Japan's Quest for Autonomy*. Princeton: Princeton University Press, 1967.
Dahrendorff, Ralf. *Society and Democracy in Germany*. New York: Doubleday, 1967.
d'Ombrain, Nicholas. *War Machinery and High Policy: Defense Administration in Peacetime Britain, 1902–1914*. London: Oxford University Press, 1973.
Emmett, W. H. *The Marxian Economic Handbook and Glossary*. London: G. Allen and Unwin, 1925.
Ermath, Fritz. *The New Germany: National Socialist Government in Theory and Practice*. Washington: Digest Press, American University Graduate School, 1936.
Field, G. Lowell. *The Syndical and Corporative Institutions of Italian Fascism*. New York: Columbia University Press, 1938.
Gregor, A. James. *The Fascist Persuasion in Radical Politics*. Princeton: Princeton University Press, 1974.
Hale, William Harlan. *Challenge to Defeat: Man in Goethe's World and Spengler's Century*. New York: Harcourt, Brace, 1932.
Havens, Thomas R. H. *Farm and Nation in Modern Japan: Agrarian Nationalism, 1870–1940*. Princeton: Princeton University Press, 1974.
Hofstadter, Richard. *Anti-Intellectualism in American Life*. New York: Knopf, 1963.
Hughes, H. Stuart. *Oswald Spengler: A Critical Estimate*. New York: Scribner, 1952.
Japan Biographical Dictionary and Who's Who. 2d. ed. Tokyo: Rengo Press, 1960.
Joes, Anthony James. *Fascism in the Contemporary World: Ideology, Evolution, and Resurgence*. Boulder: Westview Press, 1978.
Johnson, Chalmers. *An Instance of Treason*. Berkeley: University of California Press, 1974.
Kim Yong Mok. "Miki Kiyoshi: A Representative Thinker of His Times." Ph.D. dissertation, University of California, Berkeley, 1974.
Kinney, Anne R. "Japanese Investment in Manchurian Mining, Manufacturing, Transportation, and Communications, 1931–1945." Ph.D. dissertation, Columbia University, 1962.
Knauerhase, Ramon. *An Introduction to National Socialism, 1920–1939*. Columbus, Ohio: Merrill, 1962.
Kockelmans, Joseph J. *Martin Heidegger: A First Introduction to His Philosophy*. Pittsburgh: Duquesne University Press, 1965.
Lamprecht, Karl. *What Is History?* Translated by E. A. Andrews. New York: Macmillan Company, 1905.
Laqueur, Walter, ed. *Fascism: A Reader's Guide*. Berkeley: University of California Press, 1976.

Large, Stephen S. *The Rise of Labor in Japan: The Yūaikai, 1912–1919*. Tokyo: Sophia University Press, 1972.
Lukacs, George. *Marxism and Human Revolution*. Edited and with an introduction by E. San Juan, Jr. New York: Dell, 1973.
McClellan, David. *Marx before Marxism*. Suffolk: Penguin Books, 1972.
Maier, Charles S. *Recasting Bourgeois Europe: Stabilization in France, Germany, and Italy in the Decade after World War I*. Princeton: Princeton University Press, 1975.
Mandel, Ernest. *An Introduction to Marxist Economic Theory*. New York: Pathfinder Press, 1973.
Marshall, Byron K. *Capital and Nationalism in Prewar Japan: The Ideology of the Business Elite*. Stanford: Stanford University Press, 1967.
Maruyama, Masao. *Studies in the Intellectual History of Tokugawa Japan*. Translated by Mikiso Hane. Princeton: Princeton University Press, 1974.
——— . *Thought and Behavior in Modern Japanese Politics*. Edited by Ivan Morris. New York: Oxford University Press, 1963.
Marx, Karl. *Capital*. Edited by Frederick Engels. Translated by Samuel Moore and Edward Aveling. New York: Random House, 1906.
Miller, Frank O. *Minobe Tatsukichi: Interpreter of Constitutionalism in Japan*. Berkeley: University of California Press, 1965.
Milward, Alan S. *The German Economy at War*. London: Athlone Press, 1965.
Mitchell, Richard H. *Thought Control in Prewar Japan*. Ithaca: Cornell University Press, 1976.
Mosse, George L., ed. *International Fascism: New Thoughts and New Approaches*. London: Sage Publications, 1979.
Najita Tetsuo. *Japan*. Englewood Cliffs, N.J.: Prentice-Hall, 1974.
Nathan, Otto. *The Nazi Economic System: Germany's Mobilization for War*. Durham: Duke University Press, 1944.
Nolte, Ernst. *Three Faces of Fascism*. Translated by Leila Vennewitz. New York: Holt, Rinehart, and Winston, 1966.
Ogata Sadako. *Defiance in Manchuria: The Making of Japanese Foreign Policy, 1931–32*. Berkeley: University of California Press, 1964.
Peattie, Mark R. *Ishiwara Kanji and Japan's Confrontation with the West*. Princeton: Princeton University Press, 1969.
Pierson, John D. *Tokutomi Sohō: A Journalist for Modern Japan, 1863–1957*. Princeton: Princeton University Press, 1980.
Pyle, Kenneth B. *The New Generation in Meiji Japan*. Stanford: Stanford University Press, 1969.
Roberts, David D. *The Syndicalist Tradition and Italian Fascism*. Chapel Hill: University of North Carolina Press, 1979.
Rōyama Masamichi. *Japan's Position in Manchuria*. Tokyo: Institute of Pacific Relations, Japan Council, 1929.
——— and Takeuji Tatsuji. *The Philippine Polity: A Japanese View*. Translated by Takeuji Tatsuji. Edited by Theodore Friend. New Haven: Yale University, Southeast Asian Studies, 1967.
Ruggiero, Guido de. *The History of European Liberalism*. Translated by R. G. Collingwood. Boston: Beacon Press, 1959.
Scalapino, Robert. *Democracy and the Party Movement in Prewar Japan*. Berkeley:

University of California Press, 1953.
Schacht, Hjalmar. *My First Seventy-six Years*. London: Allan Wingate, 1955.
Searle, G. R. *The Quest for National Efficiency: A Study in British Politics and Political Thought, 1899-1914*. Oxford: Basil Blackwell, 1971.
Smethurst, Richard J. *A Social Basis for Prewar Japanese Militarism*. Berkeley: University of California Press, 1974.
Smith, Henry D. *Japan's First Student Radicals*. Cambridge: Harvard University Press, 1972.
Soucy, Robert J. *Fascist Intellectual: Drieu La Rochelle*. Berkeley: University of California Press, 1979.
Spengler, Oswald. *The Decline of the West*. Translated by Charles Francis Atkinson. 2 vols. New York: Knopf, 1926-28.
Steinhoff, Patricia Golden. "Tenkō: Ideology and Societal Integration in Prewar Japan." Ph.D. dissertation, Harvard University, 1969.
Sweezy, Paul M. *The Theory of Capitalist Development: Principles of Marxian Political Economy*. New York: Monthly Review Press, 1964.
Tannenbaum, Edward R. *The Fascist Experience: Italian Society and Culture, 1922-1945*. New York: Basic Books, 1972.
Totten, George. *The Social Democratic Movement in Prewar Japan*. New Haven: Yale University Press, 1966.
Turner, Henry A. *Reappraisals of Fascism*. New York: New Viewpoints, 1975.
United States, Department of State. *Foreign Relations of the United States-Japan, 1931-1941*. Washington, D.C., 1943.
Uyehara, Cecil H. *Checklist of Archives in the Japanese Ministry of Foreign Affairs, Tokyo, Japan, 1863-1945: Microfilms for the Library of Congress, 1949-1951*. Washington, D.C.: Photoduplication Service, Library of Congress, 1954.
Varga, Eugen. *The Great Crisis and Its Political Consequences*. New York: Howard Fertig, 1974.
Von Klemperer, Klemens. *Germany's New Conservatism: Its History and Dilemma in the Twentieth Century*. Princeton: Princeton University Press, 1968.
Weber, Eugen. *Varieties of Fascism: Doctrines of Revolution in the Twentieth Century*. Princeton: Van Nostrand, 1964.
Weiss, John. *The Fascist Tradition: Radical Right-Wing Extremism in Modern Europe*. New York: Harper and Row, 1967.
Wilson, George M., ed. *Crisis Politics in Prewar Japan*. Tokyo: Sophia University Press, 1970.
———. *Revolutionary Nationalist in Japan: Kita Ikki, 1883-1937*. Cambridge: Harvard University Press, 1969.
Woolf, S. J., ed. *European Fascism*. Reading, Eng.: University of Reading, 1968.
———. *The Nature of Fascism*. London: Weidenfeld and Nicholson, 1968.
Yanaga Chitoshi. *Japan since Perry*. New York: McGraw-Hill, 1949.
Young, John. *Checklist of Microfilm Reproductions of Selected Archives of the Japanese Army, Navy, and Other Government Agencies, 1868-1945*. Washington, D.C.: Georgetown University Press, 1959.

Articles
English Language

"Address by Prince Fumimaro Konoye [sic] at the First Session of the Preparatory Committee for the New National Structure, August 29, 1940." *Contemporary Japan* 9 (October 1940): 1366–69.

Allardyce, Gilbert. "What Fascism Is Not: Thoughts on the Deflation of a Concept.' *American Historical Review* 85 (April 1979): 367–98.

Baba Tsunego. "Hostilities and Parliament." *Contemporary Japan* 7 (March 1938): 590–600.

Berger, Gordon Mark. "Changing Historiographical Perspectives on Early Shōwa Politics: 'The Second Approach.' " *Journal of Asian Studies* 34 (February 1975): 473–84.

———. "Japan's Young Prince: Konoe Fumimaro's Early Political Career, 1916–1931." *Monumenta Nipponica* 29 (Winter 1974): 451–75.

Cassels, Alan. "Janus: The Two Faces of Fascism." In *Reappraisals of Fascism*, edited by Henry H. Turner, pp. 69–92. New York: New Viewpoints, 1975.

Chō Yukio. "From the Shōwa Economic Crisis to Military Economy." *Developing Economies* 5 (December 1967): 568–97.

———. "An Inquiry into the Problem of Importing American Capital into Manchuria: A Note on Japanese-American Relations, 1931–1941." In *Pearl Harbor as History: Japanese-American Relations, 1931–1941*. Edited by Dorothy Borg and Shumpei Okamoto, pp. 377–410. New York: Columbia University Press, 1973.

Crowley, James B. "A New Deal for Japan and Asia: One Road to Pearl Harbor." In *Modern East Asia: Essays in Interpretation*, edited by James B. Crowley, pp. 235–64. New York: Harcourt, Brace and World, 1970.

———. "Imperial Japan and Its Modern Discontents: The State and Military in Prewar Japan." In *Military and State in Modern Asia*, edited by Harold Z. Schiffrin, pp. 31–59. Jerusalem: Jerusalem Academic Press, 1976.

———. "Intellectuals as Visionaries of the New Asian Order." In *Dilemmas of Growth in Prewar Japan*, edited by James W. Morley, pp. 319–72. Princeton: Princeton University Press, 1972.

Duus, Peter. "Nagai Ryūtarō and the 'White Peril,' 1905–1944." *Journal of Asian Studies* 31 (November 1971): 41–48.

———. "Nagai Ryūtarō: The Tactical Dilemmas of Reform." In *Personality in Japanese History*, edited by Albert M. Craig and Donald H. Shively, pp. 399–424. Berkeley: University of California Press, 1970.

———. "Ōyama Ikuo and the Search for Democracy." In *Dilemmas of Growth in Prewar Japan*, edited by James W. Morley, pp. 423–58. Princeton: Princeton University Press, 1972.

———, and Daniel I. Okimoto. "Fascism and the History of Prewar Japan." *Journal of Asian Studies* 39 (November 1979): 65–76.

Fridell, Wilbur M. "Government Ethics Textbooks in Late Meiji Japan." *Journal of Asian Studies* 29 (August 1970): 829–33.

Furuta Tokujirō. "Factors behind Establishment of a New Political Structure." *Contemporary Opinions*, no. 345 (September 5, 1940): 10–12.

Gregor, A. James. "Fascism and Modernization: Some Addenda." *World Politics* 26 (April 1974): 370–84.

———. "The Ideology of Fascism." In *Transformation of a Continent*, edited by Gerhard S. Weinberg, pp. 253–89. Minneapolis: Burgess, 1974.

Harootunian, H. D. "Introduction: The Sense of Ending and the Problem of Taishō." In *Japan in Crisis*, edited by Bernard S. Silberman and H. D. Harootunian, pp. 3–28. Princeton: Princeton University Press, 1974.

Hashikawa Bunsō. "Japanese Perspectives on Asia: From Dissociation to Coprosperity." In *The Chinese and Japanese: Essays in Political and Cultural Interactions*, edited by Akira Iriye, pp. 328–55. Princeton: Princeton University Press, 1980.

Hayashi Kentarō. "Japan and Germany in the Interwar Period." In *Dilemmas of Growth in Prewar Japan*, edited by James W. Morley, pp. 461–88. Princeton: Princeton University Press, 1972.

Ishihama Tomoyuki. "Book Review." *Contemporary Japan* 9 (August 1940): 1057–59.

Itō Takashi. "The Role of Right-Wing Organizations in Japan." In *Pearl Harbor as History: Japanese-American Relations, 1931–1941*, edited by Dorothy Borg and Shumpei Okamoto, pp. 487–509. New York: Columbia University Press, 1973.

Keene, Donald. "Japanese Writers and the Greater East Asian War." *Journal of Asian Studies* 23 (February 1964): pp. 209–55.

Kimura Kihachirō. "Financial Control and Defeat of Capitalists." *Contemporary Japan* 10 (January 1941): 102–8.

Marsh, Susan H. "Chou Fo-hai: The Making of a Collaborator." In *The Chinese and Japanese: Essays in Political and Cultural Interactions*, edited by Akira Iriye, pp. 304–27. Princeton: Princeton University Press, 1980.

Miki Kiyoshi. "The China Affair and Japanese Thought." *Contemporary Japan* 6 (March 1938): 601–10.

Minobe Yōji. "The Principles of the New Economic Structure." *Contemporary Japan* 10 (February 1941): 178–88.

Mitchell, Richard H. "Japan's Peace Preservation Law of 1925: Its Origins and Significance." *Monumenta Nipponica* 28 (Autumn 1973): 317–45.

Morley, James W. "Introduction: Choice and Consequences." In *Dilemmas of Growth in Prewar Japan*, edited by James W. Morley, pp. 3–30. Princeton: Princeton University Press, 1972.

Mosse, George L. "Towards a General Theory of Fascism." In *International Fascism: New Thoughts and Approaches*, edited by George L. Mosse, pp. 1–41. London: Sage Publications, 1979.

Mussolini, Benito. "Fascism: Doctrine and Institutions" (1935). Reprinted in *Mediterranean Fascism, 1919–1945*, edited by Charles F. Delzell, pp. 91–96. New York: Walker, 1970.

Najita Tetsuo. "Nakano Seigō and the Spirit of the Meiji Restoration in Twentieth Century Japan." In *Dilemmas of Growth in Prewar Japan*, edited by James W. Morley, pp. 375–421. Princeton: Princeton University Press, 1972.

Passin, Herbert. "Intellectuals in the Decision-Making Process." In *Modern Japanese Organization and Decision-Making*, edited by Ezra F. Vogel, pp. 251–83. Berkeley: University of California Press, 1975.

———. "Modernization and the Japanese Intellectual: Some Comparative Observations." In *Changing Japanese Attitudes toward Modernization*, edited by Marius B. Jansen, pp. 447–88. Princeton: Princeton University Press, 1965.

Patrick, Hugh T. "The Economic Muddle of the 1920's." In *Dilemmas of Growth in Prewar Japan*, edited by James W. Morley, pp. 211–66. Princeton: Princeton University Press, 1972.

Piovesana, Gino K. "Miki Kiyoshi: Representative Thinker of an Anguished Generation." In *Studies of Japanese Culture*, edited by Joseph Roggendorff, pp. 143–61. Tokyo: Sophia University Press, 1963.

Pyle, Kenneth B. "Advantages of Followership: German Economics and Japanese Bureaucrats, 1890–1924." *Journal of Japanese Studies* 1 (Autumn 1974): 127–64.

Reischauer, Edwin O. "What Went Wrong?" In *Dilemmas of Growth in Prewar Japan*, edited by James W. Morley, pp. 489–510. Princeton: Princeton University Press, 1972.

Rocco, Alfredo. "The Political Doctrine of Fascism." In *International Conciliation: Documents*, pp. 389–445. New York: Carnegie Endowment for International Peace, 1926.

Ryū Shintarō. "Domestic Commodity Prices." *Contemporary Japan* 6 (September 1937): 248–56.

———. "Japanese Thought in Post-Meiji Times." *Japan Quarterly* 3 (April–June 1966): 157–71.

———. "Problems of North China Development." *Contemporary Japan* 7 (September 1938): 259–68.

Saitō Takao. "Political Parties Urged to Replace Bureaucratic Government." *Contemporary Opinion*, no. 308 (December 7, 1939): 13–15.

Schumpeter, Elizabeth B. "Industrial Development and Government Policy, 1936–1940." In *The Industrialization of Japan and Manchukuo, 1930–1940*, edited by Elizabeth B. Schumpeter, pp. 789–864. New York: Macmillan, 1940.

Scott, Charles E. "Heidegger and Consciousness." In *Martin Heidegger in Europe and America*, edited by Edward G. Ballard and Charles E. Scott, pp. 91–108. The Hague: Martinus Nijhoff, 1973.

Seton-Watson, Hugh. "The Age of Fascism and Its Legacy." In *International Fascism: New Thoughts and Approaches*, edited by George L. Mosse, pp. 357–76. London: Sage Publications, 1980.

Silberman, Bernard. "The Political Theory and Program of Yoshino Sakuzō." *Journal of Modern History* 31 (December 1959): 310–24.

Smith, David G. "Liberalism." In *International Encyclopedia of the Social Sciences*, edited by David L. Sills, pp. 276–82. New York: Macmillan, 1968.

Spaulding, Robert. "The Bureaucracy as a Political Force." *Dilemmas of Growth in Prewar Japan*, edited by James W. Morley, pp. 33–80. Princeton: Princeton University Press, 1972.

Spengler, Oswald. "Prussianism and Socialism." In Oswald Spengler, *Selected Essays*. Translated by Donald O. White, pp. 1–131. Chicago: Regnery, 1967.

Sternhell, Zeev. "Fascist Ideology." In *Fascism: A Reader's Guide*, edited by Walter Laqueur, pp. 315–76. Berkeley: University of California Press, 1976.

Takahashi Makoto. "The Development of Wartime Economic Controls." *Developing Economics* 5 (December 1967): 648–65.

Teters, Barbara S. "Matsuoka Yōsuke: the Diplomacy of Bluff and Gesture." In

Diplomats and Crisis: United States–Chinese–Japanese Relations, 1919–1941, edited by Richard Dean Burns and Edward M. Bennett, pp. 275–96. Santa Barbara: Clio Press, 1974.

Tiedemann, Arthur J. "Big Business and Politics in Prewar Japan." In *Dilemmas of Growth in Prewar Japan*, edited by James W. Morley, pp. 267–316. Princeton: Princeton University Press, 1972.

Tsurumi Shunsuke. "Cooperative Research on Ideological Transformation." *Journal of Social and Political Ideas in Japan* 2 (April 1964): 54–58.

Turner, Henry A., Jr. "Fascism and Modernization." *World Politics* 24 (July 1972): 547–64.

Wilson, George M. "A New Look at the Problem of Japanese Fascism." *Comparative Studies in Society and History* 10 (July 1968): 401–12.

Winkler, Heinrich August. "German Society, Hitler, and the Illusion of Restoration, 1930–33." In *International Fascism: New Thoughts and Approaches*, edited by George L. Mosse, pp. 143–61. London: Sage Publications, 1979.

Wright, W. Anthony. "Guild Socialism Revisited." *Journal of Contemporary History* 9 (January 1974): 165–80.

Yamamuro Sōbun. "A Call for a Peaceful Japan." In *Sources of the Japanese Tradition*, edited by Wm. Theodore de Bary, Donald Keene, and Tsunoda Jun, pp. 757–58. New York: Columbia University Press, 1958.

Index

Abe Katsuo, Admiral, 146
Abe Shigetaka, 97; participation in Education Study Group, 93
Agriculture, Ministry of, 125
Akinaga Gessan, Colonel (head of Cabinet Planning Board), 148
Alliance for a New Japan (Shinnihon no dōmei), 88, 92
Anti-Comintern Pact, 101, 102, 109, 134, 139
Aoki Kazuo (head of Cabinet Planning Board), 101, 186 (n. 24)
Apostasy (tenkō), 4, 164 (n. 6), 171 (n. 1). See also Miki Kiyoshi, and apostasy; Rōyama Masamichi, and apostasy; Ryū Shintarō, and apostasy
Araki Sadao, General, 94
Arima Yoriyasu (minister of agriculture), 90, 141, 144, 145, 187 (n. 43)
Arisawa Hiromi, 184 (n. 112)
Aristotle, 17
Arita Hachirō (foreign minister), 101, 178 (n. 51)
Army General Staff, 117, 142; plans for war, 106; opposition to China Incident, 107
Army Ministry, 51, 78, 93, 122; call for reforms, 33, 68–69, 89; policies in China, 62, 109, 110; five-year plan, 72, 117, 118–19; support for economic reforms, 149–50
Army of Japan, 10, 146, 148, 152, 155; support for Electric Power Control Law, 74, 75; difficulty of criticizing, 76; proposals for political reform, 79–80, 82, 134, 140; concerns Konoe, 94; attitude of Shōwa Research Association toward, 102; support for alliance with Germany and Italy, 134; attitude toward Konoe, 142, 144. See also Army General Staff; Army Ministry; Imperial Reserve Association; Konoe, attitude toward army; Kwantung Army; Miki Kiyoshi, contact with army, attitude toward military; Ryū Shintarō, attitude toward army
Asahi newspaper, 90, 173 (n. 2), 188 (n. 1); and Ryū Shintarō, 71, 72, 121, 153
Asō Hisashi, 69, 90

Baba Eiichi (finance minister), 72, 73, 76
Bank of Japan, 39, 40, 66, 73
Bank of Taiwan, 39
Bismarck, 6, 108
Brinkman, Rudolf, 137
Britain (England), 25, 42, 53, 54; as model of centralization, 13; policy toward Japan, 32, 101; as model of free speech, 38; attitude of Shōwa Research Association toward, 102, 109, 115; Japanese army's attitude toward, 106; as economic competition for Japan, 123; empire criticized, 123; as potential foe of Japan, 134; seen as "old imperialist," 139
British Labour party: as model, 23, 68; seen as fascist, 53
Buddhism, 85

Bureau for Temporary Industrial Rationalization, 42

Cabinet Consultative Council (Naikaku shingikai), 97; support for, 98
Cabinet Information Bureau, 135
Cabinet Investigation Bureau, 97, 101, 124
Cabinet Planning Board (Kikakuin), 122, 146; participation of members in Shōwa Research Association, 101, 121, 124, 125, 183 (n. 90); formation of, 125; proposals for new economic order, 147, 148–49, 152, 187 (n. 58); viewed as communist, 152, 153
Cabinet Planning Bureau (Kikakuchō), 72, 124, 125
Central Council of Corporations (Italian), 58
Chiang Kai-shek (Generalissimo), 29, 106; and China Incident, 107, 108, 109, 115
China, 77, 134; Japan's policies in, 61, 62, 72, 76, 106, 109, 110, 111; Japan's first war with, 76; U.S. policy in, 95; attitude of Shōwa Research Association toward, 102–3, 114–15, 155, 159; war in, 108, 130, 158, 161; as part of East Asian bloc economy, 117, 123; need for economic development of, 124; blamed for China Incident, 137; as part of cooperative body, 137. See also Army Ministry, policies in China; Chiang Kai-shek; China Incident; Kuomintang; Miki Kiyoshi, on Japan's China policy; Nanking government; Nationalist government; Rōyama Masamichi, theory of East Asian cooperative body; Ryū Shintarō, support for bloc economy; Shōwa Research Association, proposed solutions to China Incident
China Affairs Bureau (Taishiin), 108, 148
China Incident (China War), 77, 107, 108, 109, 115, 123, 125, 135, 141; interpreted by Miki Kiyoshi, 111; as opportunity for intellectuals, 114, 131–32; economic strains of, 116–17, 121, 122, 128, 131; predicted effects of, 126; and need for mobilization in Japan, 134. See also Army Ministry, policies in China; Chiang Kai-shek; China, war in, blamed for China Incident; Konoe, and China Incident; Kuomintang; Nanking government; Nationalist government; Shōwa Research Association, proposed solutions to China Incident
Chou Fo-hai, 132, 184 (n. 115)
Chūō kōron, 39, 63, 163
Clear Politics Association (Meiseikai), 92
Cole, George Douglas Howard, 14, 15
Comintern, 53, 54, 68, 69, 169 (n. 30)
Commerce and Industry, Ministry of, 42, 101, 144, 147, 149; policies to reduce inflation, 121
Confucianism, 62
Cooperative body (*kyōdōtai*): as concept based on theory of cooperativism, 112–13; as political ideal, 140, 142, 156, 161; as antimodern or promodern ideal, 157; first use as concept, 180 (n. 35); contribution of Rōyama Masamichi, Miki Kiyoshi, and Ryū Shintarō to, 185 (n. 9). See also Cooperativism; East Asian cooperative body
Cooperativism (*kyōdōshugi*), 61, 132, 136, 159; and idea of cooperative body, 112–13; goals of, 132–33
Corporatist state, 6, 70, 173 (n. 69). See also Italy, corporate state in
Council of Important Industry Cartels (Jūyō sangyō karuteru kondankai), 151
Czechoslovakia, 138; as model of occupational representation, 15

Diet, 23, 74, 83, 92, 97, 137, 144, 145; powers, 3, 10; proposed reforms of in New Order Movement, 3, 143, 146; legislation, 10, 116; evaluated by Rōyama Masamichi, 34–35, 55, 81; proposed reforms of, 59, 82, 104, 134, 139, 140, 142; opposition to army, 72, 79, 106; proposals to change electoral system of, 80, 99, 136; as obstacle to fascism in Japan, 138; as obstacle to New Order Movement, 150, 151
Doihara Kenji, Lt. General, 109, 110, 114
Dōmei news agency, 146

East Asian cooperative body (*Tōa kyōdōtai*): as ideal of Shōwa Research Association, 107, 122, 135, 142, 145, 147; Miki Kiyoshi's view of, 112–13; Rōyama Masamichi's view of, 137, 139, 159; evaluation of, 184 (n. 114)
East Asian League, 109; proposals for, 115, 131, 132
Education, Ministry of, 51, 84, 89, 93, 135; new policies in 1920s and 1930s, 93–94
Education Study Group (Kyōiku kenkyūkai), 88, 92–93, 176 (n. 2)
Election Purification Movement (Senkyo shukusei undō), 80, 98–99
Electric Power Control Law, 148; debate over, 74, 75, 76
Engels, Friedrich, 22
Esher Report, 13, 166 (n. 24)

Far Eastern Economic Review (*Tōyō keizai shimpōshi*), 43, 65, 119
Farmer-Labor party (Nōmin rōdōtō), 25
Fascism, 71, 76; appeal to intellectuals, 5, 6, 157, 161, 165 (n. 14); concept of freedom in, 49, 156; appeal to executive board of Shōwa Research Association, 104; nation in, 156; emphasis on struggle in, 156; in Japan, 163–64; appeal to socialists, 167 (n. 52). *See also* Corporatist state; Germany, Nazism in; Hitler; Italy, corporate state in, fascism in; Miki Kiyoshi, fascism as model of reform, interpretation of Japanese tradition and fascism; Nazism; Rōyama Masamichi, fascism as model of reform; Ryū Shintarō, fascism as model of reform; Sassa Hiroo, views on fascism
February 26 Incident (1936), 81, 84, 103–4
Federation of Economic Organizations (Keizai dantai renmei), 119
Feuerbach, Ludwig, 21
Finance, Ministry of, 148
Five Ministers Conference, 109
Foreign Affairs, Ministry of, 108, 155
Foreign Exchange Control Law (1933), 65, 173 (n. 58)
France, 68, 109, 189 (n. 10); seen as "old imperialist," 139; attacked by Germany, 142
Freud, Sigmund, 47
Friendly Society (Yūaikai), 9, 25
Fundamental Principles of the National Polity, 84

Gekokujō, 103
Gemeinschaft, 113, 127, 133, 157

Genro, 10, 79, 94
German-Soviet Non-Aggression Pact, 139
Germany, 16, 68, 101, 153, 173 (n. 69); Social Democratic party in, 6; as model of centralization, 13; as model of occupational representation, 15; as example of economic collapse, 45, 65, 67, 72; economic policies as model, 48, 77, 121, 123, 126, 130; foreign policies as model, 81, 138–39; seen as have-not nation, 95, 102; as ally of Japan, 101, 134, 144; attitude of Shōwa Research Association toward, 109; similarities with Soviet Union, 139; as "new imperialist," 139; attack on France, 142; Nazism in, 158, 164 (n. 4); industrial production in, 173–74 (n. 5). *See also* Hitler; Nazism
Gesellschaft, 113, 157
Gold standard: controversy over, 41–44, 48
Gondō Seikyō, 33, 133
Gotō Fumio (home minister): participation in Alliance for a New Japan, 92; participation in Education Study Group, 93; as leader of Election Purification Movement, 98; participation in Shōwa Research Association, 101, 185 (n. 5), 186 (n. 24); and New Order Movement, 143
Gotō Ryūnosuke, 90, 94, 181 (n. 43), 185 (n. 5); as organizer of Shōwa Research Association, 88, 89, 90, 101, 153; early career, 88–89; formation of Young Adult Association, 91–92; evaluation of Alliance for a New Japan, 92; participation in Education Study Group, 92; friendship with Konoe, 95; views on Cabinet Consultative Council, 96–97; support for election purification, 98–99; and funding of Shōwa Research Association, 99–100; participation in Shōwa Academy, 136; and New Order Movement, 143, 145, 146, 187 (n. 48); participation in IRAA, 150–51; view of New Order Movement, 186 (n. 40)
Greater East Asian Coprosperity Sphere (Daitōa kyōeiken), 3, 4, 144, 160
Greece, 112
Guild socialism, 5, 11, 14, 161

Hamada Kunimatsu (Diet member), 80
Hamaguchi Osaichi (premier), 41, 42, 53
Hani Gorō, 26
Hanyū Shinshichi, 143, 185 (n. 8)
Hara Kei (Takashi) (premier), 10
Harmonization Society (Kyōchōkai), 89, 124, 170 (n. 58)
Hasama Shigeki (home minister), 146
Hata Shunroku, General, 144
Hayashi Hirokichi, 185 (n. 5), 185 (n. 8)
Hayashi Senjurō, General (premier), 72
Hegel, Georg, 18, 21
Heidegger, Martin: impact on Miki Kiyoshi, 16, 18–19, 84
Hilferding, Rudolf, 39, 48
Hiranuma Kiichirō, Baron (premier, home minister), 94, 134, 151
Hirota Kōki (premier), 81; cabinet of, 72, 77, 78, 101, 103; as foreign minister, 108, 109
Hitler, Adolf, 52, 54, 71, 89, 134, 189 (n. 10)
Hitotsubashi University, 7, 19

Hoashi Kei, 124, 151-52
Home Affairs, Ministry of, 38, 51, 91, 92, 101, 135, 143, 146, 159; thought control policy of, 10; and election purification, 80, 98; and New Order Movement, 150, 151
Hōsei University, 7
Hōtokukai, 90
House, Colonel Edward M., 95
House of Peers, 59, 90, 94, 97, 140, 178 (n. 51)

Ikeda Seihin (finance minister), 73, 121, 152
Imperial Reserve Association (Teikoku zaigo gunjinkai), 10, 28, 51, 98
Imperial Rule Assistance Association (IRAA), 151, 153; as defeat for Shōwa Research Association, 150; as not a fascist movement, 158; as fascist, 163 (n. 4)
Inaba Hidezō, 185 (n. 8); participation in Shōwa Research Association, 124, 125, 185 (n. 5), 186 (n. 24); as member of Cabinet Planning Board, 125, 153; arrested, 153
Individual and society. *See* Miki Kiyoshi, views of individual and society; Rōyama, views of individual and society; Ryū Shintarō, views on individual and society
Industrial Association (Sangyō kumiai), 98
Inoue Junnosuke (finance minister), 40, 41, 44
Institute of Pacific Relations, Japan Council, 29
Intellectuals: role in Japanese society, 4-5, 7, 8; role in prewar Japan, 155, 164 (n. 5), 164 (n. 6). *See* Miki Kiyoshi, concern for role of intellectuals; Rōyama Masamichi, views on role of intellectuals; Ryū Shintarō, views on role of intellectuals
Inukai Tsuyoshi (premier): assassination of, 33, 56, 70, 79, 89, 94; cabinet of, 44
Ishibashi Tanzan, 65
Ishiwara Kanji, General, 109, 117
Italy, 81, 173 (n. 69); corporate state in, 4, 6, 58, 83, 141; fascism in, 39, 52, 54, 114, 158, 164 (n. 4); economic policies as model, 77, 121, 123, 126; seen as have-not nation, 95, 102; as ally of Japan, 134, 144; as "new imperialist," 139. *See also* Corporatist state; Mussolini

Japan Chamber of Commerce, 119
Japan Communist party, 36, 46, 169 (n. 30)
Japan Economic League (Nihon keizai renmei), 119, 124, 151; opposition to new economic order, 152
Japan Federation of Trade Unions (Nihon sōdōmei), 9
Japan Labor-Farmer party (Nihon rōnōtō), 25
Japan Labor Yearbook (*Nihon rōdō nenkan*), 25-26, 67, 169 (n. 32)
Japan League of Youth Associations (Dainihon rengō seinendan), 91
Japan Youth Hall (Nihon seinenkan), 89, 90, 91
Justice, Ministry of, 10, 51

Kagawa Toyohiko, 166 (n. 29)
Kagesa Sadaaki, Colonel, 110
Kaizō, 63
Kaji Ryūichi, 188 (n. 1)
Kamei Kanichirō (Diet member), 69, 75, 90, 98

Kanemitsu Tsuneo, 150
Karazawa Toshiki, 101, 181 (n. 43), 186 (n. 24)
Katsumata Seiichi: in Cabinet Investigation Bureau, 97; in Shōwa Research Association, 124, 185 (n. 5), 186 (n. 24); in Cabinet Planning Board, 125, 148; in IRAA, 151; arrested, 153; in Research Association for a National Movement, 185 (n. 8)
Kautsky, Karl, 25
Kawada Tetsuji, 111, 123
Kawai Eijirō, 90, 178 (n. 50)
Kawakami Hajime, 8, 10
Kawakami Jōtarō, 90, 97
Kaya Okinori (finance minister), 101
Kazami Akira (chief cabinet secretary, home minister): in Shōwa Research Association, 101, 116, 181 (n. 43); adviser to Konoe, 135, 144, 145, 151, 179 (n. 12)
Keio University, 111
Kellogg-Briand Pact, 31
Keynes, John Maynard, 43
Kimura Kihachirō, 124
Kishi Nobusuke (vice-minister of commerce and industry), 144, 149
Kita Ikki, 33, 71
Kobayashi Ichizō (minister of commerce and industry), 144, 147
Kobayashi Junichirō, Colonel, 100
Konoe Fumimaro (premier), 6, 119, 141; and New Order Movement, 3, 143, 144, 145, 146–47, 150, 151, 152, 186 (n. 40); first cabinet of, 73, 101, 121, 125, 134, 135; friendship with Gotō Ryūnosuke, 89; influence on Shōwa Research Association, 90, 94, 95–96, 132; participation in Alliance for a New Japan, 92; participation in Education Study Group, 92; views on domestic politics, 94–95; views of China policy, 95; and China Incident, 107, 108, 109, 134; declaration of new order in East Asia, 115–16; attitude toward the army, 142; second cabinet, 144, 147, 153, 160; and aims of the New Order Movement, 187 (n. 50). *See also* Shōwa Research Association, influence on Konoe
Korsch, Karl, 22
Kropotkin, 10
Kuhara Fusanosuke (Diet member), 142
Kuomintang, 29, 107, 108, 109, 110, 116. *See also* Chiang Kai-shek; Nanking government; Nationalist government
Kushida Tamizō, 8, 21, 22, 167 (n. 68)
Kwantung Army, 30, 31, 33, 57, 61, 62. *See also* Manchurian Incident
Kyōto, University of, 7, 16, 48, 89, 124

Labor-Farmer party (Rōnōtō), 25
La Rochelle, Drieu, 165 (n. 14), 189 (n. 10)
Law for the Control of Important Industries (1931), 42, 63–64
League of Nations, 77, 144; Rōyama Masamichi's view of, 28, 31; Lytton Commission, 30
Liberalism: Rōyama Masamichi's redefinition of, 49, 58; criticized by Alfredo Rocco, 56, 130; Miki Kiyoshi's redefinition of, 60–61; rejection of by Japanese intellectuals, 86, 130, 157, 160

London Naval Conference (1930), 33, 44, 77
Lukacs, George, 22

MacDonald, Ramsay (prime minister of Britain), 23, 53, 57
Machiavelli, Niccolo, 17
Machida Chūji (Diet member), 96
Maeda Tamon, 90, 97, 186 (n. 24)
Manchuria (Manchukuo), 45, 69–70, 148; Rōyama Masamichi's view of, 28–32; Japanese army's actions in, 34, 57, 72, 76, 161; need for economic development of, 106, 121, 124; demand for recognition of Manchukuo, 107, 109; as part of proposed cooperative body, 115, 135, 137; economic potential of, 117. *See also* Manchurian Incident
Manchurian Incident, 102; effect on Japanese intellectuals, 30–32, 38, 46–47; effect on Japan's economy, 44, 77, 117, 123
Maruyama Tsurukichi, 92
Marx, Karl, 17, 19, 22, 26, 43, 63
Marxism: appeal to Japanese intellectuals, 5, 11, 16, 47, 124; rejection of, 34, 49, 61, 62, 86, 130, 157, 159, 161. *See also* Karl Marx; Miki Kiyoshi, interpretation of Marxism; Rōyama Masamichi, criticism of democracy and socialism; Ryū Shintarō, interpretation of Marxism
Masaki Chifuyu: participation in Shōwa Research Association, 97, 124, 125; as member of Cabinet Planning Board, 125, 153, 183 (n. 90); arrested, 153
Matsui Haruo (head of Resources Bureau), 97, 98, 181 (n. 43); as "new bureaucrat," 97–98; participation in Shōwa Research Association, 101
Matsumoto Shigeharu, 30, 146
Matsuoka Komakichi, 90
Matsuoka Yōsuke (foreign minister), 144
Meiji Constitution, 3, 9, 34, 60, 85, 99, 143; interpreted by Rōyama Masamichi, 83, 138
Meiji Restoration, 57, 76, 81
Miki Kiyoshi, 94, 115; and apostasy, 4, 49–50, 159, 171 (n. 1); and New Order Movement, 4, 145; desire for political influence, 4–5, 23, 26–27, 70, 159–60; fascism as model of reform, 5–6, 87, 106, 113, 132, 155–57, 158, 160, 161; early career of, 7, 26; concern for role of intellectuals, 8, 23, 47–48, 111, 114; views of proletariat, 9, 18; desire for reform, 15, 28, 69, 70, 116, 133, 159, 160; interpretation of Marxism, 16–18, 20, 22–23; and concept of *form*, 17, 58, 114; views of individual and society, 18–19, 86, 112–13, 157, 160–61; criticized as revisionist, 26, 36; views on Japan's China policy, 30, 32, 62–63, 107, 110–14, 132, 137, 147, 185 (n. 9); strategy for reforms, 32–33, 34, 60, 61, 71, 102, 155, 161; sense of crisis, 45–46; arrest by police, 46; and thought of "anguish," 46–47; advocacy of "new thought," 47–48; fascination with West, 48; state as agent of reform, 51–52, 63, 70, 86–87, 132, 160; call for new liberalism, 60–61; flexibility in thought of, 70, 161; interpretation of Japanese tradition and fascism, 83, 84–86; definition of new totalitarianism, 86, 112; as leader of Shōwa Research Association, 88, 105, 110, 111–114, 123, 159, 180 (n. 21), 185 (n. 5), 185 (n. 9), 186 (n. 24); views of nation, 113–14, 130, 156; contact with army, 114; influence on Ryū Shintarō, 122, 127, 180 (n. 36); effect of Shōwa Research Association on, 132, 153–54, 155, 160;

participation in IRAA, 151; desire to continue Shōwa Research Association, 153; attitude toward Konoe, 154, 156; interpretation of freedom, 156; death in 1945, 163 (n. 2); protest against Nazism, 172 (n. 44); attitude toward Japanese military, 180 (n. 39)

Minobe Tatsukichi: controversy over constitutional theory of, 51, 70, 71, 79, 83, 84, 99; denunciation of interpreted as popular demand for reform, 60, 103, 161; criticism of political parties, 98

Minobe Yōji, 148, 152–53

Minseitō, 80, 90, 91, 96; cabinet of, 1929–31, 33; problems of, 34; economic policies of, 36, 41, 42, 44; position in Diet, 79, 81, 160. *See also* Hamaguchi Osaichi; Inoue Junnosuke

Mitsubishi Bank, 40

Mitsubishi Company, 100

Mitsui Company, 44, 73, 100

Miura Shinshichi, 7, 20, 167 (n. 55)

Miura Tetsutarō, 101, 128, 178 (n. 51)

Miwa Jusō, 24, 25, 139, 185 (n. 5)

Miyazaki Masayoshi, 120, 123; proposals for economic policies, 117–18, 131

Mori Hideoto, 148

Morito Tatsuo, 7, 10

Munich Agreement (1938), 134

Murase Naoki, 144, 146

Mussolini, Benito, 6, 52, 71, 155; definition of freedom, 49; influence of ideas on Rōyama Masamichi, 56, 171 (n. 86)

Mutō Akira, Major General, 146

Nakajima Chikuhei (Diet member), 142, 145

Nakayama Yū, 115

Nanking government, 102, 107. *See also* Chiang Kai-shek; Kuomintang; Nationalist government

Nasu Hiroshi, 90, 93, 101

National Council of Corporations (Italian), 141

National Essence Society (Kokuhonsha), 94

National learning school (kokugaku ha), 81

National Mobilization Law, 121

National organization, 160; as political ideal, 134, 136; Sassa Hiroo's advocacy of, 136; Rōyama Masamichi's advocacy of, 138; Shōwa Research Association's proposal for, 141; Miki Kiyoshi's support for, 145; idea criticized, 150; as fascist ideal, 158

National Policy Research Association (Kokusaku kenkyūkai), 89–90

National polity (*kokutai*): criticism of outlawed, 10; stressed by Education Ministry, 84; Ryū Shintarō's view of, 128, 156; Rōyama Masamichi's view of, 138, 156

National Socialist party (Kokka shakaitō), in Japan, 67

National Spiritual Mobilization Movement, 134–35

Nationalism: importance as perceived by Rōyama Masamichi, 30, 51, 54, 55, 56, 58; importance as perceived by Miki Kiyoshi, 46; importance as seen by Ryū Shintarō, 67; as force for reform, 70, 71. *See also* Miki Kiyoshi, interpretation of Japanese

tradition and fascism, view of nation; Rōyama Masamichi, fascism as model of reform, view of nation; Ryū Shintarō, view of nation
Nationalist government, of China: criticism of Japan's policy toward, 106, 107, 109, 134, 187 (n. 50); discussed by Shōwa Research Association, 108, 115, 132. *See also* Chiang Kai-shek; Kuomintang; Nanking government
Navy of Japan, 146; criticism of London Naval Treaty, 34; fear of Axis Pact, 134
Nazism, 111; economic policies of, 4, 6, 67, 72, 73, 77–78, 174 (n. 34); glorification of struggle in, 114; economic policies as model, 118, 119, 120, 126, 127, 128–29, 155, 159; as model of political reform, 137–38, 141; view of freedom in, 156; attraction to intellectuals, 189 (n. 10). *See also* Hitler; Germany, Nazism in
New bureaucrats, 97–98, 155; Sassa Hiroo's view of, 98; in Shōwa Research Association, 101; as viewed by executive board of Shōwa Research Association, 104. *See also* Gotō Fumio; Matsui Haruo; Yoshida Shigeru
New Friends Society (Shinyūsha), 114
New Men's Society (Shinjinkai), 11, 12
New Order Movement, 3, 151, 152, 153, 159; as fascist movement, 155, 158, 164 (n. 4); as promodern or antimodern movement, 157; interpretations of, 163 (n. 4); evaluation of, 188 (n. 1). *See also* Konoe Fumimaro, and New Order Movement; Preparation Committee for a New Order; Ryū Shintarō, influence on economic new order; Shōwa Research Association, proposals for political reform
Nietzsche, Friedrich, 85
Nishida Kitarō, 7, 16, 18
Nitobe Inazō, 88, 89, 90

Obata Tadayoshi, 146
Occupational representation: in guild socialism, 14; Rōyama Masamichi's advocacy of, 15, 59, 71, 82–83; Sassa Hiroo's advocacy of, 136; Shōwa Research Association's support for, 140, 142; and New Order Movement, 146
Ochanomizu University, 163 (n. 2)
Ogata Taketora, 71, 92, 153
Ohara Magosaburō, 25
Ohara Social Problems Research Institute (Ohara shakai mondai kenkyūjo), 7, 21, 25, 169 (n. 32)
Okada Keisuke, Admiral (premier): cabinet of, 34, 79, 96, 97, 98, 99, 177 (n. 36); escapes assassination, 71
Okada Tadahiko (Diet member), 150
Okita Saburō, 185 (n. 7)
Ōkochi Masatoshi, 97, 101, 178 (n. 51)
Okumura Kiwao, 148
Ōkura Kinmochi (Diet member), 97
Okuyama Teijirō, 97, 124, 125
Onotsuka Kiheiji, 166 (n. 21)
Open Door Policy, 10, 31, 95
Opium War, 76
Ōsaka Electric Light Company, 9
Ōsaka Free Trade Conference, 25
Ōsaka Labor School (Ōsaka rōdō gakkō), 26

Ōyama Iwao, 181 (n. 43), 184 (n. 112)
Ozaki Hotsumi, 181 (n. 43)
Ozaki Yukio (Diet member), 92

Panunzio, Sergio, 39, 165, 189 (n. 10)
Peace Preservation Law (1925), 10, 51
Plato, 37, 48
Plekhanov, George, 25
Poland, 134
Preparation Committee for the New Order, 146–47, 150
Privy Council, 59, 143, 144, 186 (n. 40)
Proletarian Science Research Center (Puroretaria kagaku kenkyūjo), 26

Research Association for a National Movement (Kokumin undō kenkyūkai), 136, 143, 185 (n. 8)
Resources Bureau, 125
Rocco, Alfredo (minister of justice, Italy), 130; explication of fascism, 56, 60, 113; influence on Rōyama Masamichi, 56, 60, 171 (n. 86)
Romantic school (roman ha), 85
Roosevelt, Franklin Delano, 119
Rōyama Masamichi, 63, 94; and New Order Movement, 4, 145; and apostasy, 4, 158–59, 171 (n. 1); desire for political influence, 4–5, 23, 26–27, 70, 159–60; fascism as model of reform, 5–6, 52, 53–54, 55–57, 58–59, 81, 87, 137–38, 155–57, 158, 160, 161, 171 (n. 86); early career of, 7, 166 (n. 21); views on role of intellectuals, 8, 24–25, 60, 61, 72; view of proletariat, 9; desire for reforms, 11–12, 28, 44, 69, 70, 159, 160; and functionalism, 12–14, 22–23; influence of guild socialism on, 14–15; views of individual and society, 19, 49, 61, 157, 160–61; view of League of Nations, 28–29, 31, 32; analysis of Manchurian Incident, 29–33; strategy for reforms, 32–33, 34, 60, 61, 71, 102, 104, 155, 161; criticism of democracy and socialism, 34–37, 54–55; state as agent of reform, 35, 38–39, 48–49, 51, 52, 58, 60, 68, 70, 81–82, 86–87, 132, 160; citizens' education and state, 37–38; view of nation, 38–39, 91, 156; sense of crisis, 45–46; fascination with West, 48; need for new ideology, 48; evaluation of Ryū Shintarō, 51; proposals for reform of Diet, 59–60; flexibility of thought of, 70, 161; support for election purification, 80, 98; proposal for new party, 80; views on Meiji Constitution, 83, 138, 185 (n. 19); as leader of Shōwa Research Association, 88, 90, 101, 104–5, 107, 135, 142, 146, 181 (n. 43), 184 (n. 5); and Konoe, 95, 154, 156; theory of East Asian cooperative body, 136–37, 146, 185 (n. 9); theory of national cooperative body, 137; views on German-Soviet pact, 138–39; endorses Greater East Asian Coprosperity Sphere, 145; effect of Shōwa Research Association on, 153–54, 155, 160; interpretation of freedom, 156; post-1945 career, 163 (n. 2); respect for Kawai Eijiro, 178 (n. 50)
Rumania, 134
Russia, 123, 152; Bolshevik Revolution, 10, 11; tsarist regime, 38; Japan's war with, 76; economic policies as model, 126. *See also* Soviet Union
Ryū Shintarō, 30, 94, 146, 151; and New Order Movement, 4; and apostasy, 4, 159, 171 (n. 1); desire for political influence, 4–5, 23, 26–27, 149, 159–60; fascism as

model of reform, 5-6, 72, 78, 87, 106, 120, 130, 132, 155-57, 158, 160, 161; early career of, 7, 25-26, 167 (n. 55); views on role of intellectuals, 8, 131-32; view of proletariat, 9; interpretation of Marxism, 16, 19-23; and Social Thought Association, 19, 167 (n. 53); as editor of *Japan Labor Yearbook*, 25-26, 67, 169 (n. 32); as teacher in labor school, 26; desire for reform, 28, 70, 116, 131, 133, 159, 160; support for bloc economy, 32, 123; strategy of reform, 32-33, 34, 48, 60, 71, 102, 104, 155, 161; criticism of Japan Communist party, 36; analysis of 1927 bank panic, 39-40; response to Great Depression, 41-45; fear of inflation, 45, 63-65, 73-74; sense of crisis, 45-46; fascination with West, 48; state as agent of reform, 51, 52, 63, 67, 68, 69, 70, 81-82, 86-87, 130, 132, 160; critique of managed economy, 65-67; view of rise of fascism in Japan, 67, 79; flexibility of thought of, 70, 161; move to *Asahi*, 71; criticism of government's economic policies in 1937, 73-74; support for Electric Power Control Law, 74-75, 76; attitude toward military, 76-77, 78-79, 131; as leader of Shōwa Research Association, 88, 105, 111, 119, 121, 123, 140, 185 (n. 9), 186 (n. 24); concern with China Incident, 107; report to Shōwa Research Association, 122; and economic research group, 124, 125-27; proposals for economic reform, 125, 127-29; views on individual and society, 128, 157, 160-61; reactions to proposals of, 129, 130, 131; view of nation, 130, 156; effect of Shōwa Research Association on, 132, 153-54, 155, 160; participation in Shōwa Academy, 136; and Miki Kiyoshi, 137, 180 (n. 36); and New Order Movement, 143; influence on new economic order, 147, 148-49, 150, 183 (n. 90), 183-84 (n. 112), 187-88 (n. 58); goes to Germany, 153; attitude toward Konoe, 154, 156; interpretation of freedom, 156; post-1945 career, 163 (n. 2); tosses diary into ocean, 164 (n. 5); and Kushida Tamizō, 167 (n. 68); participation in Research Association for a National Movement, 185 (n. 8)

Saionji Kinmochi (*genro*), 79, 94, 95
Saitō Makoto, Admiral (premier), 57, 71, 79, 95
Saitō Takao (Diet member), 80
Sakai Saburō, 110, 151, 181 (n. 43), 184 (n. 112); evaluation of Shōwa Research Association, 188 (n. 1)
Sakumizu Hisatsune, 148
Sassa Hiroo: views on fascism, 52-54, 57, 99; as leader of Shōwa Research Association, 94, 101, 121, 123, 135, 139, 181 (n. 43), 184-85 (n. 5); views on Cabinet Consultative Council, 97; view of "new bureaucrats," 98; support for election purification, 98, 99; ideas on political mobilization, 135-36; participation in Shōwa Academy, 136; and New Order Movement, 143, 145
Satō Kanji, 90, 97
Schacht, Hjalmar (minister of economics, Germany), 78, 81
Seiyūkai, 80, 90, 91, 144, 150, 160; position in Diet, 10, 79; problems of, 34; policy of noncooperation with united nation cabinet, 34, 96, 99; criticism of disarmament policy, 34; economic policies of, 36, 44
Shanghai, 45
Shiga Naokata, General, 90, 99
Shōtoku Taishi, 138
Shōwa Academy (Shōwa juku), 136, 185 (n. 7)
Shōwa Brotherhood (Shōwa dōjinkai), 136, 144, 148

Shōwa Research Association, 91, 148; and New Order Movement, 3, 4, 144, 145, 146, 157; influence on Konoe Fumimaro, 3, 108–9, 115–16, 135, 146–47, 155; participation of Miki Kiyoshi, Rōyama Masamichi, and Ryū Shintarō in, 5, 32, 38, 87, 94, 185 (n. 9); evaluation of, 88, 188 (n. 1); its start, 90; ties to Youth Association, 90, 92, 94; funding of, 90, 99–100; ties to Alliance for a New Japan, 92; ties to Education Study Group, 92–93, 94, 176 (n. 2); role of Prince Konoe in, 94–96; early organization and membership, 96–98; debate on political issues in 1934–35, 96–97, 98–99; reorganization of in 1936, 100; new bureaucrats in, 101; views of executive board on foreign policy in 1936, 101–3; attitude toward army, 102, 142, 143; views of executive board on political reform in 1936, 103–4; fascism as model of reform, 104, 141, 161; goals in 1937, 104; effect on Rōyama Masamichi, Ryū Shintarō, and Miki Kiyoshi, 105, 131–32, 153–54, 155, 160; proposed solutions to China Incident, 107–9, 114–15, 132; Cultural Problems Research Group, 110, 111–14; study of economic mobilization, 119–27; research on East Asian bloc economy, 123; plans for economic reform, 131; research on political mobilization, 135; attempts at political mobilization, 136; view of alliance with Germany, 139; proposals for political reform, 139–42; and Cabinet Planning Board Incident, 153; dissolution of, 153; interpretations of, 176 (n. 1). *See also* Gotō Fumio; Gotō Ryūnosuke; Kazami Akira; Konoe Fumimaro; Matsui Haruo; Miki Kiyoshi, as leader of Shōwa Research Association; New Order Movement; Rōyama Masamichi, as leader of Shōwa Research Association; Ryū Shintarō, as leader of Shōwa Research Association; Sassa Hiroo, as leader of Shōwa Research Association; Takahashi Kamekichi, Tazawa Yoshiharu; Yabe Teiji; Yoshida Shigeru

Social Democratic party (Shakai minshūtō), 25

Social Mass party: endorsement of war mobilization, 69, 75, 76; position in Diet, 79, 81, 82; seen as force for reform, 82, 135, 136; ties to Shōwa Research Association, 90, 101. *See also* Asō Hisashi, Kamei Kanichirō

Social Science Research Association, 124

Social Thought Association (Shakai shisōsha), 19, 23, 24, 26, 52, 53, 166 (n. 19), 188 (n. 1); participation of Rōyama Masamichi in, 12; participation of Ryū Shintarō in, 19, 167 (n. 53)

South Manchurian Railway Company, 117, 124

Soviet Union, 53, 134; as model of occupational representation, 15; as model of economic planning, 58, 77, 121; seen as threat, 62, 106; Ryū Shintarō's disappointment with, 68; attitude of Shōwa Research Association toward, 102, 109, 112; perceived by Rōyama Masamichi, 139. *See also* Russia

Spengler, Oswald, 62; his theories compared to Marxism by Ryū Shintarō, 20–23

State, the: increasing power in industrial societies, 6. *See also* Miki Kiyoshi, state as agent of reform, view of nation; Alfredo Rocco; Rōyama Masamichi, state as agent of reform, view of nation; Ryū Shintarō, state as agent of reform, view of nation; Shōwa Research Association, debate on political issues in 1934–35

Stimson, Henry L. (secretary of state, U.S.), 31

Suetsugu Nobumasa, 121

Sugiwara Masaoto, 180 (n. 35)

Sumitomo Company, 100

Supreme Command: independence of the, 3, 34, 138, 142

Suzuki Corporation, 39

Tachibana Kōzaburō, 33, 133
Tada Tokuji, Major, 142
Taira Teizō, 166 (n. 18), 181 (n. 43), 185 (n. 5)
Tajima Michiji, 90, 101
Takahashi Kamekichi, 122, 128, 152; as leader of Shōwa Research Association, 97, 101, 119–20, 121, 126, 182 (n. 66); support for election purification, 99
Takahashi Korekiyo (finance minister), 44, 48, 63, 71, 76, 117
Takano Iwasaburō, 7, 25
Takigawa Yukitoki, 48
Taki Masao (head of Cabinet Planning Board), 101
Takuma Dan, 44
Tanaka Giichi (premier): cabinet of, 53
Taniguchi Toshihiko, 101, 178 (n. 51)
Tat magazine, 189 (n. 10)
Tazawa Yoshiharu, 186 (n. 24); participation in Shōwa Research Association, 90, 101; goals for Youth Association, 91; formation of Young Adult Association, 91–92; formation of Alliance for a New Japan, 92; participation in Education Study Group, 92; formation of Election Purification Movement, 98
Temporary Foreign Trade Control Act, 116
Temporary Funds Adjustment Act, 116
Terauchi Hisaichi, General, 80
Toda Takeo, 131
Toennies, Ferdinand, 113, 161
Tōhata Seiichi, 90, 97, 110
Tokonami Takejirō (Diet member), 96
Tokyo, University of, 7, 12, 51, 93, 124, 148, 166 (n. 18), 178 (n. 50), 178 (n. 51)
Tokyo Electric Company, 44
Tomita Kenji (chief cabinet secretary), 143, 144, 145, 146
Tosaka Jun, 71
Totalitarianism (*zentaishugi*): interpreted by Miki Kiyoshi, 86, 112–13
Tsurumi Yūsuke (Diet member), 92

Ugaki Kazushige, General (foreign minister), 109
Under the Banner of New Science (Shinkō kagaku no moto ni), 26
United States (America), 68; policy toward Japan, 31, 32, 101; economic policies of, 66; attitude of Shōwa Research Association toward, 102, 109; Japanese army's attitude toward, 106; economic policies as model, 119, 121; desire of Japanese navy to avoid war with, 134. *See also* Open Door Policy; Washington Conference
Universal Manhood Suffrage, 10, 24, 34, 35, 92

Varga, Eugen, 42, 48
Versailles Treaty, 139

Wada Hiroo, 125
Wada Kōsaku, 185 (n. 8); participation in Shōwa Research Association, 124, 125, 181 (n. 43); as member of Cabinet Planning Board, 125, 153; participation in IRAA, 151; arrested, 153

Wang Ching-wei, 100, 134
Warera, 39
Washington Conference, 10, 28, 31; Nine Power Treaty, 31
World War I, 9, 76, 119
Wuhan, 114, 115, 116
Wu P'ei-fu, 110

Yabe Teiji: as leader of Shōwa Research Association, 123, 139, 186 (n. 24); proposals for political reform, 139–42, 186 (n. 24); and New Order Movement, 143, 145, 146, 147, 187 (n. 48)
Yamagawa Hitoshi, 14
Yamamoto Katsuichi, 129
Yamamuro Sōbun, 40–41
Yanaihara Tadao, 106, 107, 108
Yasui Eiichi (home minister), 144, 145, 151
Yatsugi Kazuo, 89
Yokota Kisaburō, 30, 31
Yomiuri newspaper, 46
Yonai Mitsumasa, Admiral (premier), 144, 186 (n. 40)
Yoshida Shigeru (chief cabinet secretary, head of Cabinet Investigation Bureau), 177 (n. 36); as "new bureaucrat," 97–98; participation in Shōwa Research Association, 97–98, 101, 185 (n. 5), 186 (n. 24)
Yoshida Shigeru (premier), 177 (n. 36)
Yoshino Sakuzō, 7, 11, 13, 14, 59
Yoshino Shinji (minister of commerce and industry), 101, 178 (n. 51)
Young Adult Association (Sōnendan), 91–92
Youth Association (Seinendan), 28; origins of, 10, 51, 90, 91; influence on formation of Shōwa Research Association, 88, 90, 94; Gotō Ryūnosuke and Konoe Fumimaro as leaders of, 89, 92; links to Research Association for a National Movement, 136
Yūki Toyotarō (finance minister), 72, 73, 76, 79

Zaibatsu, 44, 67, 100, 127

www.ingramcontent.com/pod-product-compliance
Lightning Source LLC
Chambersburg PA
CBHW021402290426
44108CB00010B/354